Interpreting and Translating in Public Service Settings

Policy, Practice, Pedagogy

Edited by

Raquel de Pedro Ricoy
Isabelle A. Perez
Christine W. L. Wilson

St. Jerome Publishing
Manchester, UK & Kinderhook (NY), USA

Published by
St. Jerome Publishing
2 Maple Road West, Brooklands
Manchester, M23 9HH, United Kingdom
Telephone +44 (0)161 973 9856
Fax +44 (0)161 905 3498
ken@stjeromepublishing.com
http://www.stjerome.co.uk

InTrans Publications
P. O. Box 467
Kinderhook, NY 12106, USA
Telephone (518) 758-1755
Fax (518) 758-6702

ISBN 978-1-905763-16-0 (pbk)

Printed and bound in Great Britain by
TJI Digital, Padstow, Cornwall

Typeset by
Delta Typesetters, Cairo, Egypt
Email: hilali1945@yahoo.co.uk

British Library Cataloguing in Publication Data
A catalogue record of this book is available from the British Library

Library of Congress Cataloging-in-Publication Data
Interpreting and translating in public service settings : policy, practice, pedagogy
/ edited by Raquel de Pedro Ricoy, Isabelle A. Perez, Christine W.L. Wilson.
    p. cm.
  Includes bibliographical references and index.
  ISBN 978-1-905763-16-0 (pbk. : alk. paper)
1. Public service interpreting. I. De Pedro Ricoy, Raquel. II. Perez, Isabelle, 1962-
  P306.947.I58 2009
  418'.02--dc22
                          2009011524

Interpreting and Translating in Public Service Settings
Policy, Practice, Pedagogy

Edited by
Raquel de Pedro Ricoy, Isabelle A. Perez and Christine W. L. Wilson

Translation, interpreting and other forms of communication support within public sector settings constitute a field which deals, quite literally, with matters of life and death. Overshadowed for many years by interpreting and translating in other domains, public sector interpreting and translating (PSIT) has received growing attention in recent years, with increasingly mobile populations and human rights, diversity and equality legislation shining the spotlight on the need for quality provision across an increasing range and volume of activities.

Interpreting and Translating in Public Service Settings offers a collection of analytically-grounded essays by researchers and practitioners in both translating and interpreting and in the public sector. Against a backdrop of breaking down barriers in PSIT, it aims at providing new insights into the reality of the interaction in public sector settings and into the roles and positioning of the participants by challenging existing models and paradigms. Issues of local need, but with global resonance, are addressed, and current reality is set against plans for the future. The triad of participants (interpreter/translator, public sector professional and client) is investigated, as are aspects of pedagogy, policy and practice. Empirical data supports the study of topics related to written, spoken and signed activities in a variety of professional settings. The studies presented here point to a clear need for cooperation, as well as scope for collaborative developments, across professional boundaries and international borders. Indeed, new directions in research and practice will only be fruitful if all three groups of participants come together, as decisions regarding practice should be based on theoretical tenets underpinned by empirical research.

Bringing together academics and practitioners from different countries in order to explore the multidisciplinary dimension of the subject, this collection should serve as a valuable reference tool, not only for academics and students of public sector interpreting and translating, but also for practising linguists, providers of language services and policy makers.

This volume presents an impressive international snapshot of public service interpreting policy in practice, including reference to both spoken and signed languages as well as the high status languages of Europe and the non-indigenous languages of minority migrant and immigrant communities in interpreting contexts. The authors present detailed analyses of empirical data that challenges status quo perspectives and demonstrates how academic constructs of interpreting impact on interpreter practice, and on how other stake-holders view the interpreter's role. All told, this is a key volume that clearly indicates that policy, practice and pedagogy are core pillars in PSI.

Lorraine Leeson, Trinity College Dublin, Ireland

... a welcome contribution to the growing body of empirical research on translation and interpreting in public service settings, providing plenty of food for thought on a variety of topics, from online learning environments to the concept of 'role'.

Cecilia Wadensjö, Linköping University, Sweden

This collection of papers in jargon-light language is a gold mine of clear information. It should be available wherever public service interpreting and training provision are planned; where interpreters gather; where institutional policy is made. All the bases of training, practice and policy are covered so that everybody can understand them. Buy it for your library, now.

Jan Cambridge, MCIL, RPSI, UK

Table of Contents

Preface

LORRAINE LEESON

Director of the Centre for Deaf Studies, School of Linguistics, Speech and Communication Sciences, Trinity College, Dublin, Ireland

The role of the public service interpreter is one that has received a growing amount of academic attention in recent years, and rightly so. Who amongst us would choose to have what are arguably the most significant, and potentially stressful, moments of our lives interpreted without having concern for the quality of the person doing the interpreting, their training, and the policies that underpin their practices? These three pillars are fundamentally linked, and weaknesses in any one of these has serious consequences for stakeholders across the board. This may be a simple formula, but fundamentally, without education, how ready can interpreters be to meet the demands that they will encounter? Without well educated interpreters, quality of practice is diminished and stakeholders suffer. Sadly, it is usually the most vulnerable who suffer most: those who want to get a diagnosis, get better, get educated, get asylum, get acquitted. And without strong, well-informed policy, the best pedagogy cannot be translated into best practice. Sadly, even today, it frequently requires serious errors in practice to prompt shifts in response to pedagogy and policy. Thankfully, there is also space for the academy to respond via high-level critical analyses of empirical settings. And that is what this volume does.

This collection of papers presents an impressive international snapshot of public service interpreting policy, including reference to both spoken and signed languages as well as the high status languages of Europe and the non-indigenous languages of minority migrant and immigrant communities in interpreting contexts. The authors present detailed analyses of empirical data that challenges *status quo* perspectives and demonstrates how academic constructs of interpreting impact on how interpreters practice and on how other stakeholders view their role.

Including data from a range of public service settings and a wide range of language communities that include English speakers in German asylum hearings, Francophone nurses working in Ontario (an English speaking province), English speaking tourists who encounter Italian doctors in A&E in an Italian hospital, court interpreters in Madrid, British Sign Language/ English interpreters in workplace settings, as well as consideration of the efficiency of an online programme for PSIs in Norway, where Norwegian was just one of thirteen working languages covered. At a policy level, data from Ireland, Scotland and Spain is analyzed, and a model for future implementation of public service interpreting in Scotland is presented.

Key themes addressed include the nature of interaction between participants, the notion of joint negotiation and the concept of communities of practice (Mason). The issue of asymmetry in medical encounters is presented as a the product of a complex set of factors (Merlini), while a number of authors explore how specific translation and interpreting models (machine translation model, conduit model, interactive model) impact on aspects of practice (Bot; Dickinson and Turner), while the way in which court interpreters account for their "active" role (which may be taken as practice at the other end of the machine translation or conduit model for our purposes) is scrutinized (Martin and Ortega).

Issues of gender and translation are addressed by Hébert, who demonstrates that specific discourse strategies employed by translators of French/English may be seen as detrimental to the goal of redressing inequality. Staying with linguistically driven analyses, Tillman suggests that the significance of modal particles in interpreted discourse must be given attention, arguing that the effect of the deletion of such particles by interpreters impacts negatively on the goal of interpreted encounters.

Public Service Interpreting policy responses are explored too: Spain, Ireland and Scotland are all countries that have recently investigated immigration, with the commensurate need to provide PSI services. A critical analysis of language policy and planning in these countries, with a particular emphasis on attention given to non-indigenous languages is presented by O'Rourke and Castillo, while Perez and Wilson present on a model for translation, interpreting, and communication support (TICS) that emerged from a comprehensive study of TICS providers in Scotland, the first of its kind in that country.

All told, this is a key volume that clearly indicates that policy, practice and pedagogy are core pillars in Public Service Interpreting and Translating, and one which stimulates reflection, analysis of practice, and which motivates further research in this critically important field.

Introduction

RAQUEL DE PEDRO RICOY
Centre for Translation and Interpreting Studies in Scotland,
Heriot-Watt University, Edinburgh, UK

Interpreting and translating in public-service settings (activities that are also referred to as community interpreting and translating) have become a focus of interest in academic, professional and political circles in recent years. Active campaigning on the part of formerly under-represented linguistic communities, such as the Deaf communities, as well as changes in demographic trends and patterns in western countries have triggered responses from policy makers which attempt to address the needs of increasingly multilingual, multicultural societies. As a result, there is an increasing awareness of the need for professional training, which, ideally, would be informed by empirical research.

Public-service interpreting encompasses modes that are common to other forms of interpreting: liaison (or bilateral), consecutive and simultaneous (especially in the form of *chuchotage*, or whispered interpreting, although the introduction of booths in some public-service venues, such as courtrooms, is becoming increasingly widespread). Similarly, the skills involved in translating for the public services, whether in written or oral (on-sight translation) form, are concomitant with those that translation in other settings entails. All this raises two fundamental questions: firstly, why is it necessary to investigate issues relating to Public-Service Interpreting and Translating (PSIT) separately and, secondly, what are the key issues that demand attention.

There is no doubt that the studies carried out over the years in translation and interpreting theory and the findings derived from experiments in this field are relevant to PSIT. However, public-service settings, be they hospitals, courtrooms, interview rooms, police stations or other type of venues, as well as the identity and personal circumstances of the primary interlocutors warrant specific study. Hemlin and Clarke (2003:3) claim that "Every day, community interpreters face the inherent complexity of languages and significant differences in cultures and values. But wherever interpreters may be, professionalism and respect for their code of ethics remain their prime directives". This statement is true of any interpreter, and not only of the ones working in the public services. The difference is that, arguably, failure to recognize the aforementioned "complexity of languages" or to engage with the "significant differences in cultures and values" is likely to have more significant consequences for individuals, communities and societies than comparable breakdowns in communication in other settings. Although this is also applicable to translation, it is especially relevant to interpreting, because of the singularity and immediacy of the communicative act, as well as, in some cases (for instance, in the course of a trial or during a medical examination), the relative irreparability of the statements uttered. In the event that a translation were flawed, it would be simpler to repair any errors *a posteriori*, since a record of the communicative act exists.[1] This may help explain why most of the studies concerning communication in public-service settings focus on the former activity, rather than on the latter.

As for the key issues to be addressed in terms of PSIT, it can be argued that the priority is to examine the reality of the interaction in public-service settings and the roles of the participants (including the interpreters) by challenging existing models and paradigms. The use of authentic data (hitherto difficult to obtain and, therefore, more rarely included in studies of this kind) is paramount, as are analytical approaches to the role and positioning of the participants. Angelelli (2003:15-26) makes a case for the acknowledgement of the visibility of the interpreter in her contribution to Critical Link 3. It is well known that the (in)visibility of translators and interpreters became a focus of scholarly work in the field in the latter part of the 20th century; however, it is important to underscore the importance of examining translation and interpreting in the public services as mediated communication, and to leave aside notions that translators and interpreters are neutral conduits, since their interventions play a crucial role in the communicative event. Additionally, there is a clear need for cooperation and collaborative developments in research, and it has to be emphasized that new directions will only be fruitful if all three groups of participants (public-service providers, clients and translators / interpreters) come together: theoretical tenets must be underpinned by empirical research in order to define and foster good practice; similarly, decisions as to practice should be based on theoretical tenets underpinned by empirical research.[2]

---

[1] On the other hand, interpreter-mediated exchanges are frequently unrecorded.

[2] It has been claimed that "The role of the interpreter, like other roles, derives from observed behaviour over time and from evaluation of behaviour *vis-à-vis* that expected by professional associations or other occupational or social groupings" (Gentile *et al.* 1996:31). Nevertheless, guidelines and regulations, rather than just observation and behaviour evaluation, are required in PSIT, so as to ensure the provision of a fair,

It has become commonplace to observe that studies in PSIT are relatively scarce, compared to the volume of literature on other types of translation and interpreting. Whilst this still holds true, it is also appropriate to point to the recent emergence of academic and institutional interest in this area. This book is an example of this trend. It presents a collection of critical essays on translation and interpreting in the field of the Public Services. It was inspired by the PSIT International Conference held at Heriot-Watt University under the auspices of the *Centre for Translation and Interpreting Studies in Scotland* (CTISS) in March 2005. It addresses key issues which are of crucial relevance to the field and that were, of course, discussed during the conference, but it does not constitute a volume of select proceedings.[3]

It is hoped that the present collection of essays will be of interest to translation and interpreting practitioners, trainers and researchers, as well as to the public-sector agencies, services and stakeholders. Many communities of practice have their work increasingly informed or defined by the need to manage multilingual, multicultural exchanges. The issues addressed in this book will be pertinent for: researchers in the fields of interpreting, translating, linguistics, cross-cultural communication and anthropology; trainers of public-service and sign-language interpreters and translators; public-service translators and sign-language or spoken language interpreters (practitioners, trainees and students); policy-makers with an interest in social inclusion and equality of access for people from minority and ethnic backgrounds; individuals and agencies responsible for ensuring the effective delivery of services to multilingual / multi-cultural groups; employees in public service sectors, such as the legal system and immigration, health care, local government (social work, housing, education, environmental health…), cross-cultural survey work, etc.; and organizations in the voluntary and not-for-profit sector offering support to minority language groups (including Deaf communities).

This book aims at breaking new ground in the field, by bringing together academics and practitioners in order to explore the multidisciplinary dimension of the subject. It is intended to serve as a reference tool, not only for academics, but also for practising linguists and policy makers, given the

---

high-quality service. Equally, the application of an ethical code of conduct should not be restricted to interpreters and translators, but also to the representatives of the public services that are involved in mediated exchanges.

[3] After the conference, the authors were invited to formulate their views and the results of their research in writing, rather than submit written accounts of their presentations, and other researchers were invited to contribute to the collection.

aforementioned scarcity of specialized literature. It was felt that a collection such as this would be welcome by academics who are involved in the
teaching and researching of PSIT, so as to enhance the status of a branch
of interpreting that has received comparatively little attention at higher
education level.[4] Additionally, the exploration of best practice for practitioners seeking to deliver social inclusion and equality of access across the
divides between languages and cultures, including professional cultures,
seems a worthwhile endeavour in itself and has unquestionable relevance
in the context of increasingly multilingual and multicultural societies. New
information and viewpoints regarding PSIT can be shared with the wider
community by means of works on the subject, such as this one, so as to
stimulate discussion of key issues and indicate new directions for research
in a field whose importance is paramount if diversity is to be upheld and
promoted.

The authors are an international mix of academics, practitioners of translation and interpreting (both sign and spoken languages), and public-service
professionals. Each one of them provides an insight into the subject matter
that reflects his or her own style and methodology (from empirical studies,
to heuristic research and hermeneutic approaches). Their contributions deal
with policy, theory, pedagogy and practical studies in various public-service
settings and they cover the main branches of PSIT (justice system, immigration and health services), whilst touching on other fields, thus offering the
reader a comprehensive overview, which focuses on differences, but goes
beyond them and underscores common concerns.

On policy, Perez and Wilson present the results of a comprehensive
review of current practice in relation to the provision of translating, interpreting and communication support (TICS) within the public services
in Scotland. The aim of this groundbreaking study, commissioned by the
Scottish Executive and conducted by a Heriot-Watt University team from
the *Centre for Translation and Interpreting Studies in Scotland* (CTISS),
was to move away from impressionistic assessments of needs and existing
provision. As a result, the conclusions drawn and the resulting recommendations are based on facts and evidence gathered from the language-services
providers, the relevant public sector bodies and the users of public services
and they represent a significant step forward in terms of policy developments in Scotland.

O'Rourke and Castillo present an overview of language policy and

---

[4] This was confirmed by the volume of queries concerning the potential publication of
proceedings of the PSIT International Conference mentioned above.

planning in PSI in the Republic of Ireland, Scotland and Spain. The eth-
nodemographic landscape in all three contexts has changed substantially
in recent years as a result of migratory trends. The need for the provision
of interpreting services to non-indigenous ethnic minority language groups
has been tackled in different ways in each country, but some similarities
between Ireland and Spain are noted and contrasted with the situation in
Scotland, where there is a longer history of immigration. This paper explores both institutional and grassroots initiatives and examines critically
the ideologies that are implicit in them.

In his contribution, Mason argues for the application of the notion of
"positioning" rather than that of "role" (which has been hitherto more
commonly used) to the analysis of public-service interpreting. He provides
valuable insights into the interactive nature of mediated communication
and brings into focus the effects that discursive practices have on *all* the
participants involved in any given exchange. Mason posits that, although
language is, naturally, a key element for analysis, paralinguistic and pragmatic features should not be disregarded.

Skaaden and Wattne's essay revolves around pedagogical issues. They
describe an online interpreting course offered by the University of Oslo
and evaluate the usefulness of "cybertools" in the training of interpreters.
Their analysis of the implementation of this initiative reveals very promising results: the acquisition of skills required in a public-service setting
(from linguistic expertise to the awareness of professional ethics) can be
successfully facilitated in cyberspace. Their study also points to the benefits
of integrating users of different languages in the training sessions, rather
than segregating them according to their working linguistic pair.

Merlini applies different theories to her analysis of a corpus of interpreter-mediated dialogues in the Accident and Emergency Department of an
Italian hospital, in order to provide an overview of the factors that determine
the asymmetry characterizing medical encounters. The originality of her
study resides in her choice of data: the exchanges take place between medical personnel and patients (English-speaking tourists) who are not members
of a minority and are mediated by "part-time interpreters" (i.e. linguists who
are employed to perform occasionally as interpreters, but whose remit also
includes administrative tasks).

Bot, a professional working in the field of mental health, explores two
models of interpreter and user cooperation: "the translation machine model"
and the "interactive model". Observations based on a set of empirical data
lead to a number of interesting conclusions related to these two models

and the reality of interpreter-mediated talk which are also likely to have relevance in other fields of activity.

Hébert describes an exercise, which is both empirical and reflective, aimed at assessing the reactions of Francophone nurses in Ontario to the translation of documents produced by their regulatory college in English. An interventionist strategy was applied so as to foreground the feminine in the documents in question. Interestingly, her study demonstrates that certain discursive translation strategies aimed at redressing inequalities may be perceived by some readers as detrimental. A wider conclusion drawn from the qualitative analysis of the data gathered in the course of her experiment is that gender cannot be separated from other salient social, political and economic factors.

In the context of legal settings, Martin and Ortega Herráez elaborate on the conclusions drawn from an empirical study on Spanish court interpreters' perceptions of their role and remit. Their questionnaire-based investigation reveals an interesting mismatch between what the deontological code dictates and the reality of the practice of interpreting in the courtroom: interpreters tend to go beyond their role as mediators and assume functions that lie outwith their expected remit.

Tillmann's contribution tackles the issue of modality and its relevance in dialogue interpreting. She analyzes the pragmatics of an asylum interview conducted in German and English and demonstrates how the interpreter's choices in terms of the reproduction of modal particles when working into the latter language affect the rapport between the immigration officer and the asylum applicant and the effect that this shift may have in the achievement of the goal that was set for the exchange.

Finally, Dickinson and Turner present a study of the role of sign language interpreters in the workplace. They posit that the recognition of the interpreter's visibility and of his/her role as an active communicator in mediated events is the key to fruitful communication processes. They also argue that interpreters should manage the interaction between Deaf and hearing participants in such a way that the negotiation of social identities which is implicit in such interaction is successfully reflected, as cultural (in the broad sense of the term) mediation is a crucial component of the interpreted exchanges that take place in the workplace.

This brief summary of the contents of the book is intended as an illustration of the depth and breadth of the material included here. Hopefully, readers who delve into one, more or all of the contributions will find this an enjoyable and informative experience.

References

Angelelli, C. (2003) "The Interpersonal Role of the Interpreter in Cross-Cultural Communication: A Survey of Conference, Court and Medical Interpreters in the US, Canada and Mexico", in Louise Brunette, George Bastin, Isabelle Hemlin and Heather Clarke (eds) *The Critical Link 3. Interpreters in the Community. Selected Papers from the Third International Conference on Interpreting in Legal, Health and Social Service Settings, Montreal, Quebec, Canada*, Amsterdam/Philadelphia: John Benjamins, 15-26.

Gentile, A., U. Ozolins and M. Vasilakakos (eds) (1996) *Liaison Interpreting. A Handbook*, Melbourne: Melbourne University Press.

Hemlin, I. and H. Clarke (2003) "Preface: The Complexity of the Profession", in Louise Brunette, George Bastin, Isabelle Hemlin and Heather Clarke (eds) *The Critical Link 3. Interpreters in the Community. Selected Papers from the Third International Conference on Interpreting in Legal, Health and Social Service Settings, Montreal, Quebec, Canada*, Amsterdam/Philadelphia: John Benjamins, 3-4.

A TICS Model from Scotland

A Profile of Translation, Interpreting & Communication Support in the Public Services in Scotland

ISABELLE A. PEREZ & CHRISTINE W.L. WILSON
Centre for Translation and Interpreting Studies in Scotland, Heriot-Watt University, Edinburgh, UK

Abstract. *A Heriot-Watt University team from the Centre for Translation and Interpreting Studies in Scotland (CTISS) was commissioned by the Scottish Executive to review practice in relation to the provision of translating, interpreting and communication support (TICS) within the public services in Scotland in 2004. This paper introduces the research project, which was the first to gather actual evidence to support hitherto local impressions or anecdotal views and to take account of the full range of possible TICS needs and provision across all languages. The primary objective of the project was to study TICS provision from the perspective of two of the three participants in the communication triad: the TICS providers and the public sector bodies (PSBs). The paper outlines some of the findings of a comprehensive study of TICS providers in Scotland. It also presents a brief review of findings from the study of a sample of PSBs, at both grassroots and policy levels, in a variety of types of area across Scotland and in a range of sectors. It concludes with the presentation of a model based on the recommendations that emerged from the research project and which could provide a coherent plan for future developments in TICS.*

1. Introduction

Background

The Scottish Parliament places the mainstreaming of social inclusion at the very core of its policies and requires those delivering services to the public to make sure that an equality perspective is built into all their work, planning and research. This includes equality of access to information and services.

In the period since the *Scotland Act 1998* gave powers to the Scottish Parliament in devolved areas – which include economic development, education, housing, justice and health, local government and transport – this position has been informed by many strands of research and consultation. These include language policy and planning, race and equality, disability, minority ethnic communities, the Deaf community, refugees and asylum seekers and appropriate adult[1] schemes. Scottish policies and initiatives are further grounded in legislation: the *European Convention of Human Rights* in the form of the *Human Rights Act 1998*, incorporated into domestic law; the *Disability Discrimination Act 1995*; the *Race Relations (Amendment) Act 2000*; and also the *Immigration and Asylum Act 1999*, amended by the *Nationality, Immigration and Asylum Act 2002*, which provides the legal basis for the dispersal of asylum seekers. Although immigration and asylum are matters reserved for the British Parliament at Westminster, refugees arriving in Scotland under the dispersal policy require access to and the support of the devolved services in Scotland.

Geography and people

Scotland is a small country with a population of 5,062,011 (2001 Census). Approximately 3½ million of this population live and work in the central belt of the country; the remainder live throughout the rest of the country in towns and cities mostly near the coasts, but also scattered across very remote areas and in the islands to the west and north of Scotland. Topography and weather conditions can make travel lengthy or difficult in some areas.

At any time there are individuals or communities within Scotland from a wide range of different backgrounds. One of the main industries in Scotland is tourism which means many visitors on holiday; there are also students, business people and migrant workers or those on board vessels calling at Scottish ports. Moreover, the city of Glasgow is the second city in the UK for the dispersal of asylum seekers. Whatever the reasons, the 2001 Census showed an increase in the total minority ethnic population from 1.3% of the total Scottish population in 1991 to 2.01% in 2001. There are also an estimated 1,012,000 people in Scotland with a degree of hearing loss[2] – who may or may not consider themselves to be part of the Deaf Community – and it is estimated that the prevalence of age-related hearing impairment in Scotland will rise by about 20% over the next 20 years (Scottish Executive, 2003b:3).

---

[1] In Scotland, the role of an "appropriate adult" is to provide support and reassurance to any person who requires such support and who is being interviewed by the Police as a victim, witness or accused and to ease communication with the Police. Their role is not to act as a legal representative or advocate (Thomson 2004).

[2] Figures: Scottish Council on Deafness (http://www.scod.org.uk/Statistics-i-152.html).

Language and communication

The main language in Scotland is English. However, this does not mean that English is the first or preferred language of everyone resident in the country. Some people may find it difficult, even impossible, to access information and services in Standard English. Moreover, the *Gaelic Language Act (2005)* gives Gaelic the status of an official language, alongside English, which has implications for the future as Gaelic language planning and policies are rolled out across the country.

The 2001 census did not directly collect any information about language or communication needs and preferences – with the exception of Gaelic – although a language question is being discussed in consultative groups as part of the preparatory process for the 2011 Census. The lack of formal statistical data available at present regarding the first or preferred languages or dialects and the other, additional, languages of Scottish residents, or regarding levels of literacy, means that any information is based on experience or extrapolated from studies in particular areas. However, it is clear that the following categories exist in addition to Standard English:

- indigenous languages of Scotland: Gaelic, British Sign Language (BSL) – including Scottish varieties, and (dialects of) Scots;
- languages of long-established communities: mainly Bengali, Chinese (Cantonese), Italian, Polish, Punjabi and Urdu;
- languages spoken by more recently arrived individuals or communities: evidence from earlier studies (e.g. McPake 2003) shows that these may number over 100 languages;
- languages used by visitors and temporary residents in Scotland (students, tourists and business people), which may be any of the world's spoken or sign languages.

A number of other factors also need to be taken into account. One of these relates to special language or communication needs (including issues of literacy or visual impairment) across all language groups. Another is the extent to which an individual identifies with any single group. This may be influenced by migration history, age, gender or disability; for example, deaf people born into a minority ethnic background in the UK may have learned BSL and some English, but may not have acquired the community language of their parents, which could lead to their feeling culturally excluded from that community (Perez and Wilson 2006:25).

Research study

The size of Scotland means that it is possible to conduct fairly comprehensive studies and consultation exercises, whilst the physical challenges of the land and variety of languages and backgrounds encapsulate the challenges for any coherent translation, interpreting and communication support (TICS) provision.

Research was carried out by a team from the *Centre for Translation and Interpreting Studies in Scotland* (CTISS) at Heriot-Watt University, Edinburgh in 2004 (data was collected between February and December), to provide a "snapshot" of the provision of TICS within the public services in Scotland. This research study was the first to gather actual evidence to support hitherto local impressions or anecdotal views. It was also the first study to take account of the full range of TICS needs and provision: all spoken languages (SLs), BSL and other support needs of members of the Deaf Community, as well as the communication needs of Deafblind service-users.[3] A wealth of data (quantitative and qualitative) is available in the four-hundred page final report, *Translating, Interpreting and Communication Support: A Review of Provision in Public Services in Scotland* (Perez and Wilson 2006a), and a summary in the accompanying Research Findings (Perez and Wilson. 2006b), but only some highlights can be outlined in this paper to set in context the model proposed.

The primary objective was to study TICS provision from the perspective of two of the three participants in the communication triad: the TICS providers and the public sector bodies (PSBs), as other studies had been undertaken regarding the other participant, i.e. the non-English-language user (Alexander *et al.* 2004; Kyle *et al.* 2004; Scottish Consumer Council 2005).

2. Translation, Interpreting and Communication Support (TICS) providers

The aim of the project was to investigate issues related to TICS providers as comprehensively as possible. Therefore, all agencies based in Scotland or providing significant services in Scotland (e.g. telephone interpreting providers) were approached.

---

[3] A deafblind person is someone with a dual sensory impairment (see http://www.deafblindscotland.org.uk/About_Deafblindness/FastFacts.php). The communication needs of Deafblind people may include BSL in a restricted frame or use of the Deafblind manual alphabet (see http://openscotland.gov.uk/Publications/2006/01/25141550/17).

Methodology

Telephone interviews were conducted (Phase 1) with 85 TICS providers, gathering data on the profile of each organisation, the range of services provided, TICS employees, recruitment, prior training and qualifications of the translators and interpreters employed, and quality control. In Phase 2 of the study, more detailed face-to-face interviews with staff holding senior positions within their organisations allowed for the collection of data on requests for TICS services, methods of record-keeping, details of service providers, assignments, training provided and the challenges encountered.

Profile of TICS providers

The study found that TICS providers are generally independent and commercially-based. They tend to employ freelancers (sessional workers) who are listed on the books of several agencies. The main difference between SL providers, on the one hand, and sign language or communication support providers, on the other, is that the former primarily serve the private sector whilst the latter (not-for-profit organisations in most cases) serve mainly the public sector.

It was noted that around 64% of all providers had started trading since 1990. This matched the sharp rise in demand for TICS in Scotland in the 1990s and echoed the introduction of legislation such as the *Disability Discrimination Act (1995)* and the *Human Rights Act (1998)*.

Telephone interpreting provision tends to be based outside Scotland.

Training

The study confirmed that few training and career opportunities are available specifically for freelance interpreters and translators working in the public sector; this is true both within and outside TICS agencies. Initial training provision is limited to short graduate diploma-level qualifications (such as the Diploma in Public Service Interpreting, DPSI, established by the Institute of Linguists Educational Trust in 1994),[4] though specialist

---

[4] The DPSI is accredited by the *National Qualifications Framework* (England, Wales and Northern Ireland: http://www.qca.org.uk/qca_6637.aspx) and courses generally last 150 hours. Students can prepare for this qualification in two colleges of further education in Scotland.

courses are beginning to appear at postgraduate level.[5] (An outline of the qualifications framework and training provision in Scotland can be found in Wilson and McDade 2008).

The study also found that there is hardly any continuous development training offered, nor is sufficient funding made available by agencies or, indeed, the authorities for that purpose. Yet the consensus is that in addition to advanced language skills covering both the English language and the other working language, interpreters and translators working in the public sector should acquire specialist interpreting skills – including working in two modes (consecutive and simultaneous), sight translation and *chuchotage* (i.e. "whispered" or "whispering" interpreting, which is a form of simultaneous interpreting) and advanced translation skills. They also require an understanding of standard procedures in relevant settings (for example, in the court room or in mental health consultations) and of the role of the interpreter/translator, as well as familiarity with the code of ethics and common dilemmas which may be faced.

TICS providers reported isolated and short-term provision (if any) of continuous professional development (CPD) and for the mentoring of the interpreters/translators listed on their books. In an attempt to explain the scarcity of training opportunities, they pointed to the lack of staff with adequate skills and sufficient time to provide the training, as well as a shortage of training materials and reference resources.

However, it should be noted that BSL/English interpreting is supported by a much more structured and rigorous framework – under the aegis of the *Scottish Association of Sign Language Interpreters* (SASLI) – regarding both the initial assessment and the ongoing monitoring of registered members. BSL providers generally appear better organized than their SL counterparts (agencies providing both SL and sign language services are very rare) and there is more evidence of networking and resource-sharing in the case of the former. There is also a more extensive range of training available to BSL/English interpreters, although, for obvious reasons, it only focuses on one language in combination with English. However, training focusing on BSL/English translation remains virtually non-existent.[6]

---

[5] PGDip/MSc in *Translation and Public Service Interpreting* (until 2007) and an option within MSc translation and interpreting degrees (since 2008) at Heriot-Watt University, Edinburgh.

[6] The only formal provision in Scotland is a single module within the Graduate Diploma in Interpreting Studies and Skills (BSL/English), Heriot-Watt University, Edinburgh.

Services requested

The study identified that the services most frequently requested of TICS providers are face-to-face and telephone interpreting, in particular in the areas of health, justice, education and local council services. As a variety of immigrant groups have arrived (notably, in Glasgow)[7] over time – and particularly in the ten years spanning the end of the 20th century and the start of the 21st – the number of languages and dialects for which provision is required in Scotland has risen to more than 100.[8] The focus has been on immigrant oral interaction with PSBs, as a result of which interpreting has been prioritised. However, there is also increasing recognition of the need – as yet largely unmet – for an extensive translation effort, especially in the light of legislation and policies relating to accessibility.

The demand for tangential services such as video-conferencing interpreting, interpreting involving foreign sign languages and interpreting combined with special needs support (e.g. the involvement of Appropriate Adults in police settings) is also growing. In the study, responses to researchers' questions regarding requests received for dialects and varieties of spoken/sign languages or communication support appear to demonstrate some blurring of boundaries between the different types of provision (e.g. between "conference" interpreting and "community" interpreting, as many interpreters work in both these areas of activity). The authors believe that this is a significant trend away from the existing compartmentalized structure, which undoubtedly contributes to the perception of low status and standards in the Public Service Interpreting and Translating (PSIT) professions.

Services provided

The study did show that for both SL and BSL providers, the main work areas are, in decreasing order of importance: health and legal fields, social services and education.

The overall shortage of adequately trained interpreters pervades many of the comments made by respondents in this study. This has to be understood against a background of rising and shifting demand. Since the demand is

---

[7] In recent years, Glasgow has been the second arrival city for asylum seekers under the Dispersal Policy (*Nationality, Immigration and Asylum Act* 2002).
[8] A figure of 120 languages in combination with English (excluding sign languages) was identified as having been required in Glasgow.

not systematically documented or monitored, there is a sense of *ad hoc* response on the part of TICS providers and a lack of specific planning strategies in order to cope with higher or changing demand. BSL providers are the exception and it is worth noting that they are in a better position to make contingency plans through the use of a public domain Register of translators and interpreters, which has no counterpart for SLs.

Although TICS providers claimed that they are able to fulfil requests for services in over 90% of cases, it appears – following closer examination – that a number of requests cannot be satisfied because no interpreter is available. This may be (a) because no interpreter is available for the language/dialect requested, (b) a consequence of the need to match the specific requirements of the interpreted situation (e.g. in terms of gender or dialect) or (c) due to a logistical problem, such as location or time of day or night. A notable trend that emerged from this part of the study is that the telephone interpreting service appears to be one of the main solutions adopted when other suppliers cannot meet demand (e.g. outside office hours).

Respondents clearly identify a number of issues to be considered when matching interpreters to a job. Although this is a step in the right direction in terms of awareness of the profession, the authors have to conclude that the implementation of a set policy for matching interpreters to assignments is difficult, given the complexity of certain situations. For example, the interpreter required for a police setting should normally be replaced by another interpreter if a case goes to court. However, the limited number of practitioners in certain language combinations or the challenges of certain locations can make this type of matching unrealistic. As a rule, it was reported that strategies such as "matching" or "continuity of service" are more systematically addressed by BSL than SL providers.

Overall, no clear pattern of practice emerged among TICS providers. Record keeping is not consistent across the sectors; when it is carried out, it appears to be for administrative rather than strategic purposes.

Profile of linguists

The data collected showed that freelancers registered with BSL providers will usually offer both translating and interpreting, whilst linguists accessed by SL providers usually do not provide both of these services.

Other findings supported what had been previously observed, namely that, overall, the number of female interpreters exceeds the number of male interpreters. However, there are several languages for which services could be provided only by male or only by female interpreters.

The study also found that a significant number of practitioners are aged between 30 and 59.

Overview

The research study of TICS providers working in Scotland identified gaps in provision, as well as aspects of both good and weak practice. It also highlighted particular challenges faced by providers, and identified trends in demand and in the use of new strategies and technologies (e.g. telephone and video-conference interpreting). Additional findings included evidence of the beginnings of a blurring of the boundaries between "spoken" language, sign language and communication support provision by providers, as well as between "community" interpreting and "conference" interpreting.

3.   Public Sector Bodies (PSBs)

The aim of this project was to be as representative as possible of all sectors and all locations, whilst working within the inherent constraints. The study provided actual data to support previous expectations, and the findings also revealed a wealth of new information regarding the extent to which various PSBs are ensuring equal access to information and services, and the means employed to ensure this access.

Methodology

As was the case for the TICS aspects of the study, research was conducted in two phases. In Phase 1, 108 structured telephone interviews were conducted at "grassroots level" in 12 different sectors: Primary Health Care, Hospitals, Mental Health, Justice, Police, Prisons, Local Authority, Education, Social Work, Housing, Employment and a single study in Immigration.[9] Informants

---

[9] Since the implementation of the Scotland Act (1998) full responsibility has been devolved to the Scottish Parliament for health and social work; education and training; Local Government and housing; justice and police; agriculture, forestry and fisheries; the environment; tourism, sport and heritage; economic development and internal transport. However, a number of matters are reserved to the Westminster Parliament: such matters include immigration and nationality (www.scotlandoffice.gov.uk/what-we-do/reserved-and-devolved-matters.html).

represented a spread of sub-sectors, such as A&E and Maternity, Sheriff Court and High Court, and so on. The informants were located in a variety of environments (city, other urban and rural) across Scotland, including remote areas such as the islands. Scotland was divided into 10 geographic areas for the purposes of this study. In addition, a group whose representatives had a Scotland-wide remit also participated in the study.

Phase 2 focused on 17 case studies which involved face-to-face interviews with informants at policy level and were undertaken in a representative selection of sectors (health, legal, education, council services, social work, housing and immigration) across all geographic areas.

Type of service provision

The research did not identify any PSBs with no requirement for TICS at all in the provision of services to their clients; however, the types and levels of TICS provision varied greatly: it ranged across a spectrum from the "volunteer" at one end to the "paid professional" at the other and from the "unqualified and inexperienced" to the "trained with experience in specialist fields". Only 5% of PSBs employed in-house staff specifically to provide TICS services and, generally, there was a lack of awareness that language competence did not equate to interpreting or translating skills.

Groups of providers included unpaid volunteers – even in the National Health Service (NHS) and especially for Deafblind support – and substantial use was made of family, friends and members of the local community. Indeed, 83% of PSBs were found to rely on such a service at least sometimes. Interpreting support was also provided by in-house staff that usually had expertise in a different professional area (e.g. nurses, doctors, receptionists, etc.). Finally, local educational institutions were an additional source of provision for PSBs. Thus, it was found that, overall, the majority of PSBs relied on freelance (external) provision, which was usually supplemented by another type of support.

Some PSBs did demonstrate an awareness of advisable practice regarding interpreting and a pattern emerged indicating a hierarchy of preferred provision, namely: [1] trained, professional face-to-face interpreting, [2] telephone interpreting, [3] in-house staff (with subject knowledge) and [4] family, friends, etc. The more "aware" PSBs justified the use of groups [3] and [4] on the grounds of "emergency" or "initial encounter". There is, however, a trend emerging to replace such "informal" provision by using telephone interpreting for spoken languages, but it has to be noted that the development of video-conferencing facilities for sign language interpreting has not reached the same stage of development.

The controversial policy of accepting the use of family and friends "if the client wants this" was also mentioned. However, there were indications – albeit rare – of an awareness that PSB staff, as well as the non-English-language participant, also need an interpreter in order to do their job properly and that, therefore, they need to use a professional TICS provider to ensure this.

Implementation

Overall, the level of awareness of TICS generally and even of internal organizational practices and procedures was very patchy at grassroots levels. Those with the highest levels of awareness were critical of their organization's provision. However, many PSBs were unable to answer certain questions or thought the topic did not apply to their organization (e.g. 34% of respondents could not answer questions related to the policy or procedures for payment of interpreters), thereby demonstrating internal structural weaknesses. In the study, a clear gap was identified between the development of policy and understanding at executive levels and the actual understanding and implementation of practices and procedures at grassroots level (i.e. amongst staff interacting with the public), which highlights the need to ensure information is fed down through all levels within organizations. The study also identified a breakdown in the flow of information between organizations belonging to the same sector (e.g. from primary health care practitioners to hospitals, from courts to prisons).

A practical aspect highlighted by the research was the speed with which services are usually required: in almost 12% of cases this service was required immediately or within the hour and in 46% of cases within 24 hours. However, this figure does not necessarily represent actual need. Indeed, a number of comments indicated that meetings are planned around the availability of interpreters, rather than scheduled on the basis of the clients' needs. A shortage in the supply of interpreters forced a reliance on in-house staff and family or friends, which further masked the real volume of demand for TICS as only formal provision was "counted".

Standards

In spite of the existence of National Occupational Standards[10] for both inter-preting and translation in the UK, the study found that a level of uncertainty also applied to qualifications and standards. Although most PSBs wanted TICS providers to present a suitable qualification, few had any understand-ing of what this should be. Indeed, many were totally unaware of the types of qualification available. Moreover, few PSBs (around 7%) checked the qualifications held by practitioners, but assumed (without verifying) that this had been done at a more senior level or devolved responsibility for this to the translation and interpreting agencies. There was a paradoxical contrast in attitude on the part of PSBs between, on the one hand, declaring high expectations of professional interpreters, and, on the other, being willing to use untrained, unqualified in-house staff with dubious language-com-petence or family and friends of the non-English language user. Indeed, in some cases, PSBs declared a preference for using untrained in-house staff if the interpreter had no domain-specific experience (e.g. mental health settings). PSBs in health and legal fields also emphasized the importance of an interpreter having a specialism – or at least previous experience – in their field. More generally, and as might be expected, PSBs indicated that they expected "fluency" and a "good knowledge of language" – although they often failed to relate this to *both* working languages.

As a rule, quality control tended to be neglected – especially if no "prob-lems" had apparently been encountered – and was certainly not systematic, but rather very informal or subjective (e.g. based on an impressionistic evaluation on the part of the public sector professional of the participant's facial expression as an indicator of their satisfaction or understanding): some PSBs claimed "it was easy to see if the interpreter was good based on the replies from the end-user". There was also a generalized failure on the part of PSBs to ensure that police checks[11] had been carried out. Moreover, some linguists who entered Scotland as asylum seekers may not be in possession of the paperwork required for police check purposes, or it may be impossible

---

[10] These standards have existed since 1996 in their first versions. The latest revision of the National Occupational Standards in Interpreting was launched in 2007, and the latest revision of the National Occupational Standards in Translation in 2008 (http://www.cilt.org.uk/standards/index.htm).

[11] Conducted under Disclosure Scotland to check criminal records to check the suitability of those working with people under 16 or vulnerable adults (http://www.disclosures-cotland.co.uk/index.htm).

to verify information in the country of origin. The main exceptions were the Scottish Court Service and Crown Office Procurator Fiscal Service, which do have a system in place and are working towards the monitoring of interpreters in court. This example of good practice is further illustrated by the publication of new guidelines by the Scottish Criminal Justice System (2008), which build on earlier documentation.

Type of service

Overall, it was evident that many PSBs were still struggling to provide basic TICS support and most still neglected more specialized types of support, such as provision for Deafblind people.

Interpreting was the main type of support requested and, particularly, face-to-face (liaison or dialogue) interpreting was identified as a need by 86% of respondents. There is also a demand for telephone interpreting (as declared by 34% of respondents) and an emerging one for video-conferencing interpreting (3% of respondents articulated this need). Fewer than 1% of respondents specified simultaneous interpreting (which may be perceived to relate specifically to conference work). (See Table 1 for further details).

Translation was indicated as a need by 48% of PSBs. However, only one PSB had as many requests for translation as for interpreting and the demand for communication support (CS) was higher than that for translation. It was, however, acknowledged that PSBs may be failing to make clients aware of what could be translated "on request" and, more generally, of providing access to information in languages other than English. One small, but significant, point identified in the study is that any indication that a translated version of a document is available or can be requested appears, almost without exception, at the end of the English-language document and is often only given in English.

The possibilities of alternative services (e.g. relay interpreting) or new technology were rarely addressed by PSBs. The idea of using video-interpreting was very rarely explored and machine translation was never mentioned as a potential cost-effective, quick means of giving some access to a written text (at least in gist form).

In the study, it was also observed that when a distinction was made between BSL and spoken languages, the demand for BSL was three times greater. However, it is important to reiterate that this may not reflect true need, but rather highlights the fact that BSL is more "professionalized" in the public sector and, consequently, there is more reliance on "formal" (i.e. "counted") provision. As stated above, the professional body of sign language interpreters (SASLI) is well-established and recognized and the Register held by this body is widely known – even by those who do not require any BSL provision. Nevertheless, when information is made available in "alternative formats" (e.g. Braille, large print), video/DVD versions in BSL are very rarely part of the provision.

Services	Number of responses (maximum no. of responses possible = 108)
None (formal)	7
Interpreting	3
Face-to-face interpreting	93
Simultaneous interpreting	1
Telephone interpreting	37
Video-conference interpreting	3
Sight translation	1
Translation	51
Written transcription	18
Minute-taking (different language)	2
Note-taking (same language)	9
Subtitling (different language)	2
Dubbing (voice-over)	0
Video format	2
Audio format	1
Telephoning	2
Facilitating	1

Table 1. Type of services required by PSBs

Languages

The spread of languages requested by PSBs varies from a single language (11%), through 1-5 languages (45%), up to the maximum cited of 120 languages (a single respondent in the Glasgow area).

The 20 most requested languages (at the time of study in 2004) were, in descending order: Urdu, Punjabi, Arabic, BSL,[12] Chinese (non-specified, plus Cantonese and Mandarin cited separately), French, Spanish, Russian, Turkish, Kurdish Surani, Farsi, Portuguese, Bengali, Hindi, German, Polish, Italian, Asian languages (as one category), Somali and Dutch.

---

[12] Some PSBs stated that they had also received requests for foreign sign languages (e.g. Bengali).

There is also a shift in the pattern of languages requested, which reflects the political situation at a global level (i.e. events occurring on the world stage). An increase in certain languages was reported. The five most common responses, in descending order, were: Arabic, European languages (as one category), Kurdish, Mandarin and French.[13] One of the respondents cited Arabic as a *new* language needed to interact with clients. However, the experience of a number of PSBs contradicted these findings, as they reported a decrease in Arabic and Kurdish (the top two languages cited in the languages decreasing). These findings illustrate the fluctuations in language demand at a local level, which may be attributable to the movement of people within Scotland.

PSBs tend to rely on a number of different strategies or aids to identify the languages required. Those reported (in descending order of frequency) were: language identification card, posters and other published material, such as leaflets, displaying information in several languages, referral and contacts, personal documentation of user, information provided by the telephone interpreting service or a "process of elimination". Unfortunately, the strategies adopted are not always successful. For example, PSBs relying on personal documentation tend to identify a person with a country, which can lead to errors in the language requested from TICS services. In addition, many of the language aids rely on literacy or the existence of a writing system and, consequently, these exclude non-English speakers who are illiterate or whose language has no written form. The suggestion is that an online, visual system would be more user-friendly.

Overall, the data collected pointed to an increase in demand for TICS services across languages which was explained by an increased awareness of services and less stigma felt by non-English-language users of Public Services, as well as by more awareness on the part of PSBs of the need to provide access.

Matching

Another area lacking clarity is the matching of interpreters to a particular client. Some PSBs rely on "common sense", whereas others rely on advice from TICS providers as to whether "matching" is necessary. Of those able to give an answer, only 40% of PSBs interviewed had a policy on the

---

[13] This was not limited to French as spoken in France, but includes other countries (e.g. African countries).

matching of interpreters, compared with 54% who said they had no such policy in place.[14] A practical difficulty related to matching was perceived to be the amount of information which could be disclosed in advance to facilitate the process without compromising confidentiality (especially in small or close-knit communities).

Issues taken into consideration for matching, as mentioned by PSBs, are, in decreasing order of frequency: gender, communication needs of client, ethnic, cultural and social backgrounds, suitability to setting/situation, requests or preferences expressed by users (including the PSB user), special requirements (e.g. same interpreter to ensure continuity, or need to employ someone from outside the local area), religion, age, skill level and caste. It is interesting to note the low priority given to skill level, but this may be coloured by the difficulty of obtaining a trained interpreter for certain language combinations or in rural locations, in which cases identifying a speaker of the language required becomes the key consideration.

The high priority given to gender is not unexpected, but it should be noted that emphasis was given to obtaining female interpreters for female clients, rather than male interpreters for male clients. For example, even in medical situations, it is unusual for prisons to request a male interpreter for a male inmate.

The research revealed a dilemma regarding non-discrimination: it was felt inappropriate for any interpreter to "refuse to interpret" on the basis of the ethnicity of the end-user, although end-users were permitted to raise objections with regard to the interpreter. It was, however, accepted that interpreters had the right to refuse to interpret in certain sensitive situations (e.g. termination of pregnancy).

Meeting demand

Of the 45% of PSBs that claimed that they always managed to fulfil requests for TICS services, a few qualified these claims in a way which actually suggested unsatisfied needs ("all those that are requested", received "during office hours" or provided "one way or another"), while one admitted that "in the majority of cases, TICS services were provided by the family".

The main reason for not meeting TICS requests given by the remaining PSBs was short-notice or issues linked with time scale. The shortage of interpreters was often mentioned, and not just the shortage of interpreters

---

[14] The remaining 6% of respondents did not provide an answer.

in unusual dialects, but also in long-established languages in the UK (e.g. Cantonese) and majority European languages, such as French. The lack of interpreters in the languages required, or the lack of suitable interpreters, fed into time-scale problems, geographical constraints and all the other issues, such as matching of interpreters. There were also challenges presented by the failure to flag up the need for TICS support at the appropriate point in the process.

Budgetary constraints were *not* generally cited as a barrier to TICS provision. Almost two-thirds of PSBs (60%) stated that there were no budget constraints on TICS for interpreting and that "if interpreting were needed it would be provided", even if over budget. In contrast, it was felt that there might be constraints for translation work and even problems for interpreting, if the demand for services increases.

The main barriers to using "formal" professional providers (as opposed to in-house staff or family) mentioned are: the lack of information about existing providers across all PSB representatives who were interviewed, the lack of awareness of interpreting issues (e.g. inappropriate nature of using children, other family members, or people from the community) and the misplaced belief (or misconception) that any person fluent in two languages can interpret successfully and to professional standards – or, as put forth in some cases, even "safely".

4.   Conclusions

Challenges

Many participants in the research acknowledged the lack of joined-up thinking and disparity in service provision across Scotland, expressing a wish for a coherent TICS policy and mechanisms for sharing information both within and between the organisations concerned.

A significant challenge identified is the lack of planning or strategy set against the growth of needs in TICS – both in volume and diversity – across the full spectrum of communication. This is aggravated by a lack of evidence and research to underpin strategy or inform decision-making.

An associated challenge is the lack of awareness of the needs of certain user groups. This is compounded by the failure to invest in solutions offered by new technologies or to adopt alternative means of delivering a service where beneficial.

Other challenges relate more specifically to the participants in the

TICS process, in particular the lack of information and of training for all concerned: TICS professionals and practitioners, employees in the public sector and non-English-language end-users.

Overall, it transpired that there is a lack of quality control and a need to improve assessment procedures and standards. In relation to this, the low status and lack of career prospects for those providing TICS in the public sector also needs to be addressed.

A central finding of the research is that examples of good practice are often grounded in collaborative working. Evidence also showed that it is important that developments are informed by feedback from end-users. It is also vital to include the trainers and the researchers in the debate, as practice needs to be informed by theoretical underpinning.

A TICS Model

On the basis of the research study and recommendations and observations made by contributors, the authors have drafted a model (see Figure 1) which it is proposed would respond to current and future challenges. It would also respond to the plea voiced by users of TICS for a central point for information and advice and a one-door approach for all TICS needs.

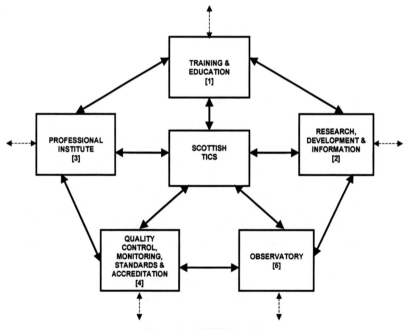

Figure 1. A TICS Model

There should be networking between all branches of this model to ensure coherence and "joined up thinking", as well as external liaison and cooperation with Scottish public sector bodies and other interested parties and with those with similar interests across the UK and internationally.

However, the model would not include the actual provision of services to maintain impartiality and objectivity and to counter fears, as expressed in the course of the data collection, about users being "held to ransom" by any powerful provider.

It is evident that adequate funding and resources must be made available for all aspects of the model.

[1]   Education and training

The role of this unit would not be to provide the actual training, but rather to provide a coherent framework for and comprehensive information about the education and training available at all levels:

- – academic: in Further Education (FE) and Higher Education (HE)
- – vocational: in the workplace or FE Colleges
- – continuing professional development (CPD): in the workplace, through private providers (both freelance individuals and organisations specializing in the provision of training) and the FE and HE sectors

This would include training especially designed for TICS providers (including bilingual workers, i.e. workers who provide a public service in the language of the service user), but also for users of TICS services: both non-English-language users and those working in the public sector.

Provision should be mapped onto a recognized system, such as the Scottish Credit and Qualifications Framework (SCQF), which already captures all school, FE and HE qualifications.[15] One function of this unit might be to help verify the level of provision as described by providers. In addition to helping source the training available and indicating its "level", this "map" would help identify where there is existing provision and where there are gaps. This, in turn, would help ensure an adequate progression of training in TICS, so as to ensure that, once the basic core skills have been addressed, the focus is shifted to other skills, thus broadening out areas of expertise.

---

[15] See http://www.scqf.org.uk/downloads/QualsCrossBoundaries_Sco.pdf.

The unit would also act as a depository or virtual catalogue or library of information regarding the teaching and learning materials available (potentially worldwide).

The remit of the unit would also be to promote the development of study programmes and learning and teaching resources – especially where gaps have been identified. One gap already identified in Scotland is the "training of the trainers".

Finally, a learning and teaching fund should be established so that grants or bursaries can be provided to facilitate training.

[2]   Research, development and information

The role of this unit would be, on the one hand, to gather and collate information and, on the other hand, to enable initiatives to be taken forward.

It would act as a depository and source of information about all aspects of research and development. A "virtual library" or index or bibliography would provide information about research work already completed or in progress, as well as relevant results and findings from around the world.

It would also provide a central point for information about conferences, funding opportunities and research grants.

Moreover, it would promote empirical research and applied research, including the development of curricula and materials. A "forward plan" of work required (short and long-term) identifying areas which need investigation could be drafted.

The unit would play a very active role in fostering a research climate in collaboration with HE institutions and other research bodies (e.g. publishing a research newsletter or journal, arranging seminars and guest speakers, and acting as a forum for discussion). As a unit, it would collaborate in research projects at national and international levels.

A research fund should be established to enable research to be taken forward.

[3]   Professional institute

The primary role of this unit would be to support members of the various TICS professions, but also to act as a source of information about the role and function of these professionals to those working in the public sector and to members of the general public. The unit would also promote good professional working practices.

The unit would seek to raise awareness of the TICS professions and be active in ensuring that the status of TICS providers working in the public sector is recognized. The unit would lobby the authorities and PSBs regarding issues of concern as appropriate.

It would collect and collate relevant data available internationally for information and comparison purposes, as well as make recommendations regarding working conditions and pay scales.

The unit would also act as a repository for examples of good practice, initiatives, new codes of practice or ethics, and so on, from around the world. A central aspect of its function would be to provide general advice to TICS professionals (e.g. regarding ethical dilemmas or problems related to work) and to be able to facilitate counselling and support for TICS personnel working in challenging areas.

More generally, the unit would act as a central information point for people seeking a TICS service – advising them and directing towards the range of appropriate providers for their needs. Consequently, it should be able to identify requests for services which cannot be met, which would aid forward planning. It would also liaise with appropriate bodies to advise members of the public regarding their rights to TICS support.

The unit could also co-ordinate the establishment of a central bibliography or bank of materials already translated or of links to these materials.

[4] Quality control, monitoring, standards and accreditation

This unit would be responsible for developing and overseeing a coherent system for quality control, monitoring, standards and accreditation.

In liaison with existing professional bodies and appropriate organisations, the unit would develop a framework for a clear career structure which would log all existing job descriptions and indicate where new levels should appear. This framework would encompass all levels of TICS practitioners, from those offering the most basic skills to the most qualified. The authors recommend the introduction of a pathway for working towards "chartered status". As some TICS professionals (e.g. translators and telephone interpreters) work across international boundaries, liaison with bodies outside Scotland would be appropriate.

The unit would collaborate in the development of tools for evaluating the skills of TICS providers and providing mentoring support. This unit would act as a governing body for the profession: a central Scottish Register of TICS practitioners would be established (but not to the exclusion of other registers) and criteria developed for continuing membership and monitoring. The unit would also take responsibility for ensuring that police checks have been completed through Disclosure Scotland[16] and would institute a system of quality control.

A central Register of TICS providers would be held by this unit and would indicate the level of accreditation, based on recruitment and selection procedures, CPD opportunities, working practices and standards, record-keeping, etc. Members would also be requested to collect a range of data to feed back to Scottish TICS (e.g. so that fluctuations and especially gaps in provision can be identified).

Acting independently of any service or training provider, employer or professional body, the unit would have the role of watchdog or ombudsman and could function as a safe, neutral point of contact for users or providers of TICS services who have a concern or complaint about any individual or organisation.

[5]   Observatory

The present reality is that a significant quantity of TICS support is provided by "informal providers". Most of the provision is not recorded and is not declared, which means that much of the real demand for TICS services is hidden below the surface. The role of this unit would be to conduct detailed and ongoing needs analyses by region, sector, type of provision, including new and emerging trends (e.g. telephone interpreting, relay interpreting, machine translation, etc.), possibly also by user-group and type of communication need. It is vital that this unit aims to identify and quantify unmet needs.

Finally, the unit would also be responsible for disseminating results to inform developments and reform policy.

[6]   Scottish TICS

The system would be centrally coordinated to ensure overall coherence and parity across the whole communication spectrum, as well as to ensure accessibility. There would be no geographic restrictions on access, as the system would primarily be virtual, which would also enable networking across national and international boundaries.

---

[16] The body which provides a "disclosure service to enhance security, public safety and the protect the vulnerable in society" (www.disclosurescotland.co.uk/index.htm).

[7]   Final comment

The proposed TICS Model could be accused of being excessively ambitious and, therefore, unrealistic or, alternatively, of being merely a wish list. However, it has the virtue of being based on a robust study which captured an extensive range and detail of quantitative, as well as qualitative, data that can stand as the evidence on which policy makers inevitably insist. The research findings reflect the views of a wide range and number of people involved in the TICS chain: a significant cross-section of employees in the public sector, at grassroots levels and at policy level, located across the entire country, and an almost comprehensive representation of all TICS providers in Scotland. They are also informed by a number of other studies collecting the views of TICS service users (Alexander *et al.* 2004; Kyle 2004; Scottish Consumer Council 2005) and supported by other recent studies, such as the recommendation by the *Scottish Refugee Integration Forum Key Action (8)* that "a national certification/accreditation body for interpreters should be established" (SRIF 2003).

It is acknowledged that the provision of TICS in the public services in Scotland (as is the case in many countries) is hugely complex and widely disparate, but a sense of movement and of positive progress has also been remarked on. It may be that the implementation of legislation (such as the *Race Relations (Amendment) Act* 2000 and the *Disability Discrimination Act* 1995) has been driving forward this progress, but the study also noted that it seems that where good practices have been introduced, these are drawing in other departments up or downstream, as well as neighbouring organizations.

However, having captured a "snapshot" of TICS provision through the study, it is important that the momentum which has built up should keep developments moving forwards in a coherent manner. Otherwise, there is a danger of various organizations spinning off in their own direction: some "reinventing the wheel" which others have already invested in creating, some inventing conflicting systems, while many gaping holes remain in the overall design. This cannot be an effective use of scarce and increasingly strained resources.

The overarching TICS Model presented in this paper incorporates the views of contributors to the research project who expressed their "manifesto" for the future. In an ideal world, the next stage must be to map the model onto a timeframe to create a forward plan.

References

Alexander, C., R. *Edwards, B. Temple, U. Kanani, L. Zhuang, M. Miah and A. Sam* (2004) *Access to Services with Interpreters. User Views,* York: Joseph Rowntree Foundation.

CILT, The National Centre for Languages (2006) *National Occupational Standards in Interpreting,* London: CILT www.cilt.org.uk/standards/interpreting.htm.

------ (2007) *National Occupational Standards in Translation,* London: CILT www.cilt.org.uk/standards/translation.htm

General Register Office for Scotland (2005) *Scotland's Census Results Online,* www.scrol.gov.uk/scrol/.

Kyle, J., A.M. Reilly, L. Allsop, M. Clark and A. Dury (2004) *Investigation of Access to Public Services in Scotland Using British Sign Language,* Edinburgh: Scottish Executive.

Lo Bianco, Joseph (2001) *Language and Literacy Policy in Scotland,* Stirling: Scottish CILT.

McPake, Joanna (2003) *Community Languages in Scotland: March 2003,* Stirling: Centre for Information on Language Teaching (CILT), www.cilt. org.uk/commlangs/policy/scotland.htm.

Perez, I.A. and C.W.L. Wilson (2006a) *Translating, Interpreting and Communication Support: A Review of Provision in the Public Services in Scotland.* Edinburgh: Scottish Executive Social Research www.scotland.gov.uk/Resource/Doc/90506/0021781.pdf.

Perez, I.A. and C.W.L. Wilson (2006b) *Translating, Interpreting and Communication Support: A Review of Provision in the Public Services in Scotland (Research Findings),* Edinburgh: Scottish Executive Social Research www. scotland.gov.uk/Resource/Doc/90537/0021782.pdf.

Race Equality Advisory Forum (2001) *Making it Real: A Race Equality Strategy for Scotland. Race Equality Advisory Forum Report. October 2001,* Edinburgh: Scottish Executive.

Scottish Association of Sign Language Interpreters (2002) *Creating Linguistic Access for Deaf and Deafblind People: A Strategy for Scotland,* Edinburgh: Scottish Association of Sign Language Interpreters.

Scottish Consumer Council (2005) *Is Anybody Listening? The User Perspective on Interpretation and Translation Services for Minority Ethnic Communities.* Glasgow: Scottish Consumer Council.

Scottish Executive (2002) *Towards an Equality Strategy: Grassroots Consultation with Ethnic Minorities,* Edinburgh: Scottish Executive.

------ (2003a) *A Partnership for a Better Scotland: Partnership Agreement,* Edinburgh: Scottish Executive.

------ (2003b) *Community Care Services for Adults with a Sensory Impairment – An Action Plan,* Edinburgh: Scottish Executive.

------ (2003c) *Making Progress: Equality Annual Report*, Edinburgh: Scottish Executive.

SRIF (2003) *Scottish Refugee Integration Forum. Action Plan*, Edinburgh: HMSO

The Working Group on Interpreting and Translation (2008) *Code of Practice for Working with Interpreters in the Scottish Criminal Justice System,* Edinburgh: Scottish Criminal Justice System, www.copfs.gov.uk/Resource/Doc/13928/0000467.pdf.

Thomson, Lindsay (2004) *An Evaluation of Appropriate Adults Schemes in Scotland. Research Findings No.78/2004*, Edinburgh: Scottish Executive.

Wilson, C.W.L. and R. McDade (2008) "From Small Acorns: The Scottish Experience of Developing Interpreter and Translator Training", in J. Napier (ed.) *Signed Language Interpreter Education and Training: A World Survey, Interpreter Education Vol. 4*, Washington, DC: Gallaudet University Press.

www.disclosurescotland.co.uk/index.htm.

Legal texts

Disability Discrimination Act 1995 (c.50). HMSO.
Human Rights Act 1998. HMSO.
Race Relations (Amendment) Act 2000. HMSO.
Gaelic Language (Scotland) Act 2005 (asp 7). HMSO.
Scotland Act 1998. HMSO.

"Top-down" or "Bottom-up"?

Language Policies in Public Service Interpreting in the Republic of Ireland, Scotland and Spain

BERNADETTE O'ROURKE & PEDRO CASTILLO

Centre for Translation and Interpreting Studies in Scotland, Heriot-Watt University, Edinburgh, UK

Abstract. *Economic prosperity along with ensuing labour shortages and a marked increase in the number of asylum seekers and political refugees have had a significant impact on the ethnic and linguistic make-up of many of our societies. The past number of years has witnessed a renewed interest in issues of language policy and planning, emerging from these changes, where nation-states are becoming more varied, diverse and at the same time more global. Language policy and planning initiatives in the area of public sector interpreting in Ireland, Scotland and Spain are examined in this paper. All three contexts offer examples of cases where there has been a marked increase in the number of economic immigrants, refugees and asylum seekers in recent years. Language policy and planning measures which regulate for the provision of interpreting services to non-indigenous ethnic minority language groups in all three contexts are critically explored. This paper explores both overt and covert "top-down" policies at government and institutional level, as well as "bottom-up" and grassroots initiatives taking place to resist, protest about or negotiate declared language policies and to propose alternatives.[1]*

1. Introduction

Over the past few years there has been renewed interest in issues of language policy and language planning as a result of changes in society's linguistic landscapes and due to nation-states becoming more varied, more diverse and more global. Although language policy is an established area of study, there has been surprisingly little research which critically explores policies that regulate the quality and provision of translation and interpreting services in multilingual communities. This paper focuses on interpreting

---

[1] We wish to acknowledge the valuable insights in relation to PSI provision in Scotland that Isabelle Perez and Christine Wilson contributed to the preparation of this article.

services, and more specifically on Public Sector Interpreting (henceforth PSI) provision in the Republic of Ireland, Scotland and Spain. The aim of the study has been to critically explore language policy which regulates for the provision of PSI to non-indigenous ethnic minority language groups in these three contexts. Both overt and covert "top-down" policies put in place by governments and at institutional levels are examined, as well as "bottom-up" and grass-roots initiatives taking place in each context. Before looking at some of the similarities and differences across the Irish, Scottish and Spanish contexts, it will be useful to look at the area of language policy research more generally and to identify key concepts which will be applied to an analysis of PSI provision in the three cases being studied.

2.   Language policy – key concepts

While noting that no single definition of "language policy" carries universal approval, Bugarski's (1992:18) provides a useful starting point. He defines language policy as "the policy of a society in the area of linguistic com-munication – that is, the set of positions, principles and decisions reflecting that community's relationships to its verbal repertoire and communicative potential". In a language policy, such positions, principles and decisions often take the form of rules, regulations or guidelines about the status, use, domains and territories of language(s) and rights of speakers of the language(s) in question. In the literature in the field (see Schiffman 1996; Spolsky 2004; Ricento 2005) language policy tends to be dichotomized into overt and covert. Overt language policy includes identifiable statements outlining the rights of an individual or language group to use their language in whatever domains they specify. This type of policy is, therefore, explicit, formalized and often *de jure* or by law. Covert language policies, on the other hand, make no explicit mention of language in any legal document or in administrative codes. Therefore, the guarantees of language rights of speakers and language users must be inferred from other policies, constitu-tions or provisions. These policies are thus implicit, informal, unstated, *de facto* and very often grass-roots.

A language policy, whether explicitly or implicitly stated, reflects the ideological views and orientations of a society, government, institutions or individuals. As Spolsky (2004:14) points out, "language ideology is lan-guage policy with the manager left out, what people think should be done [with language]". Therefore, it is possible to infer from language policy decisions or statements what the ideological orientation of a society is in relation to assumptions about a specific language or language in general. In some cases, ideologies may reflect a society's belief that linguistic homogeneity is beneficial to society and thus favour linguistic and cultural assimilation. In other cases, ideologies may reflect tolerance towards linguistic diversity.

Drawing on the above framework and concepts, the remainder of this article looks comparatively at language policy in the area of PSI in the Republic of Ireland, Scotland and Spain. In doing so, attempts are made to answer three key questions:

1. Is PSI included as an overt or covert policy in these three contexts?
2. Is language policy "top-down" or "bottom-up"?
3. What types of ideologies are reflected in language policy statements or provisions which deal specifically with the provision of PSI?

The comparative focus of this study does not lend itself to detailed analysis of the Irish, Scottish or Spanish contexts. Such analysis can be found elsewhere (see Perez and Wilson 2006 for PSI in Scotland, Phelan 2007 for PSI in the Republic of Ireland, Molina 2006 and Abril Martí 2006 for PSI in Spain). Instead, the focus of this paper is on identifying general policy trends and on highlighting broad similarities and differences across three cases which have not previously been studied from a comparative perspective. In identifying such similarities and differences, the study also draws on Ozolins' (2000) cross-national model for classifying PSI provision in different parts of the world. As Ozolins (*ibid.*:33) highlights , because PSI is still a pre-theoretical and in many instances pre-professional state of development, more extensive comparative research is required to further the development of interpreting as a profession. Through a comparative analysis of PSI provision in the Republic of Ireland, Scotland and Spain, the present article offers new insights into different models developed in countries where communication barriers exist between public sector providers and people wishing to avail of services whose language is not that of the host country.

In his proposed model, Ozolins (*ibid.*) identifies four types of responses offered by individual countries to meet the communication needs of linguistic minorities in multilingual settings. Such responses range from the most negative case scenario in which there is a total denial on the part of government administration of the need to provide PSI, to the most favourable situation in which explicit policy measures are in place to ensure that PSI provision becomes an integral part of public service provision more generally. Between these two extremes, Ozolins (*ibid.*) identifies two other response types. At the lower end of scale are government responses which provide *ad hoc* solutions to PSI provision as the need for such provision arises. At the higher end of the scale is a category which includes countries in which there is provision for linguistic services but, in difference to the highest point in Ozolins' proposed categorisation, such provision is not necessarily long term and PSI does not form an integral part of public service provision.

3.   Linguistic diversity in the Republic of Ireland, Scotland and Spain

Historically, linguistic diversity has been a characteristic of Irish, Scottish and Spanish societies. The Republic of Ireland has two official languages, Irish and English, and the island of Ireland is also home to other native languages, including Ulster Scots, Irish Sign Language and Gammon or Cant (a language historically known to and used by Irish Travellers). As well as English, which is the language spoken by the majority of the population, Scotland has two long-standing autochthonous languages, Scottish Gaelic and Scots, as well as British Sign Language, also a language native to Scotland. Similar to Ireland and Scotland, Spain has a history of linguistic diversity. Although Spanish is the official language of the Spanish State, three other regional languages hold co-official status with Spanish within their respective Autonomous Communities. These are Catalan, Galician and Basque, language communities which Turrell (2001:4) refers to as the larger "established" linguistic minorities in Spain. Spain is also home to a number of smaller established language groups including Astur-Leonés or Bable, Valencian, Occitan, Caló (the language spoken by the Gitano or Gypsy community), as well as the different varieties of Judeo-Español, labelled Ladino in Spain and Jaletía in Ceuta and Melilla.

Over recent decades, as a result of increased migration into these three countries, new modes of linguistic change have begun to appear on their respective languages markets. Indeed, in a recent EU report on linguistic diversity in different EU countries (see McPake and Tinsley 2007), the three states reporting the highest number of additional languages were the UK (288), Spain (198) and Ireland (158). If we take Scotland as a separate entity within the UK, it is estimated that over 150 languages are spoken there in addition to the autochthonous ones. Because Scotland (and the UK more generally) has a long history of immigration linked to Britain's colonial past leading to the presence of languages from former colonies (such as Urdu, Cantonese and Bengali) since the 1960s, the findings of the EU report are not unexpected. In the 2001 Census, around 2% of the Scottish population claimed a minority ethnic background, describing themselves as having Indian, Pakistani, other South Asian or Chinese ethnic backgrounds (Perez and Wilson 2006:14-17).

Compared to Scotland, which, as stated above has a somewhat longer history of immigration and non-indigenous ethnic minority languages, increased linguistic diversity in the Republic of Ireland and Spain is a much more recent phenomenon. For most of the 20th century, Ireland and Spain were countries of emigration rather than of immigration. Up until the 1980s, Ireland, for example, reported the highest levels of emigration in the European Union. However, over the past two decades this trend has been reversed and now the country has one of highest net immigration levels in the EU. It is estimated that in the six year period between 1996 and 2002, over 250,000 people went to live in Ireland and almost fifty per cent of these were born outside Ireland. This contrasts with corresponding figures from half a century ago. Redmond (in Cronin and Ó Cuilleanáin 2002:9) notes that in 1946 only 0.5% of the population was born outside Ireland and even 50 years later this percentage was still a mere 1.5%.

In Spain and the Republic of Ireland alike, economic resurgence, coupled with global shifts in patterns of migration have brought about a marked change in their respective linguistic landscapes over a very short period of time. An indication of the level of linguistic diversity in Ireland can be gauged from looking at the national origins of the most significant groups in terms of numbers receiving work permits in the period from January to October 2002. They include Latvians (3,409), Lithuanians (3,273), Filipinos (2,680), Poles (2,676), South Africans (1,937), Romanians (2,054), Ukrainians (1,786), Czechs (957), Russians (1,037) and Malaysians (956) (Dooley, in Cronin and Ó Cuilleanáin 2002). However, as Cronin and Ó Cuilleanáin (*ibid.*) point out, this does not represent the full extent of linguistic diversity and such figures do not reflect, of course, the substantial numbers of EU nationals living and working and studying in Ireland, among whom French, German, Dutch, Italian and Spanish citizens are the most numerous.

The linguistic profile of immigrant groups in Spain is somewhat different. According to Turrell (2001) there are as many as 47 migrant minority groups in Spain. From this figure she excludes Spanish-speaking South American migrants, a group which differs culturally from the host country, but has marked similarities with the native population in broad linguistic terms. Therefore, despite differences in accent and vocabulary, the linguistic barriers which exist between South American migrants and the Spanish indigenous population are minimal. Non-Spanish speaking migrant groups are made up of European minorities – particularly people from Rumania and Bulgaria (530,786), the UK (269,460), Germany (159,922) and other EU immigrants (546,938) –, African minorities – in particular from Morocco (539,773), with other African immigrants accounting for (227,815) (see INE:2007) –, as well as communities from North America – the US (15,661) – and from South America – Brazil (5,694) – and three from Asia, namely the Philippines (11,770), China (10,816) and India (6,882) (see Turrell 2001:10).

Over several decades, the main community languages spoken in Scotland and in Britain more generally have been those of the Indian sub continent: Bengali, Gujarati, Hindi, Punjabi and Urdu. Although Scotland has a long history of additional languages, there is also evidence of increasing diversification in this trend. During the first decade of the 21st century, the policy of dispersal of asylum seekers arriving in the UK[2] (which established the Scottish city of Glasgow as the second city in the UK for the dispersal of asylum seekers) extended the range of countries from which Scottish residents come, as did the enlargement of the European Union, which has enabled more people from Eastern Europe to live and work in Scotland. Reports on educational contexts from local authorities in Scotland where Punjabi and Urdu speakers had previously made up the majority of the bilingual schools now show many more languages in use. It is now not uncommon to find a range of new languages including Polish, Portuguese, Russian, Shona and Tagalog spoken by children at these schools.

4.   Language policy provision for PSI in the Republic of Ireland, Scotland and Spain

Language policy is not new to the Irish, Scottish and Spanish contexts. All three countries have, for varying lengths of time, dealt with language policy issues, particularly in relation to their autochthonous languages. Ireland, for instance, has a history of language policy for the Irish language that dates back to the early 1920s, a period which coincided with the country's political independence and attempts to revitalize Irish as the national language (see Ó Riagáin 1997). Language policy for Irish is overt, appearing in the form of explicit statements in Article 8 of the Irish Constitution, which names

---

[2] *Immigration and Asylum Act* (1999), amended by the *Nationality, Immigration and Asylum Act* (2000).

Irish the first official language of the Irish State and, as such, guarantees its protection by the State. There have been successive language policy statements on the Irish language over the roughly eighty-year period, since the founding of the State, which explicitly express the position of various governments on the Irish language. The most recent significant change at national level has been the 2003 Official Languages Act, a piece of legislation which provides a statutory framework for the delivery of services through the Irish language.

Spain, in comparison, has a shorter history of language policy in support of its autochthonous languages. Such a policy spans a mere three decades: it was put in place in the 1980s, following socio-political changes in Spain that led to the country's transition to democracy in the late 1970s. Prior to this period, language policy statements existed, but they were in favour of a linguistically homogenous Spanish-speaking state. Although there were no policy statements which explicitly outlawed the use of regional languages such as Galician, Catalan and Basque, the very fact that these languages were not mentioned is representative of the lack of support for their use. Moreover, an implicit policy of disregard for these languages can be found in pamphlets distributed in Spanish cities during the years of the dictatorship in Spain (1939-1975), which contained popular catch-cries such as "don't be barbaric – speak Spanish" (Portas Fernández 1997), thus linking these languages with a lack of prestige and value. Since the late 1970s, explicit policy statements which recognize Spain's history of linguistic diversity can be found. For example, Article 3 of the 1978 Spanish Constitution pledges support for Spain's linguistic diversity and promotes the use of the so-called "historical" languages of Spain (Galician, Catalan and Basque) in their respective territories. Spanish is the official language of the State, but these languages hold co-official status within their autonomous communities (see Mar-Molinero 2000).

Scotland has a particular responsibility as custodian of two of its autochthonous languages, Gaelic and Scots, because these languages are seen as being closely linked to the country's cultural heritage and are deemed by the Scottish Government as making a significant contribution to Scotland. Legislation to support Gaelic has existed since 1980 and in April 2005 the Scottish Parliament passed the Gaelic Language Act, recognizing it as one of the official languages of Scotland. Moreover, six public authorities within Scotland[3] have already committed to developing language policies

---

[3] The Scottish Government, The Scottish Parliament, Highlands and Islands Enterprise, The Highland Council, Argyll and Bute Council and Comhairle nan Eilean Siar.

and strategies as part of the implementation process of the new legislation to make Gaelic a functional official language, which, according to Bòrd na Gàidhlig[4] "will mean that Gaelic users can access some public services in their language of choice. It is also expected that public authorities producing Plans will encourage people to use Gaelic when dealing with them, and will expand their organisation's Gaelic services and resources".

5.   Linguistic policy in the context of the Republic of Ireland's, Scotland's and Spain's new linguistic realities

As the previous section highlights, all three contexts have experience of language policy in relation to their autochthonous language communities. However, given the Republic of Ireland's, Spain's and Scotland's changing linguistic landscapes in more recent years as a result of increased immigration, it is of interest to look at the degree to which such changes have led to an expansion of language policy initiatives, as well as a more inclusive language policy to take stock of the changing face of each country's linguistic realities. Perhaps because of Scotland's slightly longer history of immigration (which can be traced back to the 1950s and 1960s), the Scottish Government seems to have a more strongly developed language policy in relation to the country's multilingual reality. Throughout the 1990s and early 2000s, the then called Scottish Executive,[5] encouraged by legislation (*Disability Discrimination Act* 1995, *Human Rights Act* 1998, *Race Relations Amendment Act* 2000), required the mainstreaming of equality across the public sector at local and national levels: a policy paired with a commitment to "promote bilingualism and multilingualism instead of monolingualism" (Scottish Parliament, February 2003). A consultation document entitled, *A Strategy for Scotland's Languages*, produced in 2007 by the then ruling coalition in Scotland, formed by the Scottish Labour Party and the Scottish Liberal Democrat party, also provided an explicit statement of "top-down" support for Scotland's multilingual society inclusive of the entirety of new immigrants. The document (The Scottish Executive 2007:9) states the following:

> We must ensure that existing minority ethnic communities as well as
> new migrants and refugees are able to access public services in their
> own languages where necessary. People living, working or studying

---

[4] See www.bord-na-gaidhlig.org.uk/gaelic-language-plans.html.
[5] The Scottish Executive became the Scottish Government in May 2007.

in Scotland who do not understand English have the same rights to access public sector services as English speakers. We also want to create a supportive environment so that speakers of languages other than English are able to continue to develop their skills in their first language along with English.

However, language policy does not exist in a vacuum and such a policy is always strongly influenced by socio-political and socio-economic changes in the society in which it has been originally formulated (Ó Riagáin 1997; Romaine 2002). The 2007 elections in Scotland saw the coming to power of the Scottish National Party (SNP). The outgoing government, through its working document detailing its proposed strategy for a multilingual Scotland, would seem to have been moving in the direction of consolidating an all inclusive language policy for the country. However, this document has not been taken forward as a coherent, comprehensive strategy by the SNP administration, whose linguistic focus seems to be more strongly directed towards Scotland's autochthonous languages and, in particular, Gaelic.

In the Republic of Ireland, there has been a call on the government to state its position in relation to how Ireland's new linguistic realities will be dealt with and a report containing recommendations was drawn up by a steering group and published by the Royal Irish Academy in 2007. The key recommendations outlined in the report are that Ireland should "develop a national strategy for languages... both native and foreign, in Ireland" and that "A National Advisory Body should be established to liaise with language professionals, politicians and all stakeholders in society. This body would research the changing linguistic needs of society, and propose a suitable language strategy" (see Ó Dochartaigh and Broderick 2006:9). Although government discourse would not seem explicitly unfavourable towards linguistic diversity *per se*, political debate in Ireland has often tended to frame the issue of multilingualism as a "problem which needs to be solved", seeing the acquisition of English as an additional language as the main solution to resolving "problems" associated with the management of a linguistically diverse society. At a national level, for example, there is no explicit endorsement on the part of the Irish State of immigrants' linguistic rights and the maintenance or development of their own languages.

Similarly to the situation in the Republic of Ireland, there is a lack of unified policy statements in relation to language on the part of the Spanish State. This lack of unification can perhaps be explained by Spain's decentralized political system. Policy decisions in relation to health, education, employment, housing, and even justice are, for example, made at regional level by the governments of Spain's individual Autonomous Communities. In Autonomous Communities where an autochthonous language (namely, Galician, Basque and Catalan) holds co-official status alongside the Spanish language, policies tend to centre on the maintenance or revitalization of these languages amongst members of their respective communities. However, language policies dealing with the maintenance of non-indigenous minority languages now spoken in different parts of Spain are given significantly less attention, and even less so with respect to the provision of PSI. Similar to the Irish context, as Barragán (in Abril Martí 2006:107) notes, the management of linguistic diversity has been largely limited to the teaching of Spanish as an additional language.

6.   Language policy provisions for PSI

In the absence of unified, direct statements as regards linguistic diversity, it is not surprising that, when it comes to policy specific to the provision of PSI, the Irish, Scottish and Spanish approach tends to be covert rather than overt. The governments in these three contexts would seem to rely mainly on other policy statements to deal with issues relating to the provision of services to speakers of non-indigenous ethnic minority languages. In Scotland, the establishment of the *Translation, Interpreting and Communication Support* (TICS) Group in 2000 to guide developments in the provision of PSI in Scotland provides an exception to this trend. This group commissioned two important pieces of research: a literature review of translating, interpreting and communication support services across the public sector (see McPake *et al.* 2002) and an overview of the provision of translating, interpreting and communication support in the public sector in Scotland (see Perez and Wilson 2006). The 2007 consultation document (*A Strategy for Scotland's Languages*) produced by the Scottish Executive marks another significant initiative in recognition of Scotland's linguistic diversity. It is also worth noting that an analysis of the specific recommendations within the document reveals explicit references to PSI provision. The document (*The Scottish Executive* 2007:15) states that, in Scotland, the government will ensure fair and equal linguistic access to information and services and goes on to say that:

> There are policies in place which seek to ensure that all Scottish residents for whom English or Gaelic is not a first language should have access to alternative language provisions where necessary in

order to enable them to access services and provide opportunities for them to participate in Scottish life. Scottish public bodies should seek to provide access to high quality translation, interpretation and communication support services in order to ensure fair and accessible services for everyone. It is also important that communication strategies are developed for people with communication support needs. Language should not act as a barrier to awareness of, or access to, services and opportunities by considering the needs of the target audience and ensuring that information and publicity material is available in a range of languages and formats.

Apart from this explicit reference to PSI in the Scottish context, quite generally, unified direct policy statements regarding such provision are absent in the Republic of Ireland, Scotland and Spain alike. The obligation to provide PSI is stipulated by the *European Convention of Human Rights* in the form of the *Human Rights Act* of 2003, whose Article 5.2 makes reference to a person's right to liberty and security and states that "Everyone who is arrested shall be informed promptly, in a language which he understands of the reasons for his arrest and of any charge against him". Furthermore, Article 6.3 of the same Act refers to a person's right to a fair trial and in linguistic terms is also significant stating that:

Everyone charged with a criminal offence has the following minimum rights: To be informed promptly, in a language which he understands and in detail, of the nature and cause of the accusation against him ... To have the free assistance of an interpreter if he cannot understand or speak the language used in court.

The influence of the Human Rights Act on legal specific domains may in part explain why PSI provision in the courts sector (while not reaching its full potential by any means) constitutes the public service division in the Republic of Ireland, Scotland and Spain where most provision exists (see Phelan 2007 for specific details on the Republic of Ireland; Foulquié Rubio 2002, Martin 2000 and 2004, Abril Martí 2006 and Molina 2006 for Spain; and Perez and Wilson 2006 for Scotland). Moreover, at national levels, case law and constitutional provisions which regulate for the provision of PSI (see Phelan 2007 for more details for the Irish context; Arróniz 2000, Sali 2003 and Abril Martí 2006 for Spain; Perez and Wilson 2006 for Scotland) reinforce policy initiatives in place at European level. Nevertheless, even in the area of justice, particularly in the Irish (Phelan *op. cit.*) and Spanish (Abril Martí *op. cit.*:107, 129) contexts, the effectiveness of PSI provision is sometimes questionable. Although the related area of policing receives a relatively high level of provision in Scotland (see Perez and Wilson 2006), such provision is considerably less regulated by national policy statements in the cases of the Republic of Ireland and Spain. Phelan (2007), for example, notes that although in theory the *European Convention on Human Rights Act* stipulates the right to an interpreter in a Garda Síochána (Irish police) station, there is no explicit mention of this right in the 1984 *Criminal Justice Act* and, although regulations introduced in 1987 mention the provision of interpreting services for sign languages, non-indigenous ethnic minority language groups are not mentioned. Even though later documents and guidelines make reference to the provision of interpreting services, in practice such guidelines are not always followed through. This, therefore, signals mixed messages about any possible intention to take real action relating to the provision of interpreting services in Irish policing. It is worth noting, for example, that there is no mention of interpreting in the *Garda Síochána Corporate Strategy* 2005-2007. In a somewhat similar vein, Abril Martí (2006:117) notes in the case of Spain that, although immigrants detained by the police have the legal right to an interpreter, in practice, there is little formal regulation in place in terms of the quality of PSI provision and it is often the case that, rather than sourcing qualified interpreters, the institutions use the linguistic resources of other immigrants, asylum seekers or local volunteers in dealings with the police.

Health and education are sectors where explicit policy statements regarding the provision of PSI in the Republic of Ireland, Scotland and Spain are even more scant. Instead of national-based policies and guidelines, policy relating to the provision of PSI in the health sector, for instance, has tended to be institutionally-based and such provision varies from one hospital or health care centre to another. In the absence of top-down policies, the health care sector has tended to be an area in which there have been a considerable number of initiatives at grassroots level through, for example, the creation of booklets in different languages, bilingual leaflets and cards. While such bottom-up policy measures have gone some way towards improving communication between non-indigenous minority language speakers and medical staff, the lack of coordinated guidelines and plans across the health sector means that such practices have not tended to be shared across hospitals, and in some cases even across units within the same hospital.

7.   Ideologies reflected in policy (or lack of policy) for PSI provision

The lack of unified and direct statements on policy in relation to the provision of PSI, particularly in the Irish and Spanish contexts, reflect the belief that the language barriers created by increased immigration to these countries are temporary in nature and the "problems" linked to increased linguistic diversity in the country will be resolved, because eventually everyone will learn the host language.

Even a cursory analysis of reference to PSI in the Irish press provides numerous examples of the "problem-centred" discourse associated with PSI provision. There are, for example, frequent references to the cost of interpreting services. Such costs tend to be exaggerated, with the implication that such spending is a waste of taxpayers' money. Taken one step further, this argument leads to the rationale that, if interpreting is costing the state so much money, then those requiring interpreters should be asked to pay for this service themselves. This opinion was voiced in February 2008 by a justice spokesman from Ireland's main political opposition party, Fine Gael, who reacted strongly to hearing the costs of the interpreting services in Irish courts and called for defendants who are found guilty to be made to shoulder the cost of interpreting themselves (*ITIA Bulletin* 2008:7). While the proposal was rejected following the Immigrant Council of Ireland's questioning of the legal and discriminatory aspects of the proposal, these and other such comments point to the "double" punishments which powerful members of society are prepared to inflict on those who do not speak the language of the host country. The underlying message in this argument is that committing a crime deserves punishment, but a crime committed by a speaker of a language other than that of the host nation deserves extra punishment. A person's need for an interpreter is also linked to laziness and lack of effort on the part of the ethnic minority language speaker to learn and gain competence in the host language.

In 2004 an Irish District Court Judge commented that it was "absolutely ridiculous" to think that anyone living in Ireland for five years could not speak the language and refused to certify for an interpreter for the accused (Galway Advertiser, 11th January 2007, cited in Phelan *op. cit.*:26). The comments of the judge clearly highlight the lack of linguistic understanding on the part of officials, who tend to underestimate the time it takes to master a language, particularly the type of language required for something as specific as the legal domain. Such comments also reflect a deeply engrained monolingual English-language mindset with very little understanding of what it means to learn another language or the need to adapt to the speech variety of another individual or group.

While the above examples are by no means representative of all Irish people's views on how linguistic diversity should be managed, they do nonetheless suggest there are powerful sectors (politicians, judges and the media) within Irish society which undervalue the need for interpreting services. Such attitudes are not specific to the Irish context and Abril Martí's (*op. cit.*: 107) analysis of PSI provision in Spain points to similar ideologies about linguistic diversity, noting that:

> ... for those who do not speak Spanish, the Administration seems to shut its eyes. The attitude is 'if they are going to settle here [in Spain], they will have to learn the language, or, if they want to use their own language then they will have to bring along their own linguistic support. (our translation)

Abril Martí (*ibid.*:111) also notes that, even when the service sectors recognize the fact that interpreters can, in fact, improve communication and break down barriers between the service provider and the person seeking the service, the underlying belief is that the real solution to the "problem" is that the immigrant population should acquire competence in the language of the host country (in this case Spanish). As pointed out above in reference to the Irish case, such a view shows little awareness of the lengthy process and difficulties involved in learning a new language. El-Madkouri and Soto (2002:108), for example, highlight the long term linguistic difficulties encountered by Moroccan immigrants in Spain (even those with high levels of education) who, after spending years in the country, do not achieve a high level of communicative competence in Spanish. Martin (2000:16) is of the view that, in presenting acquisition of the host language as the key solution to managing linguistic diversity, the responsibility of establishing communication is transferred from the administrative services of the host country to the immigrant. Martin (*ibid.*) further suggests that the underlying ideology behind such a rationale is the belief that the host country should not be spending money on a "problem" that it has had no part in creating.

8.   Concluding remarks

A comparison of the relative strength of policy provisions in PSI across the key service areas including legal, educational and health in the Republic of Ireland, Scotland and Spain would seem to suggest that regulations, guidelines and provisions can be categorized as either low to moderate in the Irish and Spanish contexts and moderate to high in the case of Scotland. In line with Ozolins' (*op. cit.*) international four-point scale for assessing PSI provision for linguistic minorities, the Irish and Spanish contexts fall somewhere between the first point on the scale, which includes contexts which provide no solutions for PSI provision or simply deny the need for PSI needs, and the second point, which, while recognizing the need for PSI provision, attempts to resolve communication difficulties through '*ad hoc* solutions'. The method of PSI provision is sporadic and difficulties are dealt with as they arise, but without any real global, long-term plan or top-down policy.

Although PSI provision is to some degree *ad hoc* in many public service bodies in Scotland, more explicit reference to PSI provision in policy statements places the Scottish context closer to the third and fourth point on Ozolins' scale. As explained above, point three on this scale includes contexts in which PSI provision is made to cover (or at least some attempts are made to cover) the linguistic needs emerging from contact between ethnic minority language speakers and public service providers. The somewhat more developed policy statements in Scotland (although much of this takes the form of covert language policies) can be explained to some extent by the country's longer history of immigration. Although in earlier years there was little top-down support, there was an urgency in finding solutions on the ground to manage the new linguistic reality which public service providers were beginning to encounter on a daily basis. At times, this situation management was done in an *ad hoc* way, relying on younger family members who had picked up some knowledge of English in the education system to allow them to interpret for older language speakers. However, even though the mechanisms which were put in place to establish communication between service providers and non-indigenous minority-language speakers were somewhat improvised, they served as models that could inform the government of the kind of top-down policy required to meet the demands on the ground. It would, therefore, seem that, after a forty year period of experience with PSI, discussions about policy provisions had already begun to come to the fore in the 1990s, when the number of immigrants coming into the country saw a dramatic increase. As well as the positive effects of the *European Convention of Human Rights Act* 2003 on PSI provision, which were also felt in the Republic of Ireland and Spain, Scotland saw four other policy initiatives at a national level resulting in a multi-pronged approach, which, arguably, has led to the somewhat more enhanced level of provision of PSI that is currently in place. These policy measures include the *Disability Discrimination Act* 1995, the Scotland Act 1998,[6] the *Immigration and Asylum Act* 1999[7] and the *Race Relations Amendment Act* 2000. Through these policy initiatives, attempts have been made to build in PSI provision as an integral part of the system from the start, thus moving the Scottish context to the highest end of Ozolins' scale. Such initiatives suggest a shift in perspective in addressing communication barriers, moving from the "service provision model" to the "social inclusion model". The service provision model can be described mainly as a reactive model and it involves providing specialist services, such as interpreting and translation, to supplement established procedures. The social inclusion model, in contrast, builds on the view that everyone has a right to information and support, and provision is therefore built into the system from the start. An analysis of the Spanish and Irish[8] contexts would suggest significantly fewer attempts to move towards a social inclusion model and the provision of PSI is still largely at the stage of a service provision type model.

Implicit in the absence of unified statements on policy in relation to the provision of PSI, particularly in the Irish and Spanish contexts, is the ideology that linguistic diversity is a temporary phenomenon and communication "problems" with non-indigenous linguistic minorities will be resolved by the fact that everyone will eventually learn the host language. Based on such a rationale, governments' lack of explicit support for any unified attempt to manage linguistic diversity is, of course, justified. After

---

[6] *The Scotland Act* (1998) was an act which introduced devolution to Scotland and established the Scottish Parliament. The powers it gave to the Scottish Parliament enabled it to encourage equal opportunities and to ensure that Scottish public bodies respect equal opportunities legislation in their work in devolved areas. Such devolved areas include economic development, education, housing, justice and health, local government and transport. It was the Scottish Government's choice at the time to adopt "mainstreaming", but the Scotland Act gave it the power to implement its chosen policies.

[7] *The Immigration and Asylum Act* (1999), amended by the *Nationality, Immigration and Asylum Act* (2002), provides the legal basis for the dispersal of asylum seekers within the UK. Although immigration and asylum are matters dealt with by the central government and are reserved for the Westminster Parliament, refugees arriving in Scotland under the dispersal policy require access to and the support of the devolved services in Scotland.

[8] In the Republic of Ireland, there is a slight move towards a social inclusion model, particularly in light of its National Intercultural Health Strategy, launched by the government in February 2008, which shows initial attempts to build in PSI provision as an integral part of its intercultural health strategy.

all, why should the government invest in and develop a policy for something which it perceives as a temporary phenomenon? This rationale is undoubtedly linked to underlying monolingual linguistic ideologies, typical of many western societies which tend to view linguistic diversity as a "problem". The problem-centred approach to the management of linguistic diversity views those who do not speak the host language as a "burden" to the state and to the host society. The whole process of learning another language and making oneself understood in another language tends to be viewed from a monolingual mindset, leading to the institutionalization of linguistic discrimination. Nevertheless, in the absence of unified "top-down" intervention, similarly to what occurred in the early years of PSI provision in Scotland, there is evidence in the Republic of Ireland and Spain of grassroots initiatives taking place to resist, protest about and negotiate declared language policies, as well as to propose alternatives. In the longer term, these undeclared *de facto* policies at a local or individual level may very well affect declared higher level language policies and stimulate the "top-down" intervention which is required to bring about consolidated change in the provision of PSI.

References

Abril Martí, M. I. (2006) *La Interpretación en los Servicios Públicos: Caracterización como género, contextualización y modelos de formación. Hacia unas bases para el diseño curricular*, unpublished PhD thesis, Granada: Universidad de Granada. hera.ugr.es/tesisugr/16235320.pdf

Arróniz, P. (2000) "La Traducción y la Interpretación en la Administración de Justicia", in D. Kelly (ed.) *La Traducción y la Interpretación en España Hoy: Persepectivas Profesionales*, Granada: Comares, 157-69.

Bugarski, R. (1992) "Language in Yugoslavia: Situation, Policy, Planning", in R. Bugarski and C. Hawkesworth (eds) *Language Planning in Yugoslavia,* Columbus: Slavica, 10-26.

Cronin, M. and C. Ó Cuilleanáin (2002) *Languages of Ireland*, Dublin: Four Courts Press.

El-Madkouri, M. and B. Soto (2002) "La función de la interpretación en una sociedad de recepción (la complejidad lingüístico-cultural en el caso del inmigrante marroquí)", in C. Valero and G. Mancho (eds) *Traducción e Interpretación en los Servicios Públicos: Nuevas Necesidades para Nuevas Realidades,* Alcalá de Henares, Madrid: Universidad de Alcalá-Servicio de Publicaciones, 105-116 [CD-ROM].

Foulquié Rubio, A. I. (2002) "Interpretación social: la interpretación en la policía en Granada y Málaga", *Puentes* (1), Servicio de Publicaciones de la Universidad de Granada, 107-15.

Gaelic Language Plans (last updated 2008), www.bord-na-gaidhlig.org.uk/ gaelic-language-plans.html.

Hacia unas bases para el diseño curricular, unpublished PhD thesis, Granada: Universidad de Granada. hera.ugr.es/tesisugr/16235320.pdf.

INE (2008) Encuesta Nacional de Inmigrantes 2007, www.ine.es/jaxi/menu. do?type=pcaxis&path=%2Ft20%2Fp319%2Fa2007%2Fp01&file=pcaxis &L=0&divi=&his%20=.

ITIA Bulletin (January 2008) "Court Interpreting. Who should pay?", Dublin: ITIA. translatorsassociation.ie/component/option,com_docman/task,cat_ view/gid,33/Itemid,16/.

Mar-Molinero, C. (2000) *The Politics of Language in the Spanish-Speaking World,* London and New York: Routledge.

Martin, A. (2000) "La interpretación social en España", in D.A. Kelly (ed.) *Aspectos profesionales de la traducción y la interpretación en España,* Granada: Comares, 207-23.

------ (2004) "Investigación en interpretación social: estado de la cuestión", in Emilio Ortega Arjonilla (ed.) *Panorama actual de la investigación en Traducción e Interpretación,* volumen I, Granada: Atrio, 431-46.

McPake, J. and R. Johnson *et al.* (2002) *Translating, Interpreting and Communication Support Services across the Public Sector in Scotland: A Literature Review*, Edinburgh: Scottish Executive.

------ and T. Tinsley (eds) (2007) *Valuing All Languages in Europe. ECML Research and Development Reports Series,* Graz.: European Centre for Modern Languages.

Molina, M. (2006) "Los servicios de interpretación a disposición de las mujeres inmigrantes maltratadas y la nueva ley contra la violencia machista en España", *Translation Journal*, Vol. 10(3): accurapid.com/Journal/37violencia.htm

Ó Dochartaigh, P. and M. Broderick (2006) *Language Policy and Language Planning in Ireland. A Report from the Royal Irish Academy Committee for Modern Languages, Literacy and Cultural Studies,* Dublin: Royal Irish Academy, www.ria.ie/committees/pdfs/modlang/language_ policy&planning.pdf.

Ó Riagáin, P. (1997) *Language Policy and Social Reproduction in Ireland 1893-1993,* Oxford: Clarendon Press.

Ozolins, U. (2000) "Communication Needs and Interpreting in Multilingual Settings: The International Spectrum of Response", in R. Roberts, S.E. Carr, D. Abraham and A. Dufour (eds) *The Critical Link 2: Interpreters in the Community,* selected papers from the *Second International Conference in Legal, Health and Social Service Settings*, Amsterdam/Philadelphia: John Benjamins, 21-33.

Perez, I. A. and C.W.L. Wilson (2006) *Translating, Interpreting and Communication Support: A Review of Provision in the Public Services in Scotland,* Edinburgh: Scottish Executive Social Research.

Phelan, M. (February 2007) "Interpreting, Translation and Public Bodies in Ireland: The Need for Policy and Training", *Advocacy* Paper Number 5, National Consultative Committee on Racism and Interculturalism.

Portas Fernández, M. (1997) *Lingua e sociedade na Galiza,* A Coruña: Bahía Edicións.

Ricento, T. (ed.) (2005) *An Introduction to Language Policy. Theory and Method,* Oxford (UK): Blackwell.

Romaine, S. (2002) "The Impact of Language Policy on Endangered Languages", [online]. *International Journal on Multicultural Societies,* Vol. 4(2): www.unesco.org/most/vl4n2romaine.pdf.

Sali, M. (2003) "Traducción e interpretación en la Administración de Justicia", in C. Valero (ed.) "Traducción e Interpretación en los Servicios Públicos. Contextualización", *Actualidad y Futuro,* Granada: Comares, 147-70.

Schiffman, H. (1996) *Linguistic Culture and Language Policy,* New York: Routledge.

Scottish Executive (January 2007) *A Strategy for Scotland's Languages: Draft Version for Consultation,* Edinburgh: Scottish Executive, www.scotland. gov.uk/Publications/2007/01/24130746/2.

Scottish Parliament (February 2003) *Inquiry into the Role of Educational and Cultural Policy in Supporting and Developing Gaelic, Scots and Minority Languages in Scotland,* Edinburgh: Scottish Parliament.

Spolsky, B. (2004) *Language Policy,* Cambridge: Cambridge University Press.

Turrell, M. (2001) *Multilingualism in Spain: Sociolinguistic and Psycholinguistic Aspects of Linguistic Minority Groups,* Clevedon, UK: Multilingual Matters.

Role, Positioning and Discourse in Face-to-Face Interpreting

IAN MASON
Heriot-Watt University, Edinburgh, UK

Abstract. *Whereas "role" and "role conflict" have been key terms in the research and development of public-service interpreting, this paper proposes, following Davies and Harré (1990), to substitute the notion of "positioning" for that of "role" in order to reflect the constantly evolving nature of interaction among participants in interpreter-mediated encounters. Positioning differs from footing in that, rather than being the choice of an individual speaker, it evolves as a result of joint negotiation among all the participants (i.e. positions adopted by one participant are either accepted and adopted by other participants or rejected and replaced). The main source of data is a series of televised immigration interviews that illustrate a variety of positioning behaviours. A number of (para)linguistic and pragmatic categories will be suggested to illustrate ways in which participants, by their discursive practices, position themselves and others and are, in turn, affected by each other's positionings. These discursive practices are seen as emanating from social institutions or "communities of practice" (Wenger 1998), which play a part in shaping the perceptions, stance, behaviour and utterances of all those involved.*

1. Introduction

The research perspective within which this study is situated is (1) interactional and (2) descriptive. Instead of seeking to observe interpreter behaviour in isolation from that of the other key participants in the public service encounter, it is expected that, by close observation of interaction between all participants, we may find regularities of behaviour that will improve our understanding of the nature of such interpreter-mediated events. Research in the field of face-to-face dialogue interpreting has evolved from the prescriptive account of what does or does not fall within acceptable professional standards towards non-judgemental observation of events and detailed description of what actually happens. In this spirit, we shall not consider participant moves in terms of their professional acceptability but rather in terms of their potential impact on the event and its internal evolution.

2.   From role to positions

Roy (1990) reports an incident from a conference of practitioners, at which the topic of codes of ethics for interpreters had arisen. One delegate received warm applause for the assertion "Interpreters don't have a problem with ethics, they have a problem with the *role*". Indeed, "role" and "role conflict" are frequently cited topics in the literature on PSI (e.g. Anderson 1976; Niska 1995; Roy 1990, 2000; Pöllabauer 2004; Inghilleri 2003, 2005) and the debate between the interpreting profession and users of interpreting services about what the margins are within which interpreters operate remains unresolved. Investigations into the roles actually adopted by participants in a variety of settings are consequently a useful contribution to our understanding of the consequences of particular behaviours. Discussion of the interpreter's role can, however, give the impression that a role is a fixed stance, adopted in advance and sustained throughout an encounter. In this respect, a useful distinction is made by Wadensjö (1998), following Goffman, between "activity role" and "participation status" or "footing". Whereas an activity role involves mostly pre-determined stances deemed to be appropriate for fulfilling a particular socio-professional task, the "footing" adopted by participants is of a temporary and evolving nature. Loosely defined by Goffman (1981:128) as "the alignment we take up to ourselves and the others present as expressed in the way we manage the production or reception of an utterance", footing is perceptible through the frequent shifts enacted by participants, often within a single utterance. These shifts may be from one addressee or group of addressees to another, say, or they may have to do with the ownership or non-ownership of the meanings one seeks to express. Footing, as an analytical category, has been applied with great insight to the work of the interpreter by Wadensjö (e.g. 1998, 2004).

The distinction between the global activity role and these local shifts of footing brings to mind a similar distinction made in a seminal article by Davies and Harré (1990). "Role", they claim, is a fairly static concept, which might imply that participants are somehow locked into pre-determined patterns of behaviour. They offer the term "positioning", on the other hand, as a dynamic feature of talk, one that is constantly changing and subject to negotiation among participants. By their conversational moves, participants position themselves and others and are, in turn, positioned by others' moves. Davies and Harré's account is, in particular, about "the force of discursive practices and the way people are positioned through those practices" (*ibid.*:43). A simple example is provided by a recent event in UK politics. A Labour-government Home Secretary's use of the term "swamped" in reference to the number of claims for asylum in the UK provoked immediate controversy for its evocation of a notorious previous use of the same term in the 1960s by a Conservative politician in a speech widely condemned at the time for its racist overtones. Thus, the very use of such an emotively charged term positions the utterer. It does so in two ways. The speaker, in opting to employ the term rather than some other, wittingly or not, aligns himself with the discourse that it is associated with. And hearers, whether well-disposed or not, cannot avoid making the association if it has become part of their own socialisation. (It can, of course, be argued that not all hearers were in a position to make this association – i.e. not all of them would have been familiar with the type of discourse mentioned here – and that the media played a fundamental role in bringing the original use of the term to public attention).

More broadly, the discourses we choose to employ and the way they are reacted to by co-participants position us within the interaction. Such positioning is by no means always deliberate. Davies and Harré (*op. cit.*:55-57) provide a "worked example" of "how people can be living quite different narratives without realizing that they are doing so". Two academics, a male (A) and a female (B) meet at a conference. B is unwell and A offers to lead her to a pharmacy where she may be able to obtain medication. After a long walk they fail to find a pharmacy that is open for business. The following exchange then takes place:

A   I'm sorry to have dragged you all this way when you're not well.
B   You didn't drag me, I chose to come.

A dispute then arises between A and B as to their behaviour and intentions towards each other. What A saw as a genuine apology on his part was taken up by B as an assertion of power and control, as a positioning of B as weak and helpless. In this way, a distinction has to be made, in the analysis of speech, between **intended** meanings and **hearable** meanings, the latter depending on take-up, the hearer's disposition towards what is uttered and their reaction to it. An application of these notions to the field of dialogue interpreting becomes immediately apparent: if misunderstanding of this kind can arise naturally in a dyadic exchange between two interlocutors sharing the same language and (presumably) similar cultural backgrounds, how much more likely is it that people may "hear" each other's meanings differently in triadic exchanges where participants' attempts to represent their own and each other's meanings have to cross linguistic and cultural boundaries? Discourses signify within their own cultural environment and may not be hearable (in the way intended) by receivers whose cultural context is distinct (see for example, Sequences 9 and 10 below). By the same token, the inability (through lack of familiarity) of certain speakers to adopt particular discourses in a context in which they are the expected currency may lead to marginalization or exclusion.

Barsky (1994) gives a compelling account of the Canadian Convention Refugee Hearing, in which he suggests that the task of the asylum seeker is, in the terms of the work's title, to "Construct a Productive Other". Projecting the self, including aspects of linguistic and other behaviour imported from the culture of origin, is unlikely to lead to success in these interviews. The nature of the event is such, he suggests (*ibid.*:60), that "one (albeit cynical) hypothesis is that the hearing could be seen as a test of the claimant's ability to construct an appropriate version of the 'Convention Refugee'". In other words, what counts is projecting the right persona and adopting the right linguistic comportment – those valued by the host country – rather than those imported from the home country. If Barsky is correct, then it will be appreciated that the intervention of the interpreter in a site of linguistic (and cultural) difference such as the Convention Refugee hearing will be crucial in relaying or constructing the required image. How do refugees position themselves and how do interpreters re-position them for target-language receivers? How do participants react to each other's positionings? The interface between source language and target language evinced in the interpreter's performance throws into sharp relief the cultural relativity of language behaviour.[1]

At the interpreter's swearing-in during these hearings, s/he is enjoined to "Translate faithfully, correctly and to the best of your ability" (*ibid.*:41). How is this task to be accomplished by verbatim translation, except in an imagined world of cultural (including linguistic) uniformity? Berk-Seligson

---

[1] In a monolingual linguistics it is possible to treat language, and even language use (cf. some conversation analysis), as a culture-independent entity. In Translation Studies, on the other hand, where the raw data are situated at the interface between two languages, it is impossible (or futile) to conduct analysis independently of cultural considerations, including perceptions of power, status, role, socio-textual practices, etc. This is perhaps where the true link between Translation and Interpreting Studies and applied linguistics lies: contributing to the study of linguistic difference by providing evidence of the relativity of (cultural) factors that may be treated as constants in monolingual exchanges.

(e.g. 1990), Morris (1995), Hale (e.g. 1997) among others have conclusively demonstrated not only the impossibility but also the inadvisability of such an undertaking. Recognition of this opens up an area of sociolinguistic enquiry (of interpreter behaviour in three-way exchanges) that is still relatively neglected, despite recent pioneering work in the field (e.g. Wadensjö 1998; Inghilleri 2003).

Barsky's work points the way to a power- and discourse-sensitive linguistic analysis of such events but does not actually conduct such an analysis. The data samples in the work are all cited in English, thus effacing the question of linguistic difference, and the analysis is of content rather than discourse. Yet analysis of personal reference devices in one or two of the dialogues he cites would bring to light some interesting features. For example the contrast between the systematic use of agent-deleted passives in the Counsel's questions ("you were held", "you were beaten", etc.) and the all-encompassing "they" of the claimant's answers ("they beat me", "they asked", etc.). This non-specific third-person plural is used to refer to unidentified kidnappers and torturers, but also to employers and doctors (in the words of the claimant, "because they control everything, the people from the government", (Barsky *op. cit.*:138)). The claimant's pronominal use thus brings together (positions) in a single, undifferentiated category individuals who, from the perspective of the host culture, might be seen as belonging to very different categories.

What follows is an attempt to show, via evidence from several interpreter-mediated events, some of the ways in which all participants, by their discursive practices, position themselves and others and are, in turn, affected by each other's positionings. These acts of positioning are effected linguistically and paralinguistically. A number of discrete categories have been identified to be illustrated below: orientation to others, attempts to control responses, contextualization cues, markers of in-group solidarity, gaze and discoursal choices. The primary source of evidence is a series of immigration interviews, shown on a terrestrial television channel as part of a documentary about illegal immigration.[2] Although this is a small dataset and did not allow either participant observation or the opportunity for post-interviewing the participants, it does illustrate a variety of positioning behaviours and is thus useful for our purposes here. Other data sources are cited, here and there, to corroborate or further illustrate the point at issue.

---

[2] *Cutting Edge*, "Illegal Immigrants", broadcast on the UK's *Channel Four*, 30.09.97.

3. Orientation to others

As suggested by Reddy (1979), our use of language about language provides evidence of some of our fundamental attitudes towards communication: how we conceptualize it and how we treat it. In similar vein, a cursory observation of the terms and metaphors commonly used to refer to the interpreting process reveals an image of interpreting as an automatic process and of the interpreter as a "non-person", a mere conduit through which people speak and listen. Thus, we are often presented, on news programmes, with foreign statespersons *"speaking through* an interpreter", a metaphor which offers a belief both about the (non-)status of the interpreter and about the ability of communicators using interpreter services to make their own voice directly heard by each other. Similarly, the interpreter's task is often referred to as that of "conveying a message" in another language, as if, somehow, meaning will remain invariant and input equals output (except that the code has changed). According to this outlook, the interpreter would enjoy no power at all, simply responding automatically when prompted to do so, to a determinate stimulus.

Indeed, as attested by Berk-Seligson (1990) among others, the mode of interpreting adopted in United States courtrooms reflects this conception. Interpreters are required to give a close rendition only and are not to intervene on their own behalf. Thus, in Sequence 1 (taken from the trial for murder, in 1995, of the American football star, O.J. Simpson), it is apparent that the interpreter may not supply information which is evident to her, but must ask the witness to supply it. When the witness does so erroneously, she relays the error (of which she cannot fail to be aware).

Sequence 1

Att.   What is the name of the airline?
Int.   ¿Cuál es el nombre de la línea?
Wit.   Es TACA
Int.   It's TACA
Att.   Could you repeat that? And spell it please?
Wit.   TACA
Int.   ¿Lo puede deletrear?
       [*Can you spell it?*]
Wit.   T-A-C-K
Int.   T-A-C-K

[Key: Att = attorney; Int = interpreter; Wit = witness]

Thus, for legal reasons, the interpreter may not herself take responsibility for spelling TACA and is duty-bound to repeat the witness's misspelling. Later in the same cross-examination, the Attorney asks the witness to spell the Spanish first name "Josefina". The witness confesses she is unable to do so. The attorney continues to press the question, without success, until finally the judge intervenes and asks the witness, "Is it spelled in the normal way?", to which the witness replies in the affirmative. At no point in the exchange does the interpreter offer the spelling (which, for her, would be a wholly straightforward task), nor would she be expected to do so. She is, quite simply, not considered to be a participant in the communicative exchange. By translating "verbatim", she is deemed to be offering to the court an exact version of what has been said in another language. Let us note, in passing, that in behaving as required, the interpreter also positions herself as belonging to a "community of practice" (Wenger 1998) – the court of law – whose practices she has internalized and constantly reproduces. In such circumstances, the interpreter's own actions and those of other participants *position* her as a "non-person". At the same time, of course, this positioning positions other participants as being responsible for their own utterances. Thus, positioning can be both reflexive (i.e. positioning oneself) and interactive (as when one positions another participant by one's own moves; see Davies and Harré *op. cit.*:48).

The stance illustrated in Sequence 1 above, while it positions the interpreter as not authorized to intervene, does recognize the right of the "primary" participants to control their own responses (e.g. to make errors or to mislead) without interference. In this sense, it is, to a limited extent, empowering of witnesses or interviewees, who might be deemed to have very little power in the context of a courtroom cross-examination or a police interrogation. The instrumentality of the interpreter in allowing or disallowing this empowerment is illustrated in Sequences 2 and 3, taken not from court interpreting but from immigration encounters involving Russian/Swedish and Polish/English respectively. They show diametrically opposed interpreter stances.

Sequence 2

(An applicant for residence status in Sweden claims to have Greek nationality and suggests that her passport shows this)

Pol. [hands passport to Int] Can you show me where?
Int. [hands passport to Applicant] And can you show where?

(quoted from Wadensjö 1998:155 – cf. also Wadensjö 2004:110)
[key: Pol = police officer; Int = interpreter]

Sequence 3

Imm. [addresses Int.] So he understands why he's here.
Int. [to Imm.] Yes he does. [to PM] Pan rozumi dlaczego pan tu
jest, prawda?
   [*You understand why you're here, don't you?*]
PM. Tak
Int. Yes, he does.[3]

[key: Imm = immigration officer; Int = interpreter; PM = Polish man]

The essential difference between the two exchanges is one of footing (Goffman *op. cit.*). In each case, the initial move is made by the institutionally powerful participant (police, immigration officer), who addresses a question to the interpreter ("can you..."), referring to the other participant in the third person ("he understands...") and thus positioning the interpreter as his interlocutor. In Sequence 2, the interpreter appears to behave as animator (in that she reflects in Russian almost exactly the words uttered in Swedish by the interviewer) but in fact she alters the framework by projecting the question as if it had been posed directly to the interviewee.[4] In Sequence 3, on the other hand, the interpreter assumes responsibility for the belief expressed ("Yes, he does"), a role which Goffman designates as that of Principal. The importance of this distinction lies not so much in the categorization of interpreters' strategies and options as in the *effect* of the selected footing on the footing and status of the other parties involved. As noted, in both sequences, the interviewer initiates a particular participation framework by directly addressing the interpreter. The latter then has

---

[3] Cf. a further instance from the same data, in which an immigration officer offers pen and paper to a Polish man she is interviewing:
   Imm [to PM] – Your passport's still with this woman? Will you write down her name for me?
   Int [in Polish] – Write down her name [*takes pen offered by Imm to PM and writes*]
[4] Cf. Wadensjö (2004:115), where it is pointed out that the interpreter "authors" a new version. The police officer's "you" and the interpreter's "you" do not have the same referent and the officer's reference to himself ("can you show me") is omitted by the interpreter. As Wadensjö comments: "It also shows how interpreters can promote the primary parties' mutual attention by *positioning* the preceding speaker *as the current "principal"*, simultaneously as they withdraw from an *anticipated position of "responder"* (my italics).

the choice of prolonging this framework by responding to the interviewer (Sequence 3) or re-directing the question to the interviewee (Sequence 2). In Sequence 3, however, the interpreter, having initially accepted the dyadic exchange with the interviewer, then hastily revises her footing (perhaps out of professional conscience?). She turns to the interviewee and asks the interviewer's question, but selects her own words and syntax (question form), adopting the footing of Author – a matter to which we return below. Receiving the interviewee's reply, she relays this as Principal ("Yes, he does", rather than "Yes, I do"), thus reverting to the interviewer's and her own initial footing. While in Sequence 2 the interviewee is positioned as having full participation status by the interpreter's choice of footing, being invited to interact directly with the interviewer, the interpreter's choices in Sequence 3 set up two separate dyads: immigration officer with interpreter and interpreter with Polish immigrant. The effect of this is manifestly to exclude the interviewee from direct interaction with his interviewer, thus positioning him as a bystander.

The literature abounds with instances of such exclusion, often in the form of asides to the interpreter, which the latter is not expected to relay to the other participant (see e.g. Wadensjö 1998:256-57). The question that arises is: can other participants override the interpreter's gate-keeping by re-positioning themselves as primary interlocutors in the exchange? It would seem that they can, but only if they are recognized as having power within the exchange. Wadensjö (*ibid.*:166-75) relates the case of a patient having difficulty in expressing his venereal disease symptoms in a consultation involving a female interpreter and a female nurse. There is a long dyadic exchange between patient and interpreter, in which the patient fails to complete his utterance (describing his symptoms) while the interpreter back-channels and inserts encouragements such as "don't be embarrassed". The Swedish nurse, excluded from this dialogue in Russian, loses patience at her exclusion and interrupts, saying to the interpreter: "Would you break off and say what he says now?" She thus asserts her right to inclusion, founded no doubt upon the assumption that the social occasion (genre) of the medical consultation allows direct medical staff/patient dialogue only. The community of practice acknowledges norms and privileges to which the nurse, as the recognized medical expert in the exchange, can appeal.

The absence anywhere in the literature of any converse examples of the power-less participant (immigrant, patient, etc.) successfully intervening in this way points conclusively to an unstated assumption about positions across a range of genres within interpreter-mediated exchanges. The interpreter has power to sustain or interrupt the normal turn-taking sequence.[5] This power may, occasionally, be challenged – but only if the challenger is recognized as having the status and authority to do so. Otherwise, the third party is effectively (if temporarily) excluded and positioned as bystander. The regularity of this behaviour points to an interpreter community of practice, overlapping with the other communities of practice, of which they become part by their professional activity.

4. Attempts to control responses

In an earlier study (Mason 2005), I cited instances of shifts in the form of questions, whereby a question inviting a yes/no answer is interpreted as one which suggests a preferred response. For example, a question such as "Did you speak to immigration at Dover?" may become something like "You spoke to immigration at Dover?" – which merely seeks confirmation of an assumption. Pöllabauer (2004:155) cites a sequence, reproduced as Sequence 4 below, in which an interpreter transforms "the officer's yes/no question into a suggestive question". A refugee is asked about an incident cited as grounds for seeking asylum.

Sequence 4

    Imm   Were there dead people or anything else?
    Int   People were killed in the course of the incident or?

    [key: Imm = immigration officer; Int = interpreter]

What is striking about such cases is the frequency with which they are attested. In the literature on court interpreting, the reverse process is frequently attested. Hale (2006:210) cites an instance (reproduced here as Sequence 5) quoted in Berk-Seligson (1999:39), noting that the effect of omitting the tag ("did you not?") is to make the question put by the attorney less coercive.

---

[5] For Anderson (1976:218), the interpreter, as the sole bilingual in the exchange, enjoys "the advantage of power inherent in all positions which control scarce resources". Where the interpreter is not the sole bilingual participant, this power may be challenged: see Pym (1999).

Sequence 5

> Att   You made a report about this incident, did you not?
> Int   (in Spanish) Did you make a report about this incident?

[key: Att = attorney; Int = interpreter]

Hale (2006) also reports on research showing that Spanish-to-English court interpreters often omit question tags in this way.

From the point of view adopted in this paper, the relevant point is that participants in three-way exchanges (police officers, attorneys – and also interpreters) may from time to time seek to control the replies of their interlocutors by asking preferred-response questions. In doing so, they position themselves as making a prior assumption about the truth of some state of affairs and position their interlocutor as likely to agree with their assumption. The interlocutor can, of course, refuse to accept this positioning by denying the assumption. However, such dispreferred responses require more elaboration, rendering acquiescence with the offered positioning more likely, as in Sequence 6 below, reproduced from Mason (2005:37). Here, the interpreter's positioning of the interviewee goes much further than the immigration officer's yes/no question, suggesting a whole rationale for the interviewee's presence in the United Kingdom.

Sequence 6

> Imm. Did you look round for a job in Poland?
> Int.   [in Pol.] Did you look for work? You looked for work and there wasn't any?
> PM   Tak
> Int.   Yes, he was looking for work but there was no work.

[key: Imm = immigration officer; Int = interpreter; PM = Polish man]

In this instance, the interpreter may appear to show some solidarity with the immigrant in suggesting an appropriate response. These temporary positionings shift, however, within the exchange and elsewhere in the same interview the interpreter may appear to position herself as much closer to the immigration officer, in fact as co-investigator with the latter, as in Sequence 7.

Sequence 7

Imm   What did they say?
Int   I co oni powiedzieli?
      [*And what did they say?*]
PM   Że pojedziemy do pracy do Anglii.
      [*That we'll travel to work to England*]
Int   Co znaczy pojedziemy? Bo było więcej?
      [*What does it mean "we'll travel"? Because there were more?*]
PM   Tak
      [*Yes*]
Int   Yes they said they'd go and work in England because apparently he wasn't the only one, there were several people involved.

[key: Imm = immigration officer; Int = interpreter; PM = Polish man]

Thus, whereas "role" in the sense of activity role is generally taken by all concerned (interpreters, users of interpreting services) to be unvarying within an assignment, the evidence presented here (and in the work of other scholars) suggests that positioning shifts and, with each shift, brings about a potential realignment of the exchange.

5.   Contextualization cues

"Contextualisation cues" is the term used by Gumperz (1982:131)[6] to refer to constellations of linguistic features which signal the ways in which speakers intend and hearers accept the meanings of their utterances. They include code-switching and style-shifting, prosodic cues, lexical and syntactic choices and the use of, or deviation from, standard formulae. The meanings of these cues are not semantically encoded. They are implicit and therefore have to be inferred from the particular context in which they occur. What is typically involved is a departure from normal (unmarked) linguistic behaviour. As such, the cues frequently give rise to misunderstandings, particularly at sites of linguistic or cultural difference, where judgements are likely to differ as to what constitutes the norm and what a departure from the norm may signal.

---

[6] "Roughly speaking, a contextualisation cue is any feature of linguistic form that contributes to the signalling of contextual presuppositions".

In the set of immigration interviews drawn on here (see footnote 2), the genre is highly routine. An immigration officer, by means of a fairly standard set of questions, seeks to establish (1) that the immigrant entered the UK as a tourist, (2) that the immigrant has been in paid employment, (3) that, therefore, deception has occurred. A supplementary goal in some interviews is to discover the identity and whereabouts of any third party who may have organized travel and employment for a group of illegal immigrants. Once these facts have been established, the interview is effectively at an end. The questioning is conducted in a brisk manner and rarely departs from the routine. At a particular juncture in one interview, however, the interviewer's shift of pitch and intonation, in conjunction with multiple self-reference ("I") for the first time in the interview, appears to intend to signal a reduction of distance and a general benevolence – in striking contrast to the formality and coldly detached tone of what had preceded. This is clear evidence of reflexive re-positioning. It is as if, now that formal business is at an end, the immigration officer seeks to position herself as showing a human side and concern for the plight of the would-be immigrant.[7] These utterances by the interviewer (also discussed in Mason *op. cit.*) are reproduced here as Sequence 8, including the main paralinguistic features involved.

Sequence 8

    Imm Because I'm going to go and try to get your PASSport back off her. (…)
            [smiles] Well I'll see if she wants to give you the money before you go [nods] (.) [smiles] I think that {would be good.
    Int   {Ona, Liza, postara się o te pieniądze nim pan odleci, nim odlecisz ona, Liza, postara się o pieniądze.
            [*She, Lisa, will try to get the money before you (formal) depart, before you (informal) depart she, Lisa, will try to get the money*].
    Imm I'll tell her where you are, and I'll bring her over and see if she'll pay you (.) OK?

    Key:
    Imm = immigration officer; Int = interpreter

---

[7] It is, of course, equally possible that the officer is seeking to exhibit to *the interpreter* a human side to her character. In terms of Bell's (1984) audience design, the interpreter could be said to be influential on the speaker's style as an auditor. In Sequence 8, however, the officer's gaze is directed towards the interviewee only.

CAPS = emphasis
(...) = omitted sequence
{ = overlapping talk
(.) = brief pause
. = falling intonation
, = continuing intonation
? = rising intonation

In addition to the contextualization cues already mentioned, there is a noticeable style-shift in the relatively colloquial formulations "go and try", "get... back off her", "see if", etc. These cues appear not to have been relayed by the interpreter. Moreover, by explicitly referring to the interviewer in the third person, the interpreter makes it clear that she is adopting her own voice – as Principal – rather than the interviewer's – as Author. She positions herself as an independent actor, commenting on what has been uttered by the interviewer. On this footing, the contextualization cues, which belong to the interviewer's speech style, cannot be translated, for any attempt to do so would be attributed by the hearer to the interpreter rather than to the participant referred to in the third person. This may explain the interpreter's momentary uncertainty over which second-person form of address to use and her odd use of the officer's forename in her rendition as a way of signalling reduced distance.

It is, in any case, difficult to imagine how an interpreter could relay such cues in a manner that might communicate the intended values. Wadensjö (1998:246-8), following Goffman, makes a distinction between "display-ing" and "replaying" others' talk. In the former case, the interpreter tends to adopt neutral prosodic features, eliminating most of the expressive features of the utterance being translated and thus signalling detachment from (or non-ownership of) the words being used. Alternatively, the interpreter may seek to "replay" the expressive features, temporarily positioning herself as adopting the persona of the participant being translated. For a variety of reasons, however, such behaviour is hazardous. Crucially, it may not communicate what it intends to communicate and/or it may be perceived as disrespectful mimicry by the participant being translated. For it seems to be characteristic of many contextualization cues that they are intimately personal, belonging uniquely to the speaker, in a way that semantically encoded meanings are not. How, for example, might the interpreter in Se-quence 8 seek to replay (without over-playing) the prosodic shift and the implicatures in "I'll see if she wants to give you the money before you go, I think that would be good"? It is not surprising, in such circumstances, that the interpreter adopts here an explicit third-person footing. Yet again, though, the interpreter becomes the arbiter of which discourses are and which are not relayed. An attempt by the Immigration Officer to reduce distance and establish more direct contact with the interviewee has failed because the re-positioning has not been taken up. A further way in which attempts at direct communication fail is examined under section 8 below.

6.   In-group solidarity

Consideration of Sequence 8 also suggests another parameter affecting communication rights. It will have been noted that the interpreter makes use of the T-pronoun when interpreting the interviewer's question to the Polish interviewee. Most dialogue interpreters would no doubt consider this to be entirely non-standard, or even unethical, behaviour. But this anomalous use brings to light another area where power differentials are signalled. Expression of power, deference, solidarity, distance may all be either signalled or filtered out and taken up or ignored. Hearable meanings depend on take-up. Berk-Seligson (1988) cites the case of the use of honorifics by monolingual Spanish-speaking witnesses in US courtrooms. She notes the inevitable in-group solidarity of interpreters and witnesses who belong to the same ethnic group in a (largely) monocultural event and notes that interpreters often initiate a "cycle of politeness" by using honorifics (*señor, señora*) in addressing the witnesses. But they may or may not translate the same honorifics, uttered by the witness, when interpreting for the benefit of the court. Berk-Seligson's research suggests that the presence or absence of these markers of deference (i.e. interactive positioning) makes a great deal of difference to the perception by jurors of how trustworthy and convincing the witness is.

It is a commonplace of studies of the use of T/V pronouns, ever since Brown and Gilman (1960), that speakers' choices are affected by, and at the same time affect, perceptions of power and solidarity. In our data, the same intra-ethnic solidarity that Berk-Seligson perceived in her interpreters may have motivated the Polish interpreter to address her fellow-countrymen and women with T, even though these were no doubt total strangers to her prior to the encounter described here. Corroborating clues lie in the (non-source-text-motivated) use of colloquialisms here and there by the interpreter, signalling a reduction of distance in the interaction (perhaps unwanted by the interviewee). Yet, whatever the real motivation for the use of T by the interpreter (in Sequence 8, but also throughout the interview), the effect of non-reciprocated use of T in situations of unequal power can only serve to reinforce the power differential. Indeed it may be perceived as an attempt by the interpreter to place on record a difference of status. Here too, the issue of footing is involved. Were contemporary English to involve a T/V distinction, it is inconceivable that the immigration officer would, herself, initiate a cycle of T-address. The tenor of her questions is formal throughout. Therefore the interpreter's use of T concerns *her own* relationship with the addressee: the translated voice cannot be that of the immigration officer. The interpreter is in fact presenting evidence that she is speaking in her own voice – positioning herself as Principal in Goffman's terms – thus establishing direct communicative contact between herself and the interviewee, rather than facilitating contact between officer and immigrant. The interviewee is thus positioned as a direct interlocutor of the interpreter (only), in that a communicative norm is established of two dialogues, between interviewer and interpreter and between interpreter and interviewee but not, crucially, between interviewee and interviewer. In section 7, we find further evidence of the Polish interviewees' acceptance of this impoverished participation framework.

7.   Gaze

The potential of such paralinguistic features as gaze to signal not only a participation framework but also the negotiation of turn taking has long been recognized in studies of face-to-face interpreting. In a pioneering study, Lang (1978) recorded evidence of gaze, posture and gesture among participants in court proceedings in Papua New Guinea and noted in particular how inclusionary or exclusionary strategies are signalled by these means. By averting gaze while speaking, an interpreter can signal his/her own voluntary exclusion from what is deemed to be a two-way dialogue between other participants. Similarly, by not directing their gaze towards the interpreter, other participants can treat each other as addressees, relegating the interpreter to the role of auditor, a ratified participant whose role is to relay others' speech as an animator of others' voices.

In our (limited) dataset, a number of behaviours can be observed. In some circumstances, for example recording basic details of identity or asking routine questions (cf. Sequence 3 above), an immigration officer may direct gaze solely towards the interpreter, who reciprocates with gaze towards the Officer, as in Figure 1.

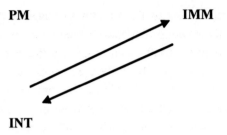

Figure 1: Speaker's gaze in an immigration interview: Option 1

Key: PM = Polish man
      IMM = immigration officer
      INT = interpreter

Such a strategy clearly excludes the linguistically-different (i.e. Polish-speaking) participant. This arrangement, however, is not the preferred option in these interviews. On most occasions, the immigration officer, when asking questions, directs gaze towards the interviewee only, perhaps reflecting a behaviour acquired through training. The interpreter, meanwhile, seeks eye contact with each interlocutor in turn as she translates from English to Polish and from Polish to English. To do this, she has to turn her head from one interlocutor to the other. She thus signals her want to be included as a participant in triadic exchange. The Polish-speaking interviewee is seated facing the Immigration Officer on the opposite side of a table. In two of the interviews, there is a distinct tendency for the interviewees (male and female) to direct gaze to the interviewer only when being addressed *but not when speaking*. In responding to questions, these interviewees invariably turn their gaze towards the interpreter. The pattern of speaker's gaze is as illustrated in Figure 2.

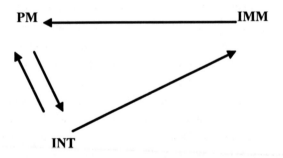

Figure 2: Speaker's gaze in an immigration interview: Option 2

On this evidence, the interviewees position the interpreter as their only interlocutor. The possible motivations for such behaviour are many and varied. Prominent among them may be simple linguistic insecurity, a lack of confidence in their ability to communicate with anyone except in their own language. (The immigration officer's stance in Figure 1 could be attributed to the same cause). But whatever the real reasons for the pattern of gaze shown in Figure 2, the effect is to deny the interviewees any chance of projecting a persona of their own to the immigration officer. By their gaze-shift, they position themselves as excluded onlookers and, by implication, interactively position the immigration officer and the interpreter as joint deciders.

8. Relaying discourses

In section 5 above, it was seen that a number of contextualization cues combined to signal a discoursal shift on the part of the interviewer, from official interrogator to conciliatory sympathizer. The shift could not be relayed to the interviewee by an interpreter adopting the footing of Principal. As I have reported elsewhere (Mason 2004), the interpreter also controls the selection of which discourses are represented and which are not. A lexical item which is reiterated no fewer than seven times in the responses of the Polish woman and man in the two major interviews featured here is *szkoły* (lit. "school"). This is partly accounted for by the fact that attending an educational course may, in certain circumstances, be counted as a legitimate reason for seeking entry to the UK. Yet the word is also used (see Sequence 10) to refer to activities undertaken in Poland before leaving that country. The item clearly covers a wide range of educational activities, from the academic to training in manual skills. But the frequent reiteration of the same term adds a discoursal value to it. Education (*szkoły*) becomes an aspiration, an activity which it is good to be engaged in, and thus, an element of self-esteem for these deportees, who have, prior to the interview, been positioned as illegal and deceitful. Sequences 9 and 10 exemplify this reflexive positioning and show how it is at least attenuated, if not effaced, in translation.

Sequence 9

Imm   How is it that you're still IN this country?
Int   Dlaczego tutaj dalej jesteś?
      [*Why are you still here?*]

PW   Bo chciałam iść tutaj do szkoły, do tej pory udało mi się, musiałam zarobić pieniądze, żeby iść do szkoły bo szkoła jest dosyć droga,
[Because I wanted to go to school here, till now I've managed to, I had to earn money to go to school because school is quite expensive.]

Int   I had to/ my intention was to attend an English course here, but I didn't have enough money so I had to earn the money in order to pay for the course.

PW   I do tej pory (.) chodzę do szkoły, chodziłam raz w tygodniu (.) niestety.
[And I still go to school, I did go to school once a week, unfortunately.]

Int   And I have been attending an English course once a week,

[key: Imm = immigration officer; Int = interpreter; PW = Polish woman]

Sequence 10

Imm What were you doing before that in Poland.

Int   A coś robił przed przyjazdem tutaj do Anglii w Polsce.
[And what were you doing in Poland before coming here to England.]

PM   Znaczy (.) uczyłem się w szkole.
[I was learning at school.]

Int   Jako student?
[As a student?]

PM   Nie, mechanik samochodowy.
[No, a car mechanic.]

Int   Right um he was attending (.) um a course um a car mechanics course.

[key: Imm = immigration officer; Int = interpreter; PM = Polish man]

The dissipation of the cohesive device of reiteration, in conjunction with other interpreter selections (e.g. deletion of "wanted to", "managed to", "unfortunately" in Sequence 9) combine to restrict the meaning potential offered in the Polish utterances to something more instrumental and non-committal in English. One plausible reading of this sequence would be that the immigrant positions himself as having been in full time education, the interpreter asks him to specify whether this involved intellectual or manual activity and then re-positions him to the officer as a manual worker.

Perceptions of status and value attaching to education and manual labour may well be involved. Significantly for our purposes here, the interpreter in Sequence 10, by her independent question to the interviewee, re-positions herself once more as co-investigator. This is reinforced by her use of the utterance-initial "Right", suggesting a successful outcome to her initiative.

9. Conclusion

In this short study of participant behaviour in a small set of data from inter-preter-mediated encounters, I have sought to highlight the range of moves, both linguistic and paralinguistic, which may signal attempts at reflexive and interactive positioning and the take-up of these by other participants. Gate-keeping, footing, manipulation of preferred/dispreferred responses, contextualization cues, in-group identity, gaze and lexical choice were all seen to be involved in the process. Following Davies and Harré (*op. cit.*), we have suggested that positioning provides a useful alternative to the rather static notion of "role" and we have sought to widen our focus from the interpreter's role to the positions adopted by and suggested to *all* participants in the ex-change. Positions evolve as an exchange develops and are the subject of joint negotiation among all involved. In some ways, then, positioning is similar to footing. The latter, though, may be treated as a choice of an individual speaker (like, say, code-switching in conversation) whereas, in the treatment of po-sitioning here, I have sought to stress its interactive nature: positionings are either accepted and adopted by other participants or rejected and replaced.

In the particular interviews that have formed the main focus of our atten-tion, the interpreters' strategic choices were unlikely to affect the outcome of the events, which was more or less pre-determined. "Illegal immigrants" had been arrested and were about to be deported, immediately following a routine interview that was little more than a legal requirement. The inter-viewees accept without demur the positioning of them offered by the other participants. However, the same linguistic and paralinguistic parameters are involved in situations (such as those described by Barsky *op. cit.*) where there is altogether more at stake. The positions adopted and accepted by participants, it has been suggested here, may exert considerable influence on the likely development of the exchange. Yet the impact of participants' choices remains under-investigated. Indeed, large-scale empirical investiga-tions of actual participant behaviour in interpreter-mediated face-to-face exchanges are still relatively few (e.g. Berk-Seligson 1990; Wadensjö 1998) and much work remains to be done, both in the ethnography and in the linguistics and pragmatics of such communicative events.

References

Anderson, R. Bruce (1976) "Perspectives on the Role of the Interpreter", in R. Brislin (ed.) *Translation: Applications and Research*, New York: Gardner Press, 208-28.

Barsky, Robert (1994) *Constructing a Productive Other. Discourse Theory and the Convention Refugee Hearing*, Amsterdam and Philadelphia: John Benjamins.

Bell, Allan (1984) "Language Style as Audience Design", *Language in Society* 13: 145-204.

Berk-Seligson, Susan (1988) "The Impact of Politeness in Witness Testimony: The Influence of the Court Interpreter", *Multilingua* 7(4): 411-39.

------ (1990) *The Bilingual Courtroom. Court Interpreters in the Judicial Process*, Chicago: University of Chicago Press.

------ (1999) "The Impact of Court Interpreting on the Coerciveness of Leading Questions", *Forensic Linguistics* 6(1): 30-56.

Brown, R. and A. Gilman (1960) "Pronouns of Power and Solidarity", in T. Sebeok (ed.) *Style in Language*, Massachusetts: MIT Press.

Cameron, D. (2001) *Working with Spoken Discourse*, London: Sage.

Davies, Bronwyn and Rom Harré (1990) "Positioning: The Discursive Production of Selves", *Journal for the Theory of Social Behaviour* 20(1): 43-63.

Goffman, Erving (1981) *Forms of Talk*, Oxford: Basil Blackwell.

Gumperz, John (1982) *Discourse Strategies*, Cambridge: Cambridge University Press.

Hale, Sandra (1997) "The Interpreter on Trial: Pragmatics in Court Interpreting", in Silvana Carr, Roda Roberts, Aideen Dufour and Dini Steyn (eds), *The Critical Link: Interpreters in the Community*, Amsterdam and Philadelphia: John Benjamins, 201-11.

------ (2006) "Themes and Methodological Issues in Court Interpreting Research", in Erik Hertog and Bart van der Veer (eds) *Taking Stock: Research and Methodology in Community Interpreting*, *Linguistica Antverpiensia*, new series 5: 205-28.

Inghilleri, Moira (2003) "Habitus, Field and Discourse: Interpreting as a Socially Situated Activity", *Target* 15(2): 243-68.

------ (2005) "Mediating Zones of Uncertainty. Interpreter Agency, the Interpreting Habitus and Political Asylum Adjudication", *The Translator* 11(1): 69-85.

Lang, Ranier (1978) "Behavioural Aspects of Liaison Interpreters in Papua New Guinea: Some Preliminary Observations", in David Gerver and H. Wallace Sinaiko (eds) *Language Interpretation and Communication*, New York and London: Plenum, 231-44.

Mason, Ian (2004) "Discourse, Audience Design and the Search for Relevance in Dialogue Interpreting", in G. Androulakis (ed.) *Proceedings of Translating in the 21ˢᵗ Century: Trends and Prospects*, Aristotle University of Thessaloniki, September 2002.

------ (2005) "Projected and Perceived Identities in Dialogue Interpreting", in Juliane House, M. Rosario, Martín Bueno and Nicole Baumgarten (eds) *Translation and the Construction of Identity, IATIS Yearbook 2005*, 30-52.

Morris, Ruth (1995) "The Moral Dilemmas of Court Interpreting", *The Translator* 1(1): 25-46.

Niska, Helge (1995) "Just Interpreting: Role Conflicts and Discourse Types in Court Interpreting", in M. Morris (ed.) *Translation and the Law*, Amsterdam and Philadelphia: Benjamins, 293-316.

Pöllabauer, Sonja (2004) "Interpreting in Asylum Hearings. Issues of Role, Responsibility and Power", *Interpreting* 6(2): 143-80.

Pym, Anthony (1999) "'Nicole Slapped Michelle': Interpreters and Theories of Interpreting at the O.J. Simpson Trial", in Ian Mason (ed.) *Dialogue Interpreting*, Special Issue of *The Translator* 5(2): 265-83.

Reddy, Michael (1979) "The Conduit Metaphor: A Case of Frame Conflict in our Language about Language", in Andrew Ortony (ed.) *Metaphor and Thought*, Cambridge: Cambridge University Press.

Roy, Cynthia (1990) "Interpreters, their Role and Metaphorical Language Use", in A.L. Wilson (ed.) *Looking Ahead: Proceedings of the 31stAnnual Conference of the American Translators Association*, Medford, N.J.: Learned Information, 77-86.

------ (2000) *Interpreting as a Discourse Process*, New York and Oxford: Oxford University Press.

Wadensjö, Cecilia (1998) *Interpreting as Interaction,* London and New York: Longman.

------ (2004) "Dialogue Interpreting – A Monologising Practice in a Dialogically Organised World", *Target* 16(1): 105-24.

Wenger, Etienne (1998) *Communities of Practice: Learning, Meaning and Identity*, Cambridge: Cambridge University Press.

Teaching Interpreting in Cyberspace
The Answer to All Our Prayers?

HANNE SKAADEN
Oslo University College, Norway

MARIA WATTNE
Norwegian Union of Municipal and General Workers (Fagforbundet)

Abstract. *An internet-based course on public sector interpreting was developed and tested by the authors for the University of Oslo and the Norwegian Directorate of Immigration in 2004. A mixed-gender group of 116 students (the majority of whom were immigrants) attended the online course, in which 13 working languages (including Norwegian as the common denominator) were represented. Drawing on this experience, the authors critically discuss both the advantages and the challenges of taking the interpreting student into the cyber-classroom, and illustrate that interpreting competencies and subject-specific knowledge can be successfully acquired in cyberspace. The pedagogical approach is inspired by experiential learning theory (Kolb 1984, cf. Boyatzis et al. 1995). Taking the importance of interpreter training as a starting point and using examples from the cyber-learning environment created for the course, the authors demonstrate the applicability of this pedagogical approach to the instruction of interpreters in general and its relevance in the context of an online-based approach in particular.*

1. Introduction: The need for interpreter training

Public sector interpreting[1] enables professionals and public servants to guide, inform and "hear" the parties in the case at hand, despite language barriers (Skaaden 2001:171). In the type of institutional dialogue commonly associated with public sector interpreting, such as the police interview or the doctor-patient consultation, the interlocutors' legal safeguard largely depends on the quality of the interpreting. The possibility of monitoring interpreting quality in public sector settings is restricted, however, due

---

[1] We prefer the term **public sector interpreting** to the term "community interpreting" and define public sector interpreting as inclusive of interpreting in legal settings. For discussions on the term **community interpreting**, see e.g. Mikkelson (1996); Gentile (1997); Skaaden (2001).

to factors of professional secrecy and the sensitivity of the information exchanged. Furthermore, few interpreters practising in this type of setting have been given the opportunity to document or enhance their qualifications. At least this is the case in Norway, where only 250 interpreting students, covering 15 languages, received university level training between 1985 and 2003. Given the fact that there is a registered need for interpreting in approximately 100 languages in Norway, this number is far too low.

The need for enhancing the practising interpreters' qualifications is, moreover, documented both by qualitative analyses of interpreted discourse (Nilsen 2000) and the bilingual screening of practitioners' lexical knowledge (Skaaden 2003). In 2003, the Norwegian authorities launched a project to improve the availability of interpreter training through the development of university level, online-based courses. Four educational institutions were involved in a two-year project. This article describes the solution developed at the University of Oslo.

2. Why bring the interpreting student into the Cyber-Classroom?

Regardless of setting and language combination, interpreting requires the mastery of a diversity of skills. In addition to the basic requirement for a high degree of bilingual proficiency, the interpreter relies on a high level of stress tolerance, concentration and stamina, along with factors such as good hearing, pronunciation and diction, as emphasized by Moser-Mercer (1994:60-61). Moreover, thorough understanding of the interpreter's function in the communicative process and his or her area of expertise are required to ensure interpreting quality.

Interpreter training is definitely a skills-based subject – it is something you do, not just something you may read and talk about. Hence, the question arises as to whether it is at all possible to take the interpreting student into the cyber-classroom so as to acquire the required skills. When teaching interpreting, one is faced with a number of pedagogical challenges, even in on-campus training programs, such as the integration of practice and theory into the curriculum (Gentile 1995). In distance learning, technology may present additional challenges of its own to students and teachers (Steyn 1999:18). Moreover, the teaching of multi-language groups (including languages as diverse as Amharic, French, Mandarin, Sorani and Thai), which requires the use of several alphabets, presents challenges concerning the existing cyber-learning platforms.

In the case of Norway, the application of cyber solutions was born out of necessity. Despite its low number of inhabitants (4.5 million), Norway is a large country, covering more than 300 000 square kilometres. Norway's geography, moreover, makes travel time-consuming and expensive. Therefore, earlier attempts to organize on-campus training for interpreters did not have the desired effects. After spending 1-2 semesters in the training course, the interpreting students would often remain in the Oslo area, or would return home to another part of the country only to find their job occupied by someone else (Skaaden 1999:36). Furthermore, when planning interpreter training, it is necessary to take into account the fact that interpreters tend to be freelancers. Hence, the interpreter's career path in the public sector is determined by the market's need for his or her particular language combination. In terms of duration, the interpreter's career may often resemble that of an athlete's (i.e. 5-10 years of active service). The flexible learning options of online technology offer a unique opportunity to respond to some of these challenges.

3.   The course: its students and the pedagogical approach

The current data emerge from a group of 116 students who attended the online-based course at the University of Oslo from January to December 2004.[2] The group had 12 working languages: Albanian, Amharic, Dari, French, Mandarin, Persian, Somali, Sorani, Thai, Turkish, Urdu and Vietnamese. The students' second working language was always Norwegian. A majority of the students were adult immigrants, some were second generation immigrants, and a few were native Norwegians. At the outset of the course, the students' age was between 19 and 59. Gender representation in the student group was 59 per cent men and 41 per cent women.

The 2004 class were recruited from a total of 246 applicants through a screening procedure that involved a bilingual lexical knowledge test and an oral aptitude test. This oral test simulated the consecutive interpreting of 15-20 short sequences in each language direction. The pass rate for the entrance tests was less than 50 per cent. Overall, the duration of the course was 32 weeks, and this equalled one semester's full time study (i.e. 30 credits). At the end of the course there were two pieces of assessment: an essay on a given topic related to professional ethics and an oral test in

---

[2] A second group of 79 students, whose languages were Arabic, Dari, Persian, Polish, Somali, Sorani, Spanish, Tamil and Urdu, followed the same course in 2005.

which the student had to consecutively interpret an institutional dialogue. These two pieces of assessment were graded separately. Of the 116 students who entered the course, 94 completed both semesters. Therefore, at 81 per cent, the course had a high completion rate (cf. Carr 2000, on online course completion rates).

In online learning, it is of primary importance to choose technology that all students may access and become comfortable with. Based on the experience gained from interpreter training by distance learning in Canada, Steyn (1999:17) recommends that the technology should be kept as simple as possible. Accordingly, in our case, all communication is carried out via the learning platform *Fronter* (see www.fronter.no). In addition, there are six weekend on-campus gatherings that are mainly devoted to practical interpreting exercises. In the on-campus exercises the students practise interpreting in role-played institutional dialogues in groups of approximately 15 students, and observe and discuss one another's performance. The on-campus classes are not further described here, but it is worth noting that their structured interpreting exercises are integrated into the thematic progression of the overall course.

The pedagogical approach applied is inspired by Kolb's (1984) notion of **experiential learning theory**, which implies that the students and their experiences are a main resource in learning (see also Boyatzis *et al.* 1995). In this approach, learning involves linking doing and thinking through structured reflection. The teacher's main task is to draw on the students' individual or group experiences in order to promote structured reflection and to facilitate learning. This basic pedagogical idea is adhered to in the organization of both the on-campus and online classes.

4.   The content of the course – what do interpreting students need to learn?

The overall aim of the course is to prepare the student for the consecutive interpreting of institutional dialogues within the framework of the Norwegian public sector. Consequently, the content of the course and its focus revolve around four basic topic areas:

a.   the interpreter's field of expertise and his or her area of responsibility: i.e. the interpreter's code of ethics and its link to basic human rights; the interpreting profession, etc.
b.   the interpreter's basic tool: i.e. addressing the questions "what is language"; "what are linguistic registers"; "what is bilingualism", etc.

    c.   general contextual or situational knowledge and models of communi-
        cation: i.e. addressing the questions "what characterizes a dialogue",
        "what characterizes an institutional dialogue", "what characterizes
        interpreted discourse", etc.

    d.   specific contextual knowledge: i.e., what does the interpreter need
        to know about the area(s) of expertise of the professionals leading
        the institutional dialogue; how to prepare for assignments, etc.

The last topic area (d) does not aim to cover all the language domains it is necessary for an interpreter to become familiar with, which are, in principle, immeasurable. The aim is rather, by way of example, to facilitate the students' development of strategies and reflective practice that they may utilize in their future interpreting careers. Hence, the spring semester addresses terminology and the frameworks of the Norwegian social and health care systems, while the autumn semester addresses the Norwegian legal and justice systems, and selected parts of public administration. The students' task is to cooperate in making comparative analyses between the societies covered by their working languages. The learning activities focusing on specific contextual knowledge (d) are therefore carried out within each language group, and the group as a whole is encouraged to share their knowledge and suggestions.

The four topic areas are interrelated, and the aim is to give the student a well founded basis for handling challenges in real life, for instance: how to recognize the boundaries of the interpreter's area of expertise and stay within them; how to optimize the interpreting tools and how to prepare for assignments; how to utilize the interpreting tools optimally in given situations and how to cooperate with the professional leading the situation; and how to utilize the strategies developed during the course when confronted with new spheres of knowledge.

5.   Organizing classes in cyberspace

For the cyber-class to succeed, **structure, predictability** and **pace** in the organization of the learning activities is a necessity. The student needs to know what to do, where and when. Being explicit about the behaviour expected online and about the students' responsibility for their own learning is also important. In the current course, these expectations, as well as the manner in which the learning activities are structured, are clearly signalled from the start. At the beginning of each semester, the students are presented with a detailed week-by-week plan for all activities. In addition, reminders pop up on the active message board. Moreover, the first on-campus meeting, organized early in the first semester, includes an introduction to *Fronter* and the structure within it that was developed for our course.

The basic structure of the online activities is reflected by two "rooms" in *Fronter*: the **auditorium** – to which all students have access – and the **language room** – to which the students of each language group have access (i.e. the Albanian room, the Amharic room, etc.). Apart from displaying information, each room has an asynchronous (forum) channel and a synchronous (chat) channel, the latter providing the opportunity for online communication in real time. The activities in the auditorium and language rooms resemble each other in structure, and follow a two-week cycle (i.e. a focus topic appears in the auditorium one week and is discussed in the chat and forum channels the following week). In the concurrent week, a focus topic appears in the language room. The topic is discussed in the chat and forum channels of the respective language rooms the following week.

A focus topic in the auditorium is a short text introducing a selected topic within the field of interpreting (e.g. interpreter impartiality and fidelity; the individual, culture and prejudice; contrastive perspectives on the expression of emotions and taboos; the interpreter's own health; etc.). The focus topic simultaneously presents questions for discussion and points to other relevant texts in the curriculum.

A focus topic in the language room presents selected newspaper texts and links to websites on the relevant subtopic (e.g. the anatomy of the human body; diagnoses and symptoms; the police interview; the asylum process; legal terminology and procedures; etc.). The students are invited to search for related texts and links in their working language, and are requested to discuss difficult terminology on the chat and forum channels the following week. In addition, each language room contains a **term bank** (i.e. a digital dictionary presenting, in Norwegian, concepts from the public sector domain with definitions). During the course, the students, working in cooperation within their language group, are required to contribute to the term bank with corresponding terminology from their other working language (i.e. not Norwegian).

5.1 Chat capability – illustrations from online learning

In their textbook on cyber-learning environments, Palloff and Pratt (1999) recommend asynchronous over synchronous communication in the cyber-classroom. In fact, they warn against the many challenges of synchronous meetings and "find that it rarely allows for productive discussion or participation and frequently disintegrates into simple one-line contributions of minimal depth" (*ibid.*:47). In our experience, however, chat capability may be utilized to promote both reflection and collaboration within the student group, and we shall illustrate that it facilitates learning both in the language room and in the auditorium. At the same time, we have found that the asynchronous forum channel is well suited to certain tasks, such as the exchange of case descriptions followed by discussion of alternative solutions and their consequences.

The chat capability was utilized effectively for discussions both in the language rooms and the auditorium. The synchronous communication, in our experience, also contributes to the dynamics of the learning environment and motivates the students to attend the cyber-classroom. Therefore, in the remainder of this essay we shall restrict description to our utilization of the synchronous sessions.

5.2   Chat capability in the language rooms

For chat sessions to be successful, Palloff and Pratt (2001:27) recommend that groups should be relatively small and that each meeting should have a clear agenda. In addition, chat sessions should not be too lengthy. Our language room chat sessions have a time frame of 90 minutes. Here, the agenda is set by the terminology topic introduced the previous week. The group may also select terminology from the "term bank" and related context knowledge for discussion. The goal is to instigate collaboration that enhances the individual's bilingual knowledge. Excerpt 1 illustrates how the students cooperate in clarifying medical terminology. The example from the French room shows the participation of four students, three women (f) and one man (m).[3]

Excerpt 1:
1.   fFren1-19:54> I found this on the web: *Centre d'Hygiène Alimentaire et d'Alcoologie (CHAA), l.m. Définition: Structure d'accueil, de soins*

---

[3] For the sake of anonymity, the student's identity is here represented by the letter *m* or *f* (indicating whether the student is male or female), then the first four letters of the student's working language and a digit that indicates the student's number of appearance in the excerpt at hand, followed by the time of posting. The digits to the far left indicate the number of postings in the excerpt. The excerpts are translated from Norwegian by the authors.

et de prévention où est assuré le suivi ambulatoire de personnes confrontées à un problème d'alcoolisation.

2. fFren1-19:55> and I thought it might be the same as "A-klinikk" [i.e. alcoholics' rehabilitation clinic]
3. fFren2-20:07> sounds right. I didn't find any better alternatives. What about the term "audiograf" [audiologist]?
4. fFren3-20:08> I've never heard of the CHAA before, but it might be the right term for "A-klinikk". Is it a public or private type of institution?
5. fFren1-20:09> I don't know. Found it on a list with terminology related to alcoholism
6. fFren2-20:09> I think they can be both private and public. The Blue Cross and the Olafia Clinic, places like that?
7. mFren1-20:10> don't know, but it sounds like an ok translation to me
8. mFren1-20:11> "anlegg"? [i.e. (pre)disposition, aptitude, tendency]
9. mFren1-20:12> some of the words are really strange
10. fFren2-20:12> *predisposition, aptitude, tendance...* What about audiologist?

One of Palloff's and Pratt's (1999) objections to chat discussions is that they may easily end up out of sync. A response may appear several lines later "due to the number of people posting or the speed of the connection" (*ibid.*:47). Moreover, "dominance in a chat session often goes to the fastest typist", according to the same authors (2001:28). Chat discourse may indeed favour the fast typist, but, in our experience, the students are good at picking up and clarifying points. An example of student persistence is found in Excerpt 1, where fFren2 posts a request for the term *audiograf* ("audiologist") in 3. When the request is ignored, she picks it up in 10, when the discussion on the term "A-klinikk" seems completed.

A moderator was present in all our chat sessions. The chat in excerpt 1 flows without the moderator's interference, however, and is thus carried out in line with the basic pedagogical idea of the course – i.e. that the students are the main resource in the learning process. In Excerpt 1, the French group includes students both with native French and native Norwegian backgrounds. This type of group diversity is an advantage in bilingual collaboration. In language groups where all students have a similar bilingual profile, in that they are all immigrants, the moderator role may become more distinctive. In this latter situation, it is of primary importance that the moderator act as a learning facilitator and not as a "lecturer" who provides the correct answers.

Excerpt 2, from the Persian room, illustrates how the moderator's role in facilitating learning can be handled. Here, the moderator has an unobtrusive presence, and only intervenes to draw attention to a distinction that needs to be emphasized. The topic of discussion in Excerpt 2 is pregnancy and the anatomy of the female body.

Excerpt 2:

1. mPers1-18:15> What are Fallopian tubes in Persian?
2. fPers1-18:16> *lolehaye tokhmdan* [Fallopian tubes]
3. mPers1-18:16> Thank you, fPers1
4. fPers2-18:16> the "egg pipes"
5. mPers1-18:17> What is ovary?
6. fPers2-18:17> *tokhmadan* [ovaries]
7. mPers2 -18:17> I totally agree
8. mPers3 -18:18> ovary is *tokhmdan* in Persian
9. mPers1-18:18> Do we have a word for vagina?
10. fPers1-18:19> yes, *wajan* [vagina]
11. moderator -18:19> There is a difference between Fallopian tubes and ovaries. Does anyone know the difference?

Again, Excerpt 2 illustrates how students can benefit from their complementary knowledge. Since both men and women attend the chat, Excerpt 2 simultaneously illustrates a virtue of the cyber-classroom and its "distant presence" – some topics are probably easier to address here than in a traditional classroom.

Finally, Excerpt 2 illustrates that the Persian group uses transcriptions in the Latin alphabet. Unfortunately, the chat tool implemented in *Fronter* could only handle the Latin alphabet. Since seven of our twelve language groups use another alphabet, transcriptions became a challenge, and forced the students to use more Norwegian than planned. The Thai group, for whom transcriptions into the Latin alphabet result in extremely long words, consequently made mostly use of the asynchronous forum. The Turkish group, as well, although using the Latin alphabet, preferred the asynchronous forum over the synchronous chat, since they found that the chat channel could not handle their diacritics sufficiently well. The problem, however, is due to the *Fronter* chat tool, and does not pertain to the pedagogical model *per se*. More sophisticated chat tools do exist, and should also be integrated into *Fronter*.

5.3   Chat sessions in mixed language groups

The basic aim of the auditorium chat sessions is to promote reflection on selected topics related to interpreter ethics and interpreted discourse. For the auditorium chats the students are divided into eight groups and are assigned to a one-hour slot every two weeks. In order to promote reflection and facilitate generalizations across languages and cultures, the groups have a maximal language mix. The organization of the chat sessions into mixed language groups in itself facilitates a learning path, since the students learn that most of the interpreter's challenges are not specific to their language and culture, but rather pertain to the interpreter's specific position in the communication.

The agenda for each chat in the auditorium is to discuss and elaborate on the focus topic presented the previous week. Again, the students are the main resource in the learning process. For the auditorium chat discussions, however, the moderator needs to plan and structure the discussion a little more than in the language rooms. When leading this type of chat, the facilitator's role needs to be clearly communicated by the moderator, who again does not hold "the right answers". In order to foster a reflective attitude among the group, it is important for the moderator to pose open-ended questions that require more than a simple "yes" or "no" answer. As suggested by Palloff and Pratt (2001:88, 121), asking the students to exemplify and draw on their own experience is another strategy that may lead to fruitful reflection. Excerpt 3 illustrates how reflection is prompted and promoted by the moderator's request for examples in a chat on the interpreter's risk of suffering from burnout.

Excerpt 3
1.   moderator - 18:24> If one of the speakers signals his or her distrust towards the interpreter, e.g. because of ethnicity. How may this drain the interpreter's energy? Any examples?
2.   mSora1 - 18:25> one thing I have noticed is that some people regard the interpreter as the client's representative. They even use the word "dere" [i.e. Norwegian you-pl. – about the interpreter and client]
3.   fSora1 - 18:26> right, I have experienced that too several times. In particular at the ODE [The Official Driving Examiners]
4.   mPers1 - 18:27> What happened at the ODE?
5.   fSora1 - 18:28> that the examiner was very sceptical, and seemed suspicious. It's something that's really annoying, and you can't help but think about it

6. mPers2 - 18:30> I have heard that some interpreters misused their position at the ODE [referring to cases where the interpreter has been accused of doing the test on behalf of the candidate]

The initial topic of the chat in Excerpt 3 is the interpreter's own health and the danger of burnout. The request to share their experiences from difficult situations leads to the categorization of previous experiences and facilitates reflection on the consequences of the interpreter's choices and professional attitude. Excerpt 4 is drawn from another group discussing the same topic. Here, we may observe how group dynamics lead to reflection and learning.

Excerpt 4:

1. mAmha1 17:25> the fact that the interpreter cannot vocalize his/her own viewpoint is taxing. You have to learn to carry your feelings and opinions inside.
2. fAmha1 17:26> what about having an opinion as long as the interpreter does not get in the way of the communication?
3. mAmha1 17:28> what do you mean by that, fAmha1?
    [...]
4. fPers1 17:33> it is important to realize that such restrictions are common to most professionals
5. fAmha1 17:35> does the interpreter have no freedom of opinion?
6. fPers1 1 17:35> If the interpreter wishes to help one party or the other, this may easily get out of hand and at odds with the purpose of the interpreter's work
7. fPers1 1 17:36> and this may in itself be taxing

Reading the chat logs we may observe a development in the students' understanding of, and attitude towards, the topics discussed. The next excerpt is drawn from a discussion on the relationship between the individual and culture, and how the interpreter's attempts at cultural brokering may contribute to, or reduce, prejudice. The excerpt is the student's response to an earlier post by a fellow student who has claimed that the interpreter should engage in cultural brokering.

Excerpt 5:

1. mAmha1- 19:43> The individual hiding behind the foreign culture may be a wonderful human being who could make himself understood

against all odds, if he/she were given the chance to do so. Here my opinion differs, in that in my opinion a minute interpretation will reduce prejudice.

2. moderator - 19:45> right, mAmha1 – and how may interpreting help the individual to be seen?

3. mAmha1 - 19:47> The professional party in the dialogue will be unable to simply sit and think about the exterior that often contributes to prejudice, but has to listen to the individual in front of him as well. In this situation the interpreter may contribute to cultural understanding by giving a correct rendition

Interpreters working in the public sector setting meet with crisis situations on a daily basis. Compared to other professions, however, they lack both the foundation of an education and a professional network in their efforts to cope. This is in itself a factor that makes the interpreter vulnerable, and the interpreting students voice the need for networks and support solutions. Elaborating on this issue, Excerpt 6 originates from a chat on the topic of professionalization:

Excerpt 6:

1. moderator - 20:43> Do you have any suggestions as to how the interpreter – in the process of adopting a professional attitude, may develop strategies to handle difficult episodes in his/her work situation?

2. mAmha1 - 20:43> interpreters from different language groups may cooperate

3. fFren1 - 20:44> Agree. Language is not crucial in such a case, since we as interpreters experience much the same, and we do have the Norwegian language in common

4. fSora1 - 20:45> mAmha1, where I work as an interpreter, there is no one to cooperate with

5. fAmha1 - 20:45> This course is an arena to become acquainted, and we may continue our collaboration, make appointments and exchange experiences

6. fFren1 - 20:46> Totally agree with you, fAmha1. The web provides an excellent opportunity to start a new way of cooperation and communication!

The excerpt illustrates that the students have detected the virtues of sharing and discussing experiences and mutual challenges across language groups.

Hence, the course seems to have achieved its goal of facilitating learning through student cooperation. Obviously, as observed by the students, the chat capability can also be utilized outside the cyber-classroom in order to facilitate much needed supervision and guidance for interpreters working in the public sector setting.

6.   Findings

In the introduction we stressed the need for the training and education of interpreters who work in the public sector setting. At the same time, we pointed to the fact that when aiming to develop functional training courses for interpreters, one is faced with a multitude of challenges, pedagogical as well as structural and organizational. An 81 per cent completion rate is considered a very good result for an online-based course. This result indicates that our course was successful in meeting the students' needs. Apart from the fact that interpreting students in general are thirsty for knowledge and keen to communicate, we believe several factors contributed to the course's success rate.

A primary factor, we believe, is found in the pedagogical approach chosen. The pedagogical idea which formed the foundation of the course is that of facilitating learning through structured reflection based on the students' own experiences. This approach appeals to the adult interpreting student, who is often a knowledgeable person with experience of a diversity of domains. The approach is, moreover, well suited to the cyber-learning environment, as it promotes interactivity and student cooperation. In accordance with the course's basic pedagogical approach, the students' responsibility for their own learning and our expectations about their online behaviour were explicitly communicated to the students from day one.

An essential factor in the success of the course is, furthermore, to be found in our structuring of the learning activities both in the online and on-campus classes. Firstly, the combination of online and campus classes promoted communication and bonds between students and between students and teachers. Secondly, the course was carefully planned as to which learning activity was suited to each channel, and this was essential to enable a safe cyber-learning environment to develop. In particular, for the online activities to succeed, predictability, structure and pace were essential. Being explicit about what to do, where and when created the motivation to meet on the Internet. Interactivity is crucial for the cyber-classroom to succeed, and a decisive factor here lies in our utilization of the synchronous chat discussions. The synchronous sessions added dynamism to the learning environment and helped motivate students to attend the cyber-classroom.

In our choice of technological options, an important rule of thumb was to "keep it simple", in order for the students' home computer technology to keep up and ensure all students equal access. Obviously, the learning effect of a highly sophisticated technological solution may be zero if the student's home technology does not allow him or her to access it. Moreover, a multitude of technological options may confuse the less cyber-wise students, rather than entice them into the activities. Hence, relative simplicity in technological solutions promotes interactivity in the cyber-classroom.

Finally, aptitude and screening tests, controlling the admitted students' basic bilingual skills, are, in our opinion, a must for any interpreter training course. In our case, the entrance test (where, as previously stated, the pass rate was less than 50 per cent) ensured a relatively high proficiency level on the part of all the students. As a result, the students admitted to the course appreciated each other's skills, and this in turn created the basis for fruitful student cooperation.

In conclusion, the cyber-classroom is a cost-efficient solution that affords freelance interpreters the possibility of enhancing their competence without giving up their career as practising interpreters. Our experience has shown that the Internet offers new possibilities for responding to some of the challenges that have characterized earlier attempts to organize interpreter training or education. We have also illustrated that a pedagogical approach in which the students and their experiences are considered a main resource in the learning process has much to offer – both to interpreter training courses and to the cyber-learning environment.

References

Boyatzis, Richard E., Scott S. Cowen and David A. Kolb (1995) *Innovation in Professional Education: Steps on a Journey from Teaching to Learning,* San Francisco: Jossey-Bass Management Series.

Carr, Sarah (2000) "As Distance Education Comes of Age, The Challenge Is Keeping the Students", in *The Chronicle of Higher Education. Information Technology,* http://chronicle.com/free/v46/i23/23a00101.htm.

Gentile, Adolfo (1995) "Translation Theory Teaching. Connecting Theory and Practice", in Cay Dollerup and Vibeke Appel (eds) *Teaching Translation and Interpreting 3*, Amsterdam: John Benjamins, 55-63.

------ (1997) "Community Interpreting or not? Practices, Standards and Accreditation" in S.E. Carr, R. Roberts, A. Dufour and D. Steyn (eds) *The*

Critical Link: Interpreters in the Community, Amsterdam/Philadelphia: John Benjamins, 109-19.

Kolb, David A. (1984) *Experiential Learning: Experience as the Source of Learning and Development,* Englewood Cliffs, N.J.: Prentice-Hall.

Mikkelson, Holly (1996) "Community Interpreting: An Emerging Profession", *Interpreting* 1(1): 125-31.

Moser-Mercer, Barbara (1994) "Aptitude Testing for Conference Interpreting: Why, When and How", in S. Lambert and B. Moser-Mercer (eds) *Bridging the Gap. Empirical Research in Simultaneous Interpretation,* Amsterdam: John Benjamins, 57-69.

Nilsen, Anne B. (2000) "Lik mulighet for å forstå og bli forstått?" [Equal opportunity to understand and being understood?], in K. Andenæs, N. Gotaas, A. B. Nilsen and K. Papendorf (eds) *Kommunikasjon og rettssikkerhet. [Communication and Legal Safeguard],* Oslo: Unipub, 23-48.

Palloff, Rena M. and Keith Pratt (1999) *Building Learning Communities in Cyberspace. Effective Strategies for the Online Classroom,* San Francisco: Jossey-Bass Publishers.

------ (2001) *Lessons from the Cyberspace Classroom. The Realities of Online Teaching,* San Francisco: Jossey-Bass Publishers.

Skaaden, Hanne (1999) "Immigration, Integration and Interpreting in Norway. Principles and Practices", *Proceedings of The 1st Babelea Conference on Community Interpreting,* London: Languageline / Babelea European Association, 30-38.

------ (2001) "Etikk og epiteter på tolkefeltet" [Ehtics and epithets in the field of interpreting], in Anne Golden and Helene Uri (eds) *Andrespråk, tospråklighet, norsk [Second Language, Bilingualism, Norwegian],* Oslo: Unipub, 164-79.

------ (2003) "On the Bilingual Screening of Interpreter Applicants", in Ángela Collados Áis, M. Manuela Fernández Sánchez and Daniel Gile (eds) *La evaluación de la calidad en interpretación: Investigación,* Granada: Interlingua, 73-85.

Steyn, Dini (1999) *Distance Education Introduction to Interpreting. Final Report,* OLT Project #69011.

Interpreters in Emergency Wards

An Empirical Study of Doctor-Interpreter-Patient Interaction

RAFFAELA MERLINI

Facoltà di Lettere e Filosofia, University of Macerata, Italy

Abstract. *This paper explores interpreting practice in the field of emergency medicine. The analysis is conducted on a corpus of tape-recorded interpreter-mediated encounters between the medical staff of an Italian hospital and English-speaking tourists. The specificity of the setting – an Accident & Emergency Ward – where patients are not members of a minority community, but feel nonetheless vulnerable because the emergency has occurred away from home, as well as the unusual profile of the interpreters who are employed on a seasonal basis as "administrative assistants", make this study an atypical investigation into public service interpreting. Through the use of different theoretical approaches – from Fairclough's distinction between powerful and non-powerful participants, to ten Have's notion of phase-specific conversational patterns, to Hall's theory of contexting – it is demonstrated that asymmetry in medical encounters is the product of a complex set of factors. More specifically, it is a shifting variable which is locally and interactionally determined through successive turns at talk by all interlocutors, doctor, patient and interpreter alike. The latter, in particular, is seen to behave as a fully-fledged social actor who makes independent choices on the basis of his or her assessment of the goals and requirements of the ongoing activity.*[1]

1. Introduction

This study is part of a wider research project designed to build a corpus of audio-recorded dialogue interpreting sessions taking place in a variety of professional fields – from healthcare to immigration services and business negotiations – which can serve as an empirical basis for investigation of real-life interpreting practices. Given the confidential nature of most of these face-to-face encounters and the consequent difficulty in obtaining authorization to record them, to date, relatively few analyses have been conducted

[1] I am indebted to Diana Unfer for the time and energy she spent in collecting the data. Without her enthusiastic commitment, this study would not have been possible.

on transcribed interpreted interactions.[2] In an attempt to contribute to this area of research, the present discussion explores the behaviour of partici-pants in medical encounters from the point of view of their contribution to and control over the ongoing activity. Taking as a starting point the by now largely accepted and documented view of the dialogue interpreter as an active participant in the interaction,[3] the following analysis will show how the interlocutors' moment-by-moment decisions concur to shape the structure of discourse at the various stages of the communicative event.

2.   The setting and the data

The data for this study were collected over a one-month period – July 2004 – by a student interpreter who worked under my supervision, Ms. Diana Unfer.[4] Since ensuring the anonymity of both the facility and the staff involved in the encounters was a *sine qua non* condition to obtain the authorization to record, it will only be said here that the setting is a National Health Service hospital, located in a popular tourist destination, a seaside resort in Northern Italy, which, every summer, attracts large numbers of holidaymakers from the United Kingdom, as well as from other countries of northern, central and eastern Europe. Given this seasonal inflow of for-eign visitors, the local health authorities operate every year, from May to September, an additional Accident & Emergency Ward specifically reserved for tourists (*Ambulatorio di Medicina Turistica*) within the Casualty Depart-ment of the general hospital.

Posts for "Administrative Assistants-Interpreters" are usually advertised every two years, following an assessment of the previous years' needs in terms of number of staff and languages required.[5] The job title is deliberately

---

[2] For a review of past studies on recorded interaction in the field of medical interpret-ing, see Bolden (2000). More recently, three full-length monographs have appeared – namely Angelelli (2004); Meyer (2004) and Bot (2005) – which draw on extensive corpora of recorded data.

[3] See Wadensjö's (1998) seminal work on the multi-faceted nature of interpreters' conduct in face-to-face interaction.

[4] Her unpublished dissertation (Unfer 2003-2004) offers a detailed, first-hand description of both the professional setting and the recorded data.

[5] The hospital in question has been operating the interpreting service for more than 15 years and is currently participating in an EU-wide research programme, which focuses on enhancing communication between medical staff and foreign patients. At the end of each consultation, the latter are routinely asked to fill in a questionnaire to evaluate

chosen to indicate that successful applicants will be asked to perform a series of administrative tasks alongside the interpreting one, such as hospital reception work, filing patients' details, providing information on services, procedures and payments, etc. Requirements for the post make no specific mention of academic qualifications in either translation or interpreting. The selection is carried out through an interview which is designed to test the applicants' knowledge of the foreign language(s). The successful candidates are then recruited on a seasonal basis for a period of 5 months. On-the-job training is provided, but only in the administrative field.

From a practical point of view, it is interesting to note that interpreters wear the same white uniform as the medical staff and could easily be mistaken for bilingual nurses by foreign patients, and all the more so because they prepare the patients' case notes, inquiring about the nature of the complaint, and sometimes even about the symptoms, before ushering them into the doctor's room. At the end of the consultation with the doctor, interpreters are once again left to deal on their own with the patients, to give them technical instructions, or simply direct them to another hospital facility or to the closest chemist. We will see that this perception of the interpreter as a member of the medical staff has an impact on the interaction.

The recorded sessions involved the following participants. The interpreters were two young women with a degree in foreign languages; they have been renamed here Tina and Teresa (i.e. names beginning with T for tourism). Out of the 9 encounters, Tina interpreted 6 (T.1, T.2, T.3, T.6, T.7, T.8) and Teresa 3 (T.4, T.5 and T.9). The doctors were all male. The patients, or at least one of the parents in the case of children, spoke English, although only in 4 cases were they British nationals and native speakers of the language. The remaining patients came from Poland (2), Denmark (2) and the Netherlands (1).

Table 1 offers a schematic illustration of the encounters. Sessions 1 to 5, highlighted by means of shaded cells in the table, will provide the exemplification for the present discussion. All the complaints reported by the patients were either minor injuries or minor ailments. Aside from the requirement of anonymity, this was the only limitation imposed on the observer, who was not allowed in the room when more serious cases were being dealt with.

---

the quality of the information they received through the interpreter. The results of the survey will be used to critically assess and improve the interpreting service.

Place	A&E Ward for Tourists, Italian NHS Hospital		
	Transcript 1 (T. 1)	Transcript 2 (T. 2)	Transcript 3 (T. 3)
Date	14 July 2004	14 July 2004	22 July 2004
Duration	10' 49"	6' 31"	14' 27"
Interpreter	Tina	Tina	Tina
Patient	Polish baby girl with her parents	English woman	English woman
Complaint	High temperature and red dots	Eye problems	Swollen ankles
	Transcript 4 (T. 4)	Transcript 5 (T. 5)	Recording 6
Date	27 July 2004	27 July 2004	19 July 2004
Duration	6'	11'	6' 22"
Interpreter	Teresa	Teresa	Tina
Patient	English girl with her parents	Polish baby boy with his parents	Young Dutch woman accompanied by her employer
Complaint	Ear pain	High temperature	Sore knee
	Recording 7	Recording 8	Recording 9
Date	22 July 2004	22 July 2004	27 July 2004
Duration	9' 10"	14'	4' 35"
Interpreter	Tina	Tina	Teresa
Patient	Danish boy with his parents	Young Danish woman	Young English man
Complaint	Nasal herpes	Stiff neck	Sore throat

Table 1: The recorded sessions

3. The medical encounter in an Accident & Emergency (A&E) Ward

Following the literature on doctor-patient interaction (see, e.g., Byrne and Long 1976; Heath 1986; Waitzkin 1991) the typical phase-by-phase structure of a medical encounter can be represented as follows:

1. opening
2. complaint presentation
3. verbal and physical examination
4. delivery of diagnosis

5. prescription of treatment and/or advice
6. closing

Within this conventional framework, ten Have (1991:151) suggests classifying sequences of talk, which he calls "episodes", according to their higher vs. lower "conversational quality", i.e.:

- type 1 episodes, in which non-medical topics are discussed;
- type 2 episodes, which have to do with medical topics that are relatively marginal to the main agenda of the consultation;
- type 3 episodes, in which the main medical agenda is explicitly developed.

In the opening phase of an encounter, parties usually engage in small talk (type 1 episodes) to establish a relationship. Type 1 and type 2 sequences may also occur whilst a predominantly non-verbal activity is being performed, such as the physical examination. Type 2 episodes tend to concentrate mainly towards the closing of the encounter (stages 5 and 6 above), as the patients may want to "clarify any residual matters" following the physician's "exposition" of the diagnosis (Tebble 1999:185), or "elicit some minor medical advice or submit some medical idea of their own, even if it is not related to the major agenda" (ten Have 1991:151). Type 3 sequences, on the other hand, are usually characteristic not only of the announcement of the diagnosis, but, prior to this, of the verbal stage of the data-gathering activity, otherwise known as history taking (or, in medical jargon, differential diagnosis).[6] This phase, which is the least "conversational" in nature, normally entails a question-answer pattern tightly controlled by the doctor, where patient-initiated topics are largely dispreferred.

Before discussing the notion of asymmetry in the questioning format, let us briefly consider the features which differentiate consultations concerning minor injuries and ailments in an A&E Ward, in particular those involving foreign patients, from similar events occurring in other healthcare settings. Unlike in the case of the "informing interview" (see Maynard 1991, 1992), when doctors meet again with patients, after the latter have gone through a series of examinations, to present the findings and deliver a final diagnosis, the doctor-patient encounter in an A&E Ward is by definition an emergency consultation. When the complaint is a minor one and the condition of the

---

[6] For extensive bibliographical references on the process of differential diagnosis, see Bolden (2000:393).

patient enables him[7] to interact with the medical staff, the encounter will typically proceed from stage 2 through to stage 6, unless the physician requires specific tests – for instance, an x-ray – and refers the patient to the relevant department, thus stopping at stage 3. In either case, the core activity being performed in this context, prior to the emergency treatment (which may be either prescribed or delivered), is the gathering of information through questioning and physical examination.

The emphasis on this phase of the interaction is further reinforced by the fact that patients and doctors are unknown to each other. This means that there is no medical history on which the doctor can base his assessment of the patient's problem, and that the production of a focused historical account becomes fundamental to the forming of an accurate diagnosis.

The urgent nature of the medical condition on the one hand, and on the other the large number of requests which must be handled especially in the summer season impose a fast pace on the encounter, where the occasion for small talk is drastically reduced, introductions are brisk and rapport-building is considered non essential. To go back to ten Have's classification, this means that type 1 episodes are either totally absent or, much less frequently, confined to the physical examination.

If we now consider the case of foreign tourists who do not speak the language of the country they are in, who, whilst on holiday, are faced with a health problem affecting either themselves or their children, who are far away from home and are unable to consult the family doctor, we can easily understand how much more vulnerable these patients must feel in a situation which is naturally stressful. Although this interactional scenario is hardly comparable to the conventional image of a community interpreting framework, where the hierarchical configuration of the participants' roles, naturally stemming from their unequal knowledge, is heightened by a marked status differential (the service users are in this case immigrants and refugees), the psychological dependence on the interpreter can be assumed as a typical trait of this kind of interaction too.

4.   Asymmetry vs. symmetry in medical interviews

As ten Have observes (1991:140), when set against the benchmark of ordinary conversation among peers, doctor-patient communication exhibits

---

[7] In the remaining discussion, doctors and patients will be conventionally referred to as 'he' and interpreters as 'she'.

at least two kinds of asymmetries. First, there is an asymmetry of topic, given that it is the patient's condition that is under examination and not the doctor's. Second, there is an asymmetry of knowledge and therefore of tasks, whereby the patient reports the complaint, answers questions and accepts the doctor's decisions, while the doctor listens to complaints, elicits specific information, makes a diagnosis, and prescribes treatment. This means that, apart from the initial decision to consult a physician and request treatment, the patient loses the initiative early on in the encounter, and the doctor takes over as the dominant party, by controlling the question-answer format.

Investigating interactional behaviour in terms of turn-taking and topic development, researchers have found that moves such as questions, which establish a conditional relevance for specific kinds of actions (i.e. answers), are mostly taken by doctors and seem to be dispreferred when taken by patients. Fairclough (1992:153) argues that this interactional dominance by the doctor results from an asymmetrical and institutionally determined distribution of "talking rights and obligations"[8] between "powerful" (P) and "non-powerful" (N-P) participants, whereby: "(i) P may select N-P, but not vice-versa; (ii) P may self-select, but N-P may not; [...] (iii) P's turn may be extended across any number of points of possible completion". What this means in practice is that the patient usually takes the floor when the doctor offers it by asking him a question. The doctor, on the other hand, is not given the floor but takes it when the patient has finished answering the question, or when he decides that the patient's response has become "irrelevant" to a strictly medical assessment of his problem. In the latter case, overlaps may be used by the doctor as a device to cut short the patient's turn. A corollary of this organization is to do with topic control. It is the doctor who introduces new topics through his questions, "polices the agenda" – the expression is again Fairclough's (*ibid.*:155) – by simply acknowledging the patient's answer without commenting on or assessing it, changes topic abruptly, or else stays on topic by reformulating a question which he thinks has not been satisfactorily answered.

This asymmetrical model is contrasted by Mishler (1984) with a more

---

[8] Drew and Heritage (1992:22) clarify that, in institutional interaction, acceptance of, or rather, adherence to "special and particular constraints on what one or both of the participants will treat as allowable contributions to the business at hand" depends on their orientation to the goals, tasks and identity of the institution in question.

symmetrical interactional format – which the author sees as morally superior and professionally more effective – where the doctor swaps the normative "Voice of Medicine", with its assertiveness, scientific objectivity and affective neutrality, for the "Voice of the Lifeworld", thus displaying a high degree of attentiveness to the patient's understanding of his problem and to his communicative needs. The effect of this alternative conversational style is that turn-taking is more collaboratively managed and topic development more extensively negotiated by the two participants. Although both Mishler and Fairclough explore the possibility of analyzing the same interaction in terms of conflict and struggle between the two voices, with the VoL intruding on the doctor's agenda, they nonetheless seem to imply that the shift in conversational models is made possible primarily by the doctor's willingness to make the floor available to the patient. Fairclough's words (1992:146) are unequivocal:

> Notice that the initiative for yielding a measure of control to the patient in medical interviews of this sort invariably comes from the doctor, which suggests that doctors do still exercise control at some level, even if in the paradoxical form of ceding control.

Looking at doctor-patient interaction from a different angle and explicitly rejecting the notion that asymmetry is simply an effect of institutionalized power relationships, ten Have (1991) suggests considering interactional control as a variable of the specific phase in the interaction. Whereas the patient has limited possibilities for requesting information during the questioning sequences of history taking, his interventions appear to be more acceptable in other phases, for instance during or after the discussion of treatment (see section 3 above).

Whilst accepting both perspectives as promising analytical tools, we would contend that equal attention needs to be devoted to the patient's conduct as a crucial factor in deciding the extent of the doctor's domination on the interaction. Building on the above-mentioned notion of a conflict of voices, what is suggested here is that the selection of a more assertive style by the patient – which may be due to personality, medical knowledge or cultural models – may act as a powerful counterweight to institutionally determined or even phase-specific asymmetries. For the purposes of the present study, let us consider in particular the impact that cultural patterns may have on interactional behaviour. Hall's theory of contexting (1976, 1983) offers an interesting paradigm to assess an individual's communicative style in terms of his or her reliance on explicit information (text) versus implicit information (context), as dictated by the conventional orientations of the culture he or she belongs to. The author's basic distinction between high- and low-context cultures has since been expanded to include other sets of related dichotomies – i.e. direct vs. indirect, and egalitarian vs. hierarchic. Figure 1 below, which is a slightly modified version of the con-texting cline suggested by Victor (1992:143), shows the positioning of the three cultures, namely Italian, British and Polish, involved in the encounters discussed in this paper.

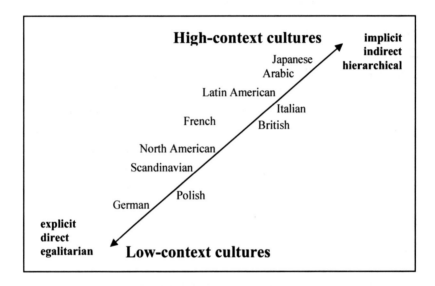

Figure 1: Contexting cline

Whilst the Italian and British cultures are somewhat closer to the Japanese end of verbal restraint and hierarchic positioning, than to the German prefer-ence for explicitness and egalitarianism, the Polish culture – which has been added to the cline following Goddard and Wierzbicka's (1997) description of Polish discourse style – endorses extreme frankness and directness. Given the marked distance between these culture-specific interactional models, a third line of investigation will thus be pursued in the analysis of the recorded sessions. This will be done in full awareness that the limited number of cases under examination cannot obviously be taken as supporting evidence for the validity of theoretical assumptions about culturally divergent patterns of interaction. Cultural modelling will be used here as a supplementary tool, to offer possible explanations of the patients' interactional behaviour, besides personal inclinations and preferences.

If one moves from monolingual settings – either culturally homogeneous or heterogeneous – to linguistically mediated encounters, the picture becomes even more complex, given that the interpreter, who is usually the sole bilingual, is in a somewhat unique position to control the content, direction and organization of the verbal exchange. Depending on her reproduction or modification of the participants' normative orientations or interactional styles,[9] the encounter can be expected to develop along different pathways and produce more or less symmetrical configurations.

5.   Analysis of the data: who leads?

In the following analysis, examples will be organized into three sections according to the party who is monopolizing the initiative at that moment. We will start from sequences where the doctor controls the question-answer cycles, the patient refrains from formulating requests and gives very short and factual answers, and the interpreter confines herself to translation acts. We will then move on to more marked interactional forms, where first the interpreter and then the patients (or their parents) are seen to deviate from their conventional roles.

5.1. The doctor leads

In T1 a Polish baby girl is taken to the emergency ward by her parents because she has had a high temperature for two days and some red dots have appeared on her body. In the following sequence the doctor is clearly seen to proceed through a pre-set agenda. He interrupts the interpreter, before she has finished translating the father's answer, to state his intention to examine the baby (line 128). He then disregards the father's attempt to explain that although the baby did not cry the night before, they as parents know that she is not feeling well (line 130), and asks the mother to hold the baby's head still, thus forcing the interpreter to translate his instruction instead of the father's comment. Lastly, he announces the diagnosis, i.e. an inflammation of the nose.

---

[9] See also Merlini and Favaron (2005).

[1]   T. 1(121-133) [10]

121   D: **allora la bambina ha pianto durante la notte↑**
           now did the girl cry during the night

122   I: did she cry during the night↑ ((the question is first addressed to the mother
123   who does not speak English then to the father)) did she cry during the night↑=

124   F: =no not at all=

125   I: =no not at all

126   F: she is rather silent because=

127   I: =è abbastanza silenziosa la bambina ⌐>°non ha pianto°<
           the girl is rather quiet | *she did not cry*

128   D: └ **va bene vorrei vedere un attimo questo**
                                            alright I would like to examine this

129   I: ⌐°she[11] wants to°
130   F: └ we know that she's ill

131   D: **le tiene ferma la testa**
           can you keep her head still

132   I: °could you keep please the head°

133   D: **va bene comunque la bambina ha in atto una una rinite**
           okay in any case the girl has an inflammation of the nose

T2 presents the case of an English woman complaining of cloudy vision. The doctor, after asking a series of questions aimed at ascertaining the symptoms she is experiencing, changes topic abruptly, cutting short the interpreter's last sentence (line 55) in what had been a long-winded and laborious translation, where the lack of an English word ("shadow") had required the joint efforts of the doctor, who kept offering synonyms for the Italian word ("ombra"), and of the patient, who kept repeating the same concept over and over. Once order is restored, an unmarked sequence follows which sees the doctor regaining total control of the question-answer mechanism (line 57). As reported in the literature on medical interviews,[12] the doctor refrains from utterances indicating his information processing. He simply acknowledges the patient's answers through discourse markers such as *yes, mhm, okay*, and proceeds to check the patient's blood pressure, without any explanation (line 64).

---

[10] Examples are numbered progressively. The acronyms T. 1, T. 2, T. 3, etc. identify the transcript from which a given excerpt has been taken, whilst the numbers in parentheses refer to the place of the reported lines in the transcript. For easier reference, the latter also appear beside each line. Idiomatic translations into English of the Italian utterances are shown in italics. Features of interest are shown in bold. For the transcription key, see appendix 1.

[11] Here, the interpreter's use of "she" instead of "he" to refer to the male doctor is simply a slip of the tongue.

[12] For a review of studies on the physicians' uses of third turns, see ten Have (1991).

[2] T. 2 (50-67)

50 I: └insomma┘ lei vede una forma ner ┌a:=
         so she sees a black shape

51 D: └sì
                                           yes

52 I: =rotonda::
         round

53 D: mhm

54 I: a black shape ┌round

55 D: └okay okay

56 P: yes round

57 D: **la signora soffre di ipertensione la signora↑**
         does the lady suffer from hypertension

58 I: do you suffer from hypertension hypertension↑

59 P: no

60 I: no

61 D: **no ha preso qualche trauma al capo↑**
         has she had any head trauma

62 I: have you got any:: any: trauma↑

63 P: ((shakes her head))

64 D.   **no va be' intanto le misuro la pressione eventualmente**
         no okay in any case I'll check her blood pressure

65 I: we check your pressure=

66 P: =okay=

67 I: =blood pressure

5.2   *The interpreter leads*

Let us now look at sequences where the translation mechanism – i.e., the conversion of each original utterance into an equivalent utterance in the target language – is dropped, and the interpreter is seen either to respond to a primary interlocutor or to take the initiative by introducing new topics. As was previously said, the first person foreign patients meet when coming to the emergency ward is the interpreter, who takes down their names and inquires about the nature of the complaints. It is, therefore, not surprising to see the interpreter introducing the patient and her problem at the beginning of the session, as shown in the following example:

[3] T. 3 (1-7)

1   D: sì
        yes

2   I: **le si è gonfiato un po' le caviglie↑**
        her ankles are a little bit swollen

3   D: come si chiama la signora ↑
        what's the lady's name

4   I: **S. ((spells the surname))**
5   D: sì (.)la signora soffre di ipertensione ↑
           yes does the lady suffer from hypertension

6   I: umm suffer do you suffer hypertension↑
7   P: no

Equally natural is the interpreter's attempt to engage the 7-year old British girl in T4, whom she has already met in the waiting room, in a brief conversation so as to make her feel a bit more relaxed while the doctor is examining her ear:

[4]   T. 4 (16-21)
16   D: si siede qua un attimo↑
           would she come and sit here

17   ((the doctor starts examining the girl))
18   I: °**how old are you C.↑**°
19   P: °seven°
20   I: °seven°
21   D: è la prima volta che le capita   ⌐ questo problema↑ ⌐
           is it the first time that she has had   *this problem*

Whilst autonomous initiatives of these kinds are almost negligible when occurring in type 1 episodes, which are characterized by a marked conversational quality, in type 2 and type 3 episodes, the interpreter's attempt at controlling the interaction may have more serious repercussions. Going back to T3, as the doctor examines the British woman's ankles, Tina, the interpreter, first addresses the latter to comment on her symptoms (line 53), then re-expresses her opinion in Italian (line 55), thus inviting the doctor to respond by selecting him as next speaker:

[5]   T.3 (53-56)
53   I: °do you think they are very swollen or (.) they don't seem to be very swollen ( )°
54   P: ⌐yeah o-on ( )
55   I: ⌐non sembrano tanto gonfie=
           they don't look so swollen

56   D:=un pochino qua mi sembra un po' gonfie qua
           a little bit here I think they are a bit swollen here

In sequence [6], the doctor's later remark, i.e. that the swelling of the left ankle is visibly due to an insect bite, is mistranslated by Tina as a diagnosis for the overall problem (line 96), to which the patient understandably asks whether the puncture on the left ankle can be the cause of the swelling in both ankles. Instead of translating back the patient's question, Tina self-selects as primary interlocutor and reiterates the diagnosis; interestingly enough, at this point she switches from reported speech ("in his opinion he says…") to the first person plural to associate herself with the diagnosis, thus projecting the idea that she is part of the medical staff (lines 98-99). The hesitations in her utterance are, however, an indicator that she sees the point the woman is trying to make. In her next turn, she therefore checks again with the doctor whether he thinks that the swelling might be caused by the insect bite. Unfortunately, she then sticks to the same statement (lines 106-107) instead of translating the doctor's intention to check the patient's pulse. It will take many more turns before the woman is explicitly told that the problem might derive from her high blood pressure.

[6]   T.3 (94-107)
94   D: ∟ qua si è gonfia:ta > perché la signora < è stata punta da un
                            here it is swollen because the lady was bitten by an

95   insetto sicuramente
            insect for sure

96   I: **in his opinion he says you have been bitten by an insect**
97   P: and would that make both ankles to swell↑
98   I: **yes we-w- yes we suppose >this is the< the reason why you are why your**
99   **ankles are so swollen**
100   P: right
101   I: tu pensi che sia così gon ⌐fio↑=
            do you think it is so swollen

102   D: ∟è molto probabile ⌐ il polso↑
                            it's very likely   *her pulse*

103   I: ∟=per una puntura
                                                because of the puncture

104   d'INSETTO↑
            of an insect

105   D: perché il problema circolatorio adesso le misuro anche la pressione ⌐però il polso
         because the circulation problem now I'll also take her blood pressure   *yet her pulse*

106   I: ∟yes he
107   **probably says you have been bitten by an insect**

In T2, the interpreter's behaviour is potentially dangerous for the patient's health.[13] The interaction has reached the stage in which the doctor is formulating a possible diagnosis, a detached retina, and decides to refer the patient to an eye specialist (lines 68-69). In subsequent sequences, and up

---

[13] For an in-depth discussion of this session, see Merlini (2007).

to the very end of the encounter, this diagnosis is never once translated into English for the patient, who is only told that she needs to see some specialist (lines 82 and 84). Tina is repeatedly found to shift topics and use her translation slots to interact as a powerful primary interlocutor with either the patient, as in [7], or the doctor, as in [8] and [9]:

[7] T. 2(68-84)
68 D: eventualmente la mandiamo a fare una visita urgente specialistica da un oculista
possibly we should make an urgent appointment for her to see an eye specialist

69 perché potrebbe essere un distacco della retina °per cui° adesso vediamo
because it could well be a detached retina so now

70 I: **so please sit here (.) how long are you** ⌜**staying**↑
71 D: ⌞>dove la mandiamo↑<=
where shall we send her

72 P: ⌜( )
73 D: ⌞>dove la mandiamo a XX ⌜X¹⁴<↑
where shall we send her to XX   ⌞ X
74 P: ⌞ back home on Saturday °go home on
75 Saturday°
76 D: può stare seduta
you can sit down

77 I: you can sit
78 D. >sit down<
79 I: yes sit down here yes just-just NOW sit può star seduta vero:↑ (.) **relax yourself**
she can sit down can't she

80 **don't worry**
81 P: ((smiles))
82 I: maybe you need a specialist to visit you
83 P: all right
84 I: you need you need to be visited by a specialist ( )

An interesting feature, aside from the patient's submissiveness (lines 81 and 83), is Tina's attempt to reassure her ("relax yourself don't worry", lines 79-80), which may indicate that the non-translation of the diagnosis is a deliberate choice on her part not to frighten the woman. This interpretation is further supported by a reiteration of the reassuring utterance a few exchanges later, as shown in excerpt [8], line 107. The sequence also contains an aside initiated by Tina, who asks the doctor to comment on the

---

¹⁴ The 3 X's stand for the name of a nearby hospital.

blood pressure reading she has just translated into English (line 97), without then conveying his answer to the patient, who is left with a meaningless string of numbers:

[8]   **T. 2 (95-107)**
95   ((the doctor checks the patient's blood pressure))
96   D: (novanta) centoquarantanove
             ninety one-hundred and fortynine

97   I: ninety one-hundred and fortynine **e com'è quindi**↑
                                                 how high is this then

98   D: leggermente altina quanti anni ha la signora↑
             slightly high how old is the lady

99   I: what how old are you↑
100   P: fiftythree
101   I: fiftythree ((smiles)) cinquantatré
                          fiftythree

102   D: cinquantatré
             fiftythree

103   I: yes
104   D: >sentiamo un attimo il cuore<
             let's listen to the heart

105   I: °he wants to check to check your heart° (.) deve togliersi la ⌐maglietta↑=
                                                      does she have to take off her │ *T-shirt*
106   D: └°sì°
                                                                                       yes

107   I: = YES >you have to ( )< °don't worry°

In [9], as the consultation is coming to a close, Tina is seen to interrupt a primary speaker and shift topics, thus exhibiting once again the behaviour of a powerful participant in Furlough's (1992) terms. Instead of translating the doctor's reiterated indication that there might be some problem with the woman's retina requiring urgent attention, she asks him to confirm the hospital facility where the patient is to be sent (line 123), and then concentrates on practical details as to the way in which the latter can reach it.

[9]   **T.2   (120-131)**
120   D: l-l'iride è normale il riflesso della pupilla è normale però e:videntemente
             the iris is normal the pupil reflex is normal but clearly

121   potrebbe esserci qualcosa a livello della retina personalmente: io la mando a fare
             there might be something wrong with the retina personally I would have her

122   una visita ⌐ specialistica=
             examined │ *by a specialist*
123   I: └ °allora la mandiamo a XXX:↑°
                         so shall we send her to XXX

124 D: =urge:nte: da un oculista
         an eye specialist through an urgent appointment

125 I: **okay (.) you have two choices (.) first possibility you're going to drive to XXX**
126   **have you got a car↑**
127 P: no
128 I: °no niente macchina okay° so you can't go to XXX because we are
         no car okay

129   all together the same hospital and we don't have the the: specialist here you have
130   to go to you have to drive to XXX OR you can go to private o può andare da
                                                                   or she can see a

131   un privato
         private doctor

Sequences [6] to [9] are clearly more of an example of how the interpreter can actually mislead rather than lead the conversation. In the following section, we will see how this incomplete and highly incoherent set of instructions spurs the British woman to change tack.

5.3   The patient leads

The sequence discussed above continues with a series of questions posed by the woman who is clearly concerned about her health and probably scared by what she perceives as a reticence to break bad news:

[10] T.2 (132-157)
132 P: **is it urgent is it urgent↑**
133 I: yes the doctor says it's urgent=
134 P: =urgent ((she turns to the doctor for confirmation))
135 D: sì ((whispered))
         yes

136 P: ⌜⌜ **where's** ⌝ X-=
137 I: ⌞⌞ facciamo: ⌟
             let's

138 P: =**where's X- where's this place X-↑**
139 I: >XXX< but come here sit down here
140 P. **(my pressure)**
141 I: it's light high than usual è un po' dico lievemente ⌜più elevata
                                    shall I say it is a bit   ⌞*higher*
142 D: ⌞sì::
                                                                yes

143 I: just a little bit
144 D: =centoquarantanove su novanta diciamo ⌜>dunque< considerando l'età:↑
         one-hundred and forty-nine over ninety ⌞*so considering her age*
145 I: ⌞one-hundred and forty-nine over

146   ninety
147   P: **my heart is okay↑>my heart is okay<↑**
148   I: il suo cuore è a posto↑
           is her heart okay

149   D: sì il cuore è a posto però il solito   ⌈ problema: ⌉ che può essere correlato ( )=
           yes her heart is okay but this   │ *problem*   │ *is usually related*
150   I: ⌊ °it's okay°   ⌋
151   D: =al momento >comunque< la pressione non è preoccupante=
           at the moment however her blood pressure is not worrying

152   I: =mhm=
153   D: =certo è che:: sarà meglio che insomma che sia vista da un medico °perché°
           in any case she'd better be examined by a specialist because

154   deve esserci un problema all'interno dell'occhio ehm un problema vascolare
           there must be a problem inside the eye a vascular problem

155   °(all'interno dell'occhio)°
           inside the eye

156   ((interpreter and patient exit the room; the interpreter makes the appointment
157   with the eye specialist and explains to the patient how to reach the other hospital))

Although, as stated earlier on, patient-initiated questions are more common in the closing stages of a medical encounter, here this typically unassertive British woman is driven to take the initiative not so much by the delivery of diagnostic news – since almost none has so far been given – as by the interpreter's behaviour. Tina's preoccupation not to alarm the patient has in fact had the opposite effect. Despite her questions, however, the patient will still leave the ward unaware that her eye problems might be due to as serious a condition as a detached retina (lines 156-157).[15]

Let us end this analysis with sequences where the parents of both the

---

[15] Investigating Spanish-speaking patients' knowledge of their discharge diagnosis at a public hospital emergency department in Los Angeles, Baker *et al.* (1996) found markedly lower subjective ratings of understanding for patients who communicated with the English-speaking healthcare personnel through an interpreter compared with those who thought an interpreter was unnecessary and did not have one. More specifically, 16% of patients for whom an interpreter was not needed and not used stated that the physician "did not say the diagnosis", compared with 29% for whom an interpreter was not used although the patient thought one should have been used, and 32% for whom an interpreter was used. In their attempt to explain the reasons why the assistance of interpreters did not improve the patients' understanding of their diagnoses, the authors point to suboptimal interpreting performances, resulting from the use of untrained interpreters, such as other hospital personnel or family members and friends. Although no such *ad-hoc* interpreters are involved in the present study, the lack of formal training in interpreting, particularly in professional ethics, is an underlying concern in our case too.

Polish baby girl (T.1) and the Polish baby boy (T.5) are seen to consistently introduce new topics throughout the two encounters. Only a few exchanges into the data-gathering phase (type 3 episodes), the father of the baby girl offers unasked-for information, as in the following example, where he self-selects as next speaker and starts producing a full account of the previous day, even though the doctor was still inquiring about the dose of Ibuprofen that had been administered to the girl to bring the temperature down:

[11] T. 1 (30-44)

```
30   D:  e gli ha dato quanti millilitri↑
             and how may millilitres did you give her

31   F:   ┌ ┌two point two point five┐
32   I:   └ └due punto cinque        ┘ ogni sei ore ha detto due virgola cinque
               two point five               every six hours he said twopoint five

33        °milligrammi° ogni sei ore
          milligrams every six hours

34        ((background noise))
35   F:   and in the night in the night=
36   I:   =yes=
37   F:   =we were on the beach after uh afternoon because he we asked if we can go=
38   I:   =°mhm°=
39   F:   =outside ( ) so we were afternoon on the beach=
40   I:   mhm
41   P:   =there were no: higher    ┌ temperatures
42   I:                             └ ah so you-you-you went to the beach with the
43        child↑
44   P:   yes
```

A few exchanges later, as the doctor is asking to examine the red dots on the baby's body, the father intervenes again to inform him that his child has an allergy:

[12] T. 1(85-91)

```
85   D:  ┌ ┌va be' vediamola un attimo
         [ [ okay let's have a look at her
86   I:  └ └°e un'altra sulla schiena°
               and another one on the back

87   F:  she's she's an allergician but umm
88   I:  s-she's a↑
89   F:  al-aller she has a-an allergy=
90   I:  =which one↑=
91   F:  =of the milk
```

Similar instances of interactional control are also found during the doctor's prescription of the therapy at the end of the physical examination.

In [13], seeing that only the temperature problem has been addressed (lines 150-151), the father brings the discussion back to the red dots, thus inviting the doctor to have a closer look at the baby:

[13] T. 1(150-157)
150 D: allora umm per il momento l'unica cosa da fare >se vuol tener la bambina< è
         now for the time being the only thing you can do can you hold the baby still is

151   quella di fare una terapia antifebbrile dandogli l'ibuprofene
         to treat her with Ibuprofen for fever relief

152 I: what we can do now is a therapy against ⌐ the fever and=
153 F: └against the fever
154 I: =that's all
155 F: **mhm mhm and the dots↑**
156 I: e queste macchioline che dice perché è venuto principalmente per quello
         and what about the dots because he says that he's come here mainly for them

157 D: sì sì eh le macchioline vediamole meglio un attimo alla luce
         yes yes the dots let's have a better look at them by the light

The father's direct and explicit questioning goes on right to the end of the encounter, when the interpreter has already started dealing with the paperwork formalities, as the sequence 14 shows:

[14] T. 1(243-248)
243 I: devo stampare↑ venticique e ottantadue non hanno titolo
         shall I stamp twenty-five eighty-two they have no title

244 F: **air conditioned can we use in the room↑ air conditioned can**
245   **⌐we use (in the room)**
246 I: └possono usare l'aria condizionata   ⌐ nella stanza↑
         can they use air conditioning   *in the room*
247 D: └ecco meglio evitare
                                                     no better not

248 I: it's better to avoid it (.) for the moment all right↑

         (257-259)
257 F: **and vitamin vitamin C**
258 D: vitamina se vuole   ⌐ gliela può dare
         if he wants to give her the vitamin │ *he can*
259 I: └ yes these vitamins you can

The same interactional style is displayed in T5 by the mother of the Polish boy. Our last example is taken once again from the closing phase of the consultation:

[15] T. 5(168-184)

168 D: il modello centoundici
            the one-hundred-eleven form

169 I: you have any copy of the: e one-hundred-eleven module so coz I left it in the
170   office
171 M: mhm
172 I: °just to see the ( ) thank you°
173 M: **and his throat is is is infected his throat↑**
174 D: è infiammata è infiammata
            it is inflamed it is inflamed

175 I: it's inflamated inflamated
176 M: **inflamated and kind of angina or so↑**
177 I: °angina°
178 D: be' è angina ma per il momento non c'è non ci sono placche digli non ci sono
            well it is angina but for the moment there are no plaques tell her that there are no

179   placche
            plaques

180 I: there's not plaques inside the throat it's not plaques
181 M: **so it's not s-serious↑**
182 I: dice se è
            she asks whether

183 D: no: ⌈ al ⌉ momento no
            no [*for*] *the moment no*
184 I: ⌊ no ⌋

Observation of sessions T.1 and T.5 would seem to reveal the above-mentioned orientation of Polish culture towards text-based, equal-to-equal communication (see section 4). This behaviour stands in stark contrast to the extremely low level of interactivity displayed not only by the two English women, but also by the English parents in T4. Throughout the latter encounter, which cannot be further exemplified owing to constraints of length, the couple never once take the initiative, and mostly confine their interventions to yes/no answers to the doctor's questions, clearly not out of inadequate knowledge of English. The fact that out of a 600-word interaction only 30 are uttered by the English parents (their seven-year-old child speaks only once to answer the interpreter's question about her age, as shown in [4] above) is particularly revealing.

6.   Conclusions

The main theoretical concern of this paper was with the identification of those factors which can determine a higher or lower degree of interactional control by any one of the participants in the medical encounter. We will therefore attempt to summarize the findings of our analysis by answering a series of questions.

Firstly, is asymmetry a function of the doctor's adherence to an institutionally determined distribution of talking rights and obligations? If in a monolingual encounter the doctor may decide to monopolize or else share his/her interactional power with the patient on the basis of his/her personal inclination towards a more or less empathic conversational style, in linguistically mediated communication his/her moves are necessarily dependent, at least in part, on the interpreter's translation choices and management of turns. Evidence of this was found in our sessions, where throughout the same encounter (see, for instance, excerpts from T.1 and T.2), the same doctor displays varying degrees of interactional dominance, as rapid and restrictive questioning alternates with more informally and cooperatively negotiated topic development.

Secondly, is asymmetry a function of a given phase in the medical consultation? As previously mentioned, the literature on medical communication indicates that patient-initiated questions are most strongly dispreferred in the data-gathering phase (type 3 episodes), whilst they are more acceptable after diagnosis and treatment have been announced (type 2 episodes). The analysis of our sessions has not produced unequivocal evidence of phase-specificity. Whilst in T.2 and T.5 patient-initiated questions did tend to appear towards the end of the encounter, in T.1 they were a constant feature throughout all the stages of the consultation, including history-taking.

Thirdly, is asymmetry a function of the patient's preference for directness vs. indirectness, possibly dictated by reference to prevailing cultural paradigms? A significantly higher concentration of patient-initiated questions and hence a less marked asymmetry were indeed observed in the encounters involving the Polish parents (T.1 and T.5), as compared with the generally passive interactional behaviour of the English participants. Although this may depend on an individual's disposition and character, rather than on adherence to a given cultural orientation, the latter hypothesis was thought to offer an interesting enough explanation, bar mere coincidence, for the recurrence of similar communicative styles in the two nationally diverse groups of patients, albeit in the restricted and statistically irrelevant confines of our sessions. At the same time, however, we have also seen a submissive British woman become progressively more assertive, as a consequence of information gaps in the interpreter's – not the doctor's – delivery of the diagnosis.

Fourthly and lastly, is asymmetry a function of the interpreter's independent assessment of the goals and requirements of the ongoing activity? Here, two different trends have been observed. On the one hand, a more empathic and less asymmetrical conversational model clearly emerged when the interpreter engaged in small talk with the patients, in particular during the physical examination. On the other hand, in less informal phases of the encounter the interpreter's attempts to exert interactional control often resulted in an increased asymmetry, as she topicalized the practical aspects of the doctor's utterances whilst leaving out more medically relevant information in the translations for the patient. This behaviour, which put the patient in a position of even greater knowledge inferiority, eventually led to a redressing of the imbalance, as the latter shifted to more assertive patterns. It is worth noting that this kind of asymmetry was recurrently found only in the encounters interpreted by Tina. This would further suggest that interpreters are fully-fledged social actors, who may have different perceptions of their roles and different views on how to organize their participation in a mediated encounter. Our study has shown that this may entail independent analyses and decisions as to what the patients should or should not be told. However, as Bolden (2000:415) warns, "given interpreters' lack of medical expertise, their interventions may have negative consequences on the quality of medical care received by patients".

To conclude, what seems to emerge from the preceding analysis is a complex interplay of different factors, which explains why symmetrical and asymmetrical configurations are in a state of constant flux within any communicative event, and are only partially determined by institutional norms or individual preference. In this view, interactional control is to be seen as a shifting variable, or rather as a "micro-political achievement, produced in and through actual turns at talk" (Frankel, in West 1984:95-96) by all interlocutors, doctor, patient and interpreter alike. The polymorphic nature of medical encounters, especially when occurring across linguistic and cultural barriers, is vividly depicted in the following quotation, which aptly summarizes the present discussion:

> Consultations are sometimes almost like conversations. At other times, they resemble interrogation. But mostly they are somewhere in between, zigzagging between the two poles in a way that is negotiated on a turn-by-turn basis by the participants themselves. (ten Have 1991:162)

APPENDIX: Transcription key

Symbols		Meaning
A B	⌈⌈ well I said ⌊⌊ Yes	utterances starting simultaneously
A B	she's ⌈ right ⌉ ⌊ huh mm ⌋	overlapping utterances
A B	I agree= =me too	latched utterances
	(.)	untimed pause within a turn
	((pause))	untimed pause between turns
	↑	rising intonation
	wo:::rd	lengthened vowel or consonant sound
	word – word	abrupt cut-off in the flow of speech
	<u>word</u>	emphasis
	WORD	increased volume
	°word°	decreased volume
	>word<	quicker pace
	((word))	relevant contextual information; characterisations of the talk; vocalisations that cannot be spelled recognisably
	(word)	transcriber's guess
	( )	unrecoverable speech

Fillers		Meaning
English	*Italian*	
umm	umm	doubt
mhm	mhm	expression or request of agreement
ah	ah; eh	emphasis
eh	eh	query
uh	ehm	staller
oh	oh	surprise

References

Angelelli, C. (2004) *Medical Interpreting and Cross-cultural Communication*, Cambridge: Cambridge University Press.

Baker, D.W., R.M. Parker, M.V. Williams, W.C. Coates and K. Pitkin (1996) "Use and Effectiveness of Interpreters in an Emergency Department", *Journal of the American Medical Association* 275(10): 783-88.

Bolden, G. (2000) "Toward Understanding Practices of Medical Interpreting:

Interpreters' Involvement in History Taking", *Discourse Studies* 2(4): 387-419.

Bot, H. (2005) *Dialogue Interpreting in Mental Health*, Amsterdam & New York: Rodopi.

Byrne, P. S. and B. E. L. Long (1976) *Doctors Talking to Patients: A Study of the Verbal Behaviour of General Practitioners Consulting in their Surgeries*, London: Her Majesty's Stationery Office.

Drew, P. and J. Heritage (1992) "Analyzing Talk at Work: An Introduction", in P. Drew and J. Heritage (eds) *Talk at Work. Interaction in Institutional Settings*, Cambridge: Cambridge University Press, 3-65.

Fairclough, N. (1992) *Discourse and Social Change*, Cambridge: Polity Press.

Goddard, C. and A. Wierzbicka (1997) "Discourse and Culture", in Teun A. van Dijk (ed.) *Discourse as Social Interaction*, London: Sage Publications, 231-59.

Hall, E.T. (1976) *Beyond Culture*, New York: Doubleday.

------ (1983) *The Dance of Life, The Other Dimension of Time*, New York: Doubleday.

ten Have, P. (1991) "Talk and Institution: A Reconsideration of the 'Asymmetry' of Doctor-Patient Interaction", in D. Boden and D.H. Zimmerman (eds) *Talk and Social Structure*, Cambridge: Polity Press, 138-63.

Heath, C. (1986) *Body Movement and Speech in Medical Interaction*, Cambridge: Cambridge University Press.

Maynard, D. W. (1991) "The Perspective-Display Series and the Delivery and Receipt of Diagnostic News", in D. Bodem and D.H. Zimmerman (eds) *Talk and Social Structure*, Cambridge: Polity Press, 164-92.

------ (1992) "On Clinicians Co-implicating Recipients' Perspective in the Delivery of Diagnostic News", in P. Drew and J. Heritage (eds) *Talk at Work. Interaction in Institutional Settings*, Cambridge: Cambridge University Press, 331-58.

Merlini, R. (2007) "L'interpretazione in ambito medico. Specialità di lessico o di ruolo?", in D. Poli (ed.) *Lessicologia e metalinguaggio. Atti del Convegno di Studi, Macerata, 19-21 dicembre 2005*, Roma: Il Calamo, 433-52.

------ and R. Favaron (2005) "Examining the 'Voice of Interpreting' in Speech Pathology", *Interpreting* 7(2): 263-302.

Meyer, B. (2004) *Dolmetschen im medizinischen Aufklärungsgespräch. Eine diskursanalytische Untersuchung zur Wissensvermittlung im mehrsprachigen Krankenhaus*, Münster, etc.: Waxmann Verlag.

Mishler, E. G. (1984) *The Discourse of Medicine: Dialectics of Medical Interviews*, Norwood, New Jersey: Ablex Publishing Corporation.

Tebble, H. (1999) "The Tenor of Consultant Physicians: Implications for Medical Interpreting", in I. Mason (ed.) *Dialogue Interpreting*, Special Issue of *The Translator* 5(2): 179-200.

Unfer, D. (2003-2004) *L'interprete delle vacanze: analisi di colloqui mediati in Pronto Soccorso*, unpublished dissertation, SSLMIT, Italy: University of Trieste.

Victor, D. A. (1992) *International Business Communication*, London: Harper Collins.

Wadensjö, C. (1998) *Interpreting as Interaction*, London & New York: Longman.

Waitzkin, H. (1991) *The Politics of Medical Encounters: How Patients and Doctors Deal with Social Problems*, New Haven, CT: Yale University Press.

West, C. (1984) *Routine Complications: Troubles in Talk Between Doctors and Patients*, Bloomington: Indiana University Press.

Role Models in Mental Health Interpreting

HANNEKE BOT

Psychiatric Hospital de Gelderse Roos / Department Phoenix, Renkum, The Netherlands / Freelance Trainer, Researcher and Counsellor in Interpreting

Abstract. *In this paper, two frequently used models of interpreter and user cooperation are described: the translation machine model and the interactive model of interpreting. The paper provides a summary of observations made on the basis of some empirical data (extracted from videotaped interpreter-mediated psychotherapeutic sessions) with regard to the adherence of participants in the communication to these models. It concludes that the translation machine model is, in essence, an ideology, but that translation machine techniques are used in practice. It also concludes that the translation machine ideology denies the interactional realities of interpreter-mediated talk, which leads to the unwarranted assumption that interpreters actually make equivalent renditions that do not need any repair strategies. The interactional approach, however, leads to the questioning of the concept of equivalence and to the use of repair strategies in the practice of interpreter-mediated talk. This ultimately leads to the mutual understanding at which this type of talk aims.*

1.   Introduction

In the Netherlands, most interpreters working in the social sector are engaged through the *Dutch Interpreter and Translator Centre* (TVcN). TVcN provides interpreters, i.e. professionals whose task is to translate the words uttered by the primary speakers – mainly healthcare providers, police personnel, lawyers, judges, and their clients – and who do not consider advocacy or cultural mediation to be part of their job. Interviewing some of these interpreters, the professionals using their services and some patients about "what aspects define the quality of interpreter-mediated dialogue" as part of my PhD research (Bot 2005), I observed, however, that within this paradigm – the interpreter as a performer of language transfer – people have different ideas about the actual involvement of the interpreter in the interaction.

I described the interpreter's roles according to two *"Ideal typische"* models: the interpreter as a "translation machine" and the "interactive interpreter". In my subsequent analysis of videotaped interpreter-mediated psychotherapeutic sessions, it turned out that interpreters and users, in reality, only partly act according to the model they say they adhere to. I also observed a position of the interpreter that had not been mentioned in the interviews: the "interpreter as participant".

I concluded – on practical and logical grounds – that the model according to which the interpreter is a "translation machine" is an ideology. In fact, within the context of the same dialogue, interpreters sometimes use the translation machine technique, act as interactive interpreters and as participants in their own right.

I noticed, however, that interpreters and users in favour of the translation machine ideology dealt with some communicative issues in a manner that was different to that used by interpreters and users who started from an interactive stance, with some specific effect on the quality of the communication. This led me to some tentatively phrased conclusions about what ideas would help to optimize interpreter-mediated talk.

My research project revolved specifically around face-to-face interpreting in psychotherapy sessions with asylum seekers in the Netherlands. However, I feel that the mechanisms I describe apply to other types of interpreter-mediated talk as well.

2.   Two models, three positions and a continuum

As stated above, I derived two *Ideal* typical models from the interviews in order to describe the role of the interpreter and subsequently of the user of his/her services (Bot 2005:88-91). They are explained below.

2.1   *The translation machine interpreter*

Very generally, this model includes the following patterns: the health professional does his/her job: i.e. organizes his/her consultation, interview or other type of communicative event as he/she would do in a monolingual situation. The only difference is that the professional allows the interpreter time to translate. The interpreter "walks in and translates" without any specific introduction to the communicative situation at hand.

In this model, the professional primary speaker is in charge of the dialogue. This implies that he/she is the chairperson of the session: he/she introduces the speakers to each other and decides when someone gets a turn to speak.

The emphasis is on the interpreter's skills. The interpreter translates as closely to the original utterance as possible. "Equivalence" of translation (the production of a complete translation and the use of a direct form of translation, i.e. one that keeps the perspective of the primary speakers) is considered to be of the utmost importance. Included in this approach is the notion that an "equivalent" translation lies within the reach of every professional interpreter. As such, equivalence is not seen as a problematic issue. A translation machine interpreter will not ask "unprompted" questions, the only exception being situations in which the interpreter may ask for clarification in the event that he/she has not heard or understood what was said. The interpreter will simply translate whatever the primary participants say. Interpreters operating as translation machines will not intervene when they feel there is a misunderstanding, nor will they adapt the primary speakers' use of language to prevent any confusion from occurring.

Primary speakers can make it easier for the interpreter to work as a translation machine by putting effort into formulating short and grammatically-correct phrases, by facing and looking at each other, addressing each other and, in general, by paying little attention to the interpreter.

Working according to this model means that differences in attitude, behavioural norms or conversational techniques between various settings are not deemed problematic. No need is felt for specialization, for example, in legal or medical settings, except with regard to terminology. Interpreters will emphasize their non-partisan approach and their neutral attitude: they will show no emotions, let alone express value-judgements about the content of the conversation. Additionally, a seating position "away" from the primary speakers, which could even be behind one of them, underscores the interpreters' detachment.

In this kind of scenario, the interpreter will be wary of social interaction with the primary speakers. Consequently, he/she may, for example, emphasize the need for waiting facilities separate from those of his/her clients and will not appreciate a "debriefing" session with a therapist even after an emotionally charged session.

At an institutional and organizational level, this model can be supported by various measures. For instance, in the Code of Conduct for interpreters, the notion of the interpreter as a translation machine is embodied in the emphasis that is placed on "neutrality" and "non-involvement", as well as in the advice against any meta-communication about the task and the absolute lack of attention paid to the importance of "communicational cultures" in the different settings in which an interpreter may work. So much so, that it may even be the case that interpreters are advised not to mention their names when greeting the patient.

This tendency also becomes apparent when users have no choice regarding the interpreter who will be contracted and/or when the Centre (TVcN) will not reveal the interpreter's name. TVcN decides to whom an assignment will be assigned and their choice is based on practical issues such as availability and planning. In principle, the interpreter is treated as a nameless person – an "invisible non-person".

In this model, the quality of the interaction is defined by the linguistic and translational skills of the interpreter, his/her vow of secrecy and his/her neutral, non-judgemental stance.

2.2   *The interactive model of interpreting*

In general terms, the interactive model is characterized by the recognition that the primary speakers and interpreter alike are present as people, albeit in their various professional roles. The importance of an "equivalent" translation is recognized, but that alone is not considered to be sufficient to make communication successful. This approach also recognizes that the concept of equivalence is very complex and problematic.

Just as it matters who the professional working with a client is (a lawyer or a therapist will not simply ask any colleague to stand in for him or her at the next session with his/her client), the interpreter who is present also matters. The professional chooses the interpreter in accordance with the needs of the dialogue that needs to be interpreted. In some situations, the decision to engage an interpreter can even be made in consultation with the patient and the professional may try to book the same interpreter for the following sessions with a given client. Attention may be paid to the issue of "trust", both in relation to the professional primary speaker and the interpreter. Furthermore, the interpreter is there as a person with a name.

When, in the course of an ongoing series of interpreter-mediated events, a "new" interpreter becomes involved, this new interpreter may be briefed about the previous sessions by the professional to help him/her understand the ongoing process. To maintain the client's feelings of trust, it is preferable that this is done in the client's presence and that it is translated both ways.

The interpreter is there to translate the words that are being uttered, but it is recognized that he/she, by being present, exerts some influence on the conversation, which can be put to use to facilitate the communicative process. For example, the interpreter's attitude will play a part in discouraging or encouraging the primary speakers to speak freely. In health care, "empathy" on the part of both the health care provider and the interpreter is seen as a prerequisite for therapeutic communication. It is regarded as important that the interpreter has some understanding of the general attitude and techniques that characterize the type of communication at hand. It is also regarded as important that all three participants have a good rapport, as this will encourage free communication. Having said that, "neutrality" and "non-partisanship" can be very problematic concepts in relation to "empathy". Non-verbal communication, which is also part of the interpreter's communicative behaviour, plays an important role in creating an atmosphere of trust. People working according to this model see the communication as the product of the cooperation of all three participants (interpreter, professional user and non-professional user). As expressed by a therapist, "when there is a misunderstanding, you have to make an effort to find out whether the patient does not understand your intervention, or whether something went amiss in the interpretation".

In this model, there is recognition of the therapist as the "director" of a session, i.e. the leader of the communicative event. However, the therapist can sometimes delegate his/her leadership to some extent. As the interpreter has "superior knowledge" of the content of the conversation, the turn-taking, for example, can be partly delegated to him/her. The importance of an accurate and complete transfer of content is understood, but, at the same time, the complexity of the concept of "equivalent translation" is recognized and it is accepted that not the entirety of the translation will be "equivalent" to the original utterances. It is also understood that the primary speakers themselves will notice all manner of extra-textual features. For example, when a story is told by the interviewee in a halting manner, it is assumed that the professional will notice this, even when the interpreter renders the content of the speaker's words in a coherent fashion. There is less emphasis on keeping the same personal perspective in the rendition of the content of the primary speaker's turn and meta-communication between two participants is not seen as problematic: it is understood that sometimes it may be useful to explore and clarify what has been said before an utterance can be rendered in the other language. In a trustful relationship, "transparency" is important, but it is not an absolute prerequisite for open communication.

2.3 *The interpreter as participant*

Upon examination of the material that I collected, I noticed that at times in the professional encounter, the interpreter no longer acted as an "interpreter", but rather engaged in the dialogue as a participant in his/her own right, with his/her own "text". When the interpreter acts as a participant he/she does not "translate" the words of the primary speakers. I found examples of this interpreter's position in my material and also in my own work as a psychotherapist in interpreter-mediated sessions. A typical scenario for the interpreter to act as a participant would occur in waiting-room talk between him/her and a patient, or in instances of small talk between the interpreter, the therapist and the patient. In my data, there was considerable evidence of small talk about the quality of the coffee provided in the institute that took place before the session and also about the (very stormy) weather, after the session had formally ended. But even in the course of a dialogue an interpreter can act as an active participant. It is worth noting that I did not find examples of this kind of behaviour in my research data; however, I do encounter such examples in my own professional practice. I can cite, for example, requests for a glass of water or for a window to be opened, as well as requests for participation in the planning of the following session to take account of the interpreter's availability. In addition (and perhaps more significantly), I have also encountered emphasized agreement with a primary speaker's words and remarks about the topic at hand that bear no translational relationship to a turn of the primary speaker. As an example of this type of interpreter's behaviour, I can cite the occasion when a health professional was talking to a patient about how he could improve his sleep-ing pattern and the interpreter told the other participants about how *he* dealt with this problem himself, thus suggesting a coping mechanism derived from his own experience as a potential solution to the problem raised in the exchange.[1]

2.4 *Normative constructs versus everyday practice*

The models that I derived from the data gathered in the course of these interviews are normative constructs: one assumption leads to the next and, thus, a logical system emerges. The analysis of practice in interpreted-mediated encounters, however, turned out to be more complicated. Not only did I encounter examples of the interpreter acting as a participant, but I also noticed that, in reality, and quite independently of the norms

---

[1] At this point it is worth noting that I am aware that interpreters and patients may also meet socially, away from the institutional setting in which the interpreter and patient meet formally.

that interpreters and users assume have to be applied, the participants in a conversational exchange act in ways that can be related to a number of positions within a single assignment. As each of the models considered involved varying degrees of "interactiveness" or "machineness", a continuum could be constructed. In practice, the interpreter and the professional user move along this continuum within one assignment, adopting different positions that depend on the immediate communicative context and on their own (normative) ideas about how to behave.

2.5 Continuum of interaction

This continuum illustrates the degree of involvement of the interpreter as a person in the dialogue:

translation machine.....interactive interpreter.....interpreter as participant

Although this continuum is very simple, I feel it is a rather helpful tool for understanding and classifying interpreter behaviour. It contributes to an understanding of interpreter behaviour within the overall assumption that the key task of the interpreter is to interpret the words of the primary speakers. In fact, it can be argued that it can serve as a basis to describe which degree of involvement best suits each type of exchange and the various kinds of communicative situations in which exchanges take place.

Depending on which normative construct one subscribes to, the different positions are evaluated and judged differently. Seen from the point of view of the translation machine model, that the interpreter as participant takes part in arranging an appointment may be seen as "all right", but he/she engaging in small talk, not to mention adding his/her own coping mechanisms to the discussion or meeting socially with the non-professional participant, is not acceptable.

From the perspective of the interactive interpreter, small talk and even the interpreter's own additions are not seen as being problematic *per se*. For example, in therapeutic work, this kind of interaction may serve the purpose of what is known as "joining" (Menuchin and Fischman 1981), a strategy in which a therapist familiarizes himself/herself with a patient's family in order to build up a working relationship. From this point of view, social interaction between the various participants outside the session is also not necessarily a "boundary violation"[2]; on the contrary, it can be seen as

---

[2] Gutheil and Gabbard (1993) distinguish between "boundary crossings" and "boundary

useful in the development of the therapeutic relationship or in terms of the development of the patient's social network. In the same vein, self-disclosure by the interpreter can be used as an acceptable technique in therapy, just as it can in the case of the therapist.

In different institutional settings, there will be different normative judgements about these positions. In police interviews, court settings and other adversarial situations, the position of the interpreter as participant is very restricted – interpreters will try to steer away from the participant end of the continuum and try to stay as close as possible to the translation machine end. In healthcare, however, the interactive position is often preferred and the interpreter as participant is allowed.

As for the translation machine end of the continuum, it is worth mentioning that, if applied in its extreme form, the interpreter would not have any influence as a person, but rather would interpret the words of the primary speakers in a fully equivalent manner. Apart from the fact that it is impossible to translate without having any "shifts" because of linguistic reasons (e.g. different grammatical rules, lexical asymmetry), social science has shown that it is also "impossible not to communicate" (Watzlawick *et al.* 1967). The simple fact that an interpreter is not a machine makes it impossible to apply the translation machine model in its extreme form. In this sense, the translation machine model is an ideology. On the other hand, it is possible to act as a translation machine, to try to closely follow the model, to use it strategically. This would imply emphasizing neutrality, but it would also mean that the interpreter focuses periodically on an "exact translation", for example, when interpreting dates, numbers, legal evidence or other textual features in relation to which precision is paramount. Hence, the translation machine end of the continuum should be understood as a technique.

3.   From models to practice

In my research I analyzed sessions from three therapist-interpreter-patient groups, adhering to different models of interpreting. I observed that, irrespective of the model the participants said they adhered to, the interpreter's behaviour could be seen as shifting along the continuum. The translation machine therapist and interpreter did establish social contact (materialized

---

violations" in therapeutic behaviour. A "crossing" is a descriptive term, neither laudatory nor pejorative, and is used to describe *any* divergence in behaviour from a set of formal rules. "Violation" is used to refer to the harmful crossing of a boundary.

in, for example, small talk and conversations about how to cooperate) outside the formal sessions. The therapist made as much of an effort to engage the interpreter as interactively-oriented health professionals did. Analyzing the tapes, I discovered that, although the translation machine therapist made shorter turns (15 words per turn, compared to 20 and 30 with the other two therapists) and had the interpreter seated in a position to facilitate his "instrumental" task in the communication in accordance with the translation machine ideology, this did not result in noticeably fewer divergent ("non-equivalent") renditions than those observed in the case of the interactively oriented groups.

3.1 *Reactions to divergent renditions*

In general, the number of divergent renditions was high: between 10 and 40 % of the number of turns per session were interpreted divergently. Having observed this made me pose the following questions: what happens when a large proportion of the renditions in a session is divergently rendered? Does this have a dramatic effect in the communicative act? This made me investigate sequences of turns focusing on a third question, namely: "what happens after a divergent rendition?"

I noticed a number of points. Firstly, I noticed that divergent renditions often occur without any observable effect. The primary participants may raise a metaphorical eyebrow, but all that can be observed is that such renditions often go unchecked. I noticed that this happened especially when the source text related to a tangential subject or something that was, apparently, considered not to have particular significance. A possible explanation for this is that some notion of "economy" comes into play: in order to keep the communication going, one cannot dwell on every misunderstanding.

Secondly, I noticed that sometimes the primary speakers were not in a position to notice that a rendition was divergent, either because the communicative exchange was coherent in each language, in spite of the differences in content between both languages, or because a certain divergence occurred systematically. These unnoticed divergent renditions happened in all sessions, irrespective of the purported theoretical stance (in terms of the interpreting models) of the participants.

Thirdly, I frequently observed situations in which that the primary speakers gave the impression that they had noticed the divergence. Of course, this is difficult to ascertain, as they cannot really detect the causes of the problems that may affect the communication process. However, what I observed is that, on several occasions, primary speakers seemed to have sensed that "something was not quite right". Although this could be the result of divergence in the interpreting, instances of misunderstanding, mishearing or deliberate divergence on the part of the primary speaker are also possible causes. Sometimes, this resulted in a rather vague reaction to a long story in which all kind of information had been divergently rendered, emphasizing the main ideas and feelings, while the details were left out. When this happened, the divergence was brushed over and any misunderstanding was not explored. Nevertheless, it is worth noting that instances of a different reaction to divergence, namely, repair strategies (e.g. giving or asking for feedback, rephrasing questions and asking clarifying questions), were also common. Occasionally, divergence occurring in one turn would be repaired in the following turn, but at times a repair action would occur much later in the same session or could even happen in the following session. In this way, divergent renditions were counteracted and mutual understanding was created. The issue of repair strategies will be dealt with more specifically in the following section.

4.   Divergence and repair: a royal couple

Does all this have anything to do with the models, i.e. with the notions that interpreters and the users of their services have in mind when working together? The answer is: yes, it can be strongly argued that it does.

An interesting aspect that I found in my material was that the translation machine therapist and interpreter did not use any repair strategies. The interpreter never asked a clarifying question, although there were several occasions when a clarifying question would have been appropriate, because the primary utterance was not only highly ungrammatical, but also incomprehensible. In principle, the translation machine model allows for seeking clarification; however, from my observations can be inferred that the emphasis on translation machine behaviour and the assumption that equivalence is non-problematic discourage the interpreter from asking questions.

In the interactive working groups, the interpreter asked or signalled short questions such as "sorry, I do not understand" several times, upon which the therapist or patient repeated (apparently assuming the interpreter did not hear properly) or rephrased (apparently assuming the interpreter did not understand) their previous utterance.

Additionally, the therapists working from an interactive stance returned to their previous questions or interventions when they got a reaction that did not fully match their expectations. An example of this strategy is included below. In the session from which the example is taken, there had been some talk about the patient's worries about his expired residence permit and, after the practical issues had been dealt with, the therapist asks: "what does it mean to you, that you do not have it yet?", which is rendered by the interpreter as: "what problem does this cause to you?". To this the patient replies that he is worried that his house will be taken away from him. The therapist then says: "but that is not really what I meant" and rephrases his intervention. And after a few turns, he says: "You have done everything that should be done, but you still do not trust the situation, isn't that it?" After this question, which was rendered accurately, the patient starts to talk about his lack of trust in all kinds of things and a therapeutic theme emerges.

We see here that the patient's first reply refers to purely practical matters, in accordance with the question he has heard from the interpreter. However, the therapist had aimed at probing psychological issues and, faced with the patient's response, it is conceivable for the former to have concluded that the latter did not appear to be interested in reflection. He might even have concluded: "see, this patient is from another culture, so he does not understand mentalization". Instead, and in line with the interactive model, the therapist pursues his quest for a therapeutic approach to the issue: he rephrases his question and probes further, until a therapeutic theme that can be explored further emerges.

I noticed in my material that it is the use of this kind of repair strategies that ultimately makes the difference between a translation machine approach and an interactive approach. In the translation machine dyad, the interpreter never asked questions and neither did the therapist. It would appear, thus, that the emphasis on the importance of equivalent renditions – and the concomitant belief that equivalence is a resolvable problem – leads to the **assumption** that all renditions are equivalent. Ultimately, this is the basis of the translation machine model: the influence of the interpreter is negligible, the renditions are equivalent and the communication is between therapist and patient alone. This means that the difference between this model and the interactive one is not that translation machine leads to better interpretations, but rather that renditions are assumed to be equivalent by the participants.

Not surprisingly, I noticed that in the sessions of the translation machine group, misunderstandings occurred and were not resolved. I concluded that this was not the result of the lower quality of the renditions (the interpreter did not do any better or worse than the other interpreters), but that rather it was due to the absence of repair strategies.

5.   Conclusions

As I have mentioned earlier, the evidence I have presented here is not based on a large volume of data and, therefore, I have to present my conclusions in a tentative fashion. Nevertheless, it is possible to infer that most of my observations are not specific to this data and can equally apply to material gathered from other communicative situations when the mediation of an interpreter is required.

In agreement with Wadensjö's (1998) and Pöchhacker's (2004) work, I concluded from the findings of my study that the translation machine model leads to the deployment of useful techniques, but that the interactive paradigm should be the point of departure for interpreter-mediated encounters. I reached this conclusion, firstly, on theoretical grounds, because of the above-mentioned impossibility of not communicating, and, secondly, because the interactive stance includes the use of repair strategies, which are vital in dealing with the unavoidable divergent renditions given by interpreters. In fact, repair strategies are the means that lead to the creation of the mutual understanding between therapist, patient and interpreter that is ultimately sought.

References

Bot, H. (2005) *Dialogue Interpreting in Mental Health*, Amsterdam & New York: Rodopi.

Gutheil, Thomas G. and Glen O. Gabbard (1993) "The Concept of Boundaries in Clinical Practice", *American Journal of Psychiatry*: 150, 188-196.

Minuchin, S. and C. Fischman (1981) *Family Therapy Techniques*, Cambridge: Harvard University Press.

Pöchhacker, F. (2004) *Introducing Interpreting Studies*, London & New York: Routledge.

Wadensjö, C. (1998) *Interpreting as Interaction*, London & New York: Longman

Watzlawick, P., J.H. Beavin and D.D. Jackson (1967) *Pragmatics of Human Communication*, New York: Norton and Company.

Feminization
A Socially and Politically Charged Translation Strategy

LYSE HÉBERT
York University, Toronto, Canada

Abstract. "Language [consists] of socially and politically situated practices that are differentially distributed on the basis of gender, class, race, ethnicity and other phenomena" (Briggs 1996:4). Discursive features can index, at times simultaneously, a number of social and political positions and identities. One such position/identity is gender. As a salient social category, gender is discursively foregrounded through a variety of utterances and silences and, in certain languages, through mandatory grammatical markers. This paper presents the results of a study aimed at assessing the reactions of Francophone nurses in Ontario (a Canadian English-speaking province) to translated documents produced by their regulatory college. More specifically, the purpose of the study was to determine the impact of the feminization of texts directed to a predominantly female readership. This qualitative analysis focused on respondents' attitudes toward the feminization strategies used by translators, but also produced surprising data regarding reactions to gender neutral texts in either English or French. The study demonstrates that certain discursive/translation strategies aimed at redressing inequalities may be perceived by some readers as detrimental. In fact, results show that gender cannot be separated from other salient social, political and economic factors.

1. Introduction

Ethnographic and sociological reflections on translation and interpreting have been increasing in number and in scope in the past few years. I refer in particular, but not exclusively, to the special issue of *The Translator*, in 2005, entitled "Bourdieu and the Sociology of Translation and Interpreting", and to Daniel Simeoni's earlier article in *Target* 10(1) on "The Translator's Habitus". This theoretical framework is especially useful for reflecting on choices made by translators of public sector documents.

This article is based on a study conducted in 2002-2003.[1] It analyzes the decision to "feminize" the translation of so-called gender neutral source texts and presents the results of field research on the reception of these feminized texts.[2] The readership thereof is a relatively small group of Francophone nurses in Ontario[3] who receive all documents from their professional regulatory body in French. This regulatory body, the College of Nurses of Ontario (CNO), sets criteria for registration and establishes practice standards which it also enforces. Since 1989, I have been a member of the team that provides translation and interpreting services to the College.[4]

The research project was first and foremost a reflexive one: as one of those responsible for translating the College of Nurses' documents into French, and for deciding to "feminize" them, I wondered about the judiciousness of this strategy and its impact on readers. My own ambivalence toward the strategy was one of the principal motives for this study and, while I hoped that the interview subjects might have a less equivocal position, I suspected that the large number of factors influencing readers' perceptions, especially grammatical dogma, might produce unexpected results. In fact, most of the nurses interviewed are acutely aware of the role language plays in expressing identity. Grammatical constraints are generally the least of their concerns; they engage in very thoughtful discussions on the gendered nature of their profession and on the language used to describe and define it.

2. Translation of governmental documents in Ontario

In Ontario, the systematic translation of governmental and paragovernmental texts from English to French is a relatively recent phenomenon that stems from the passage, in 1986, of the *French Language Services*

---

[1] Hébert, Lyse (2003) *Pour une traduction-affirmation: les textes de l'Ordre des infirmières et infirmiers de l'Ontario*, unpublished M.A. thesis, Toronto: York University.
[2] The source texts discussed here were produced in English, and the target language is French. Interviews with research participants were conducted in French and excerpt responses reproduced here are translated by the author.
[3] There are approximately 140,000 professional nurses in Ontario, of whom slightly more than 1,600 (1.2%) self-identify as Francophones.
[4] My thanks to Dominique Joly, translator, revisor and business partner for her unfailing support.

Act (FLSA), by which "the Legislative Assembly recognizes the contribution of the cultural heritage of the French-speaking population and wishes to preserve it for future generations [and] guarantee the use of the French language in institutions of the Legislature and the Government of Ontario" (*French Language Services Act, R.S.O.* 1990, Chapter F.32, Preamble).

All provincial laws passed since then have been translated into French, as have been most other documents produced for wide public distribution. The FLSA also provides for regulations to designate certain organizations as public service agencies, thus requiring them to comply with the Act. It was in this context that the College of Nurses, along with large numbers of agencies whose mandate or activities were provincial in scope, began to translate its publications and offer some of its services in French. It should be pointed out that some of these activities are partly subsidized by the Ontario Ministry of Health and Long-Term Care.

3.   Feminization

As English is the administrative language in the Ontario public service, almost all governmental and paragovernmental documents published in French are translations. In the absence of prescriptive rules for gender inclusive writing (guidelines have been produced by the Ontario public sector but are not strictly enforced), it is to translators that the task falls of ensuring the presence of women in these documents. These translators, whether they work in-house or on a contractual basis, are nonetheless expected to follow the guidelines, whose initial purpose was to redress traditional inequalities in both society and discourse.

In Ontario government documents, the terms *féminisation* and *rédaction non sexiste* are used interchangeably. While the strategy itself was meant, initially, to foster equality between the sexes, these terms reflect two very different standpoints. In this paper, the two terms are not synonymous. Non-sexist writing refers to strategies ensuring the visibility of both women and men in texts, and specifically administrative and academic writing, whereas feminization applies to the use of feminine nouns as generic forms.

Non-sexist writing, as a public sector policy, is therefore the norm in Ontario. In English, a language that is not morphologically marked for gender, simply ensuring the presence of both pronouns "she/he" and "her/his" or replacing them with the unmarked "they" and "their" is usually considered sufficient to signal a desire for inclusiveness. In languages that have grammatical gender, such as French, non-sexist strategies can give rise to new discursive forms that are marked with respect to established norms.

Regardless of morphology, however, all languages express and create default, or unmarked, categories in the minds of speakers and hearers, writers and readers. This is a function of societal factors, not grammatical conditioning. Consider the following, excerpted from a letter of thanks to a healthcare facility:

> During the last two weeks of my mother's life, the nurses continued to support her by offering her food and encouraging her to drink. When she finally became bedridden, they gently turned her every two hours. They moistened her mouth and lips, massaged her skin and talked to her.[5]

It is likely that most readers would conclude that the nurses in this situation were women. Indeed various studies (see for example Fecteau *et al.* 1992) have shown that the nursing profession is perceived as a female one. Thus, regardless of the language used, the word "nurse" is filed in our minds under the category feminine. Despite all best efforts and intentions, all speakers and readers at some time or other revert to "default" categories of this type. Non-sexist writing is thus part of a global social project to discourage such essentializing habits and to ensure the inclusion and visibility of all members of society.

Feminization, on the other hand, is a consciously extremist strategy that is marked in the current social context because it appears to run counter to this goal of inclusiveness, since only one of two social categories – male and female – is being represented. Not surprisingly, this strategy raises a number of ethical dilemmas for translators and, presumably, for readers.

The decision to adopt this practice in translating the documents of the College of Nurses of Ontario (CNO) was made by the translators in consultation with the client. CNO, which regulates the nursing profession in the province, is one of 21 such bodies established by the Ontario government[6] and is mandated by a provincial legislative framework. As such it is bound by the same norms as are all governmental and paragovernmental agencies.

Non-sexist writing has been the norm in the Canadian public sector for several decades. As early as 1978 the government of Canada (Employment and Immigration Canada) published a comprehensive list of "feminized"

---

[5] CNO (2006) 'In Praise of Nurses', *The Standard*, March: 35.
[6] *Regulated Health Professions Act*, Schedule 1, 1991:18.

professional titles in French. Since then, provincial governments in Ontario and Québec have published policies on gender inclusiveness that reflect those adopted by the federal public service.

The translators' initial objective in rejecting these norms in favour of a feminizing strategy was to solve some of the problems attending non-sexist writing in French, chief among which is the constant repetition, not only of both feminine and masculine nouns, but also of all modifiers. The chosen solution was not merely based on linguistic factors however, but a function of the translators' social and political standpoint.

In Ontario, the majority of nurses (96%) are women. In such a context, the translators argued that the use of the generic masculine form, even with an explanatory note, would be unjustifiable, if not absurd, since the inclusion of the masculine form *infirmier*: nurse in a doublet produces a text written in the masculine. Instead of reproducing the non-sexist style used in the original English texts through the use of the doublet *les infirmières et les infirmiers*, they opted for the generic feminine with an explanatory note.[7] This was done even in instances where the masculine was added in the source text. Neutral forms such as *le personnel infirmier*: nursing staff, and epicenes, or collective nouns, such as *membres de la profession*: members of the profession, were not avoided, but could not be considered as a universal solution to the problem.

The following examples demonstrate the translation strategy adopted.

1. The **nurse's** primary accountability is to the client. This means that the **nurse** is accountable for **her/his** decisions and actions related to client care, including decisions about access to care when this is a component of the **nurse's** role.
   La responsabilité première de l'infirmière est envers son client. Ceci signifie qu'elle est responsable de ses gestes et de ses décisions relativement aux soins qu'elle prodigue, y compris les décisions sur l'accessibilité des services si cela fait partie de son rôle. (*Communiqué*, 27(1) 2002:12)

2. What is new is the growing government interest in the concept that an RN, RPN or RN(EC) working to **her/his** full scope of practice will have a profound and positive effect on the healthcare system.

---

[7] The note reads: *Dans le présent document, le mot « infirmière » est employé sans préjudice et désigne à la fois les hommes et les femmes.* (In this document [the feminine form of] the word "nurse" is used without prejudice and refers to both men and women).

> *Ce qui est nouveau, c'est que le gouvernement s'intéresse de plus en*
> *plus à l'idée que l'IA, l'IAA ou l'IA (cat. spéc.) qui met en œuvre toute*
> *la gamme de ses compétences puisse influer profondément et posi-*
> *tivement sur le réseau de la santé.* (*Communiqué*, 27(4) 2002:4)

3. **Nurses** use the designations RN for **Registered Nurse**, and RPN for
   Registered Practical Nurse. Nurses with Temporary registrations
   use the designation RN (Temp) or RPN (temp). RNs in the extended
   class, working in the **primary healthcare nurse practitioner** role,
   use the designation RN(EC).
   *L'infirmière utilise le titre IA, pour **infirmière autorisée**, ou IAA,*
   *pour **infirmière auxiliaire autorisée**. Les **personnes** qui détiennent*
   un certificat d'inscription temporaire emploient le titre IA (temp.) ou
   *IAA (temp.). Les **membres** de la catégorie spécialisée qui exercent à*
   *titre d'**infirmière praticienne en soins primaires** emploient le titre*
   IA (cat. spéc.). (*Normes sur la tenue de dossiers*, 2002:13)

In the first excerpt, the English text specifies "her/his decision" in order
to explicitly add the seme masculine to the term nurse. Yet, rather than
translating this by the doublet *l'infirmière ou l'infirmier*, which would have
been a more "faithful" rendering, the translators opted for the feminine form
only, thus removing a lexical element from the translation.

The second excerpt demonstrates the neutralizing effect of abbreviations.
Once again, the English writer inserts the masculine after the abbreviated
titles to underscore the presence of men. In French these abbreviations are
not marked for gender and the translators have produced a text that, taken
out of context, could be judged gender inclusive.

The last example demonstrates the economy of the feminizing strategy.
To understand the impracticability of the doublet, one merely needs to
rewrite the French version inserting *l'infirmière ou l'infirmier* in all cases
where the translators opted for the feminine only.

Although non-sexist writing has drawbacks, these are not sufficient to
justify the choices made by the translators who, as feminists, were aware
that feminization may be directed at a politicized, female readership or it
can be used to develop, or train, such a readership.

4.   Feminization and identity

Feminist and poststructuralist theorists insist on the need to read between
the lines, to listen for the unspoken. Critical discourse analysis further

heightens our awareness of the fact that language at once embodies and constitutes ideology. Discursive features can index, at times simultaneously, a number of social and political positions and identities. One such position/identity is gender.

The strategy adopted by feminist translators is part of an overt social project: foregrounding the reality of women's lives and its representation. This reformist strategy has been the subject of some very challenging theorizing, especially on the part of Canadian translators, writers and academics. Barbara Godard, Suzanne de Lotbinière-Harwood, Sherry Simon and Luise von Flotow, among others, have not only broken new ground: they have sown the seeds of a new culture in translation. Some of these women take an aggressive stance: they hijack the source text, both literally and figuratively. Whether one agrees with their position or not, their practice and their reflections have irrevocably changed the theoretical paradigm.

For feminist translators in the public sector, the goal is to discover, in the original text, signs of "gendered agency" (Spivak 2000:397). But this alone is not adequate: feminist translators, as social agents, must then choose amongst a finite series of alternatives ways of foregrounding these signs. They might, for example, choose a new palette of metaphors in order to avoid shading a text in paternalist, violent, or sexist hues. They might determine the relevance of some elements in the source text based on their own feminist principles. And they might reflect on the presence and representation of women, in both source texts and in their own translations.

Expressing feminine identities in texts and translations is not limited to avoiding sexist language: it is part of the sociopolitical process of affirmation. Thus the goal in foregrounding the feminine in texts directed at nurses was to counter the neutralizing effect of non-sexist writing. In so doing, the translators consciously intervened in the way in which Francophone nurses perceive, speak and live their profession.

Is this strategy valid? Or does it exemplify the double standard decried by Rosemary Arrojo (1994)? If the goal of non-sexist writing is to increase the visibility of minority segments (i.e. women) in all sectors of social activity, can a feminizing strategy that decreases the visibility of men (a minority in this particular sector) be justified? Does the desire to affirm, or celebrate, women's identity and contributions to a particular profession and to society in general constitute acceptable grounds for violating current norms? To answer these questions, we must situate translation in a sociological framework.

According to André Lefevere (1990:26), translation, as an activity and as a product, contributes to **image making**. And re-enunciating a message is never a neutral exercise. In this case, the strategy runs counter to *doxa*, as it emphasizes gender. In functionalist terms (Nord 1997:28-29), transforming non-sexist texts into feminized translations demonstrates an intention that was absent from the source. If the end justifies the means, then the strategy would appear to be valid, at least from a feminist perspective.

Pierre Bourdieu's concept of reflexivity as a method of sociological inquiry is particularly useful in this context. Translation, as a practice, implies choice: each translation problem requires that the translator select among the range of solutions her *habitus* provides her with in a given field. In other words, what I call translation-affirmation is a function of the environment in which it is practised.

5.   Research results

5.1 *Affirmation of nursing as a female profession*

Thirteen nurses (12 women, 1 man) responded to the call for research participants. While this is not a statistically significant sample, the objective was to obtain and analyze qualitative, rather than quantitative data. In view of the very small percentage of men in the nursing profession (4%), I was fortunate to receive a positive response from one male nurse. Although his presence in the sample might artificially weight his responses, the qualitative differences in his speech and in his opinions are significant enough to warrant their inclusion.

One the most salient aspects of the respondents' discourse was their exclusive use of the feminine form *infirmière*. The male respondent, who occasionally used the doublet *les infirmières et les infirmiers*, was the only exception. Very early in the process, it became evident that members of the nursing profession speak in the feminine.

Some of the attitudes, beliefs and concepts expressed by respondents demonstrate the internalization of stereotypes. A majority of respondents made unabashedly negative remarks on the "chattiness" and "gossiping" that characterize a workplace where women are the majority, as well as more oblique references to essentializing feminine traits such as caring, compassion, listening, and helping that apparently make women particularly suited to the nursing role. Yet, regardless of their attitudes toward women, a majority also expressed a concern for affirming their profession or ensuring its recognition.

Respect for others and a concern for their well-being were the two primary characteristics of nursing cited by respondents and were linked to the expression of discomfort regarding the feminizing of texts. Of the 12 respondents who cited these characteristics, 8 were either ambivalent or strongly opposed to feminizing, which they perceived as unjust.

Of the 12 women interviewed, 8 affirmed the genderedness of their profession, but in most cases the terms used were revealing:

- I wouldn't want to be quoted, as old fashioned, you know, but it's almost like a maternal side, taking care of people.
- I think women are more caring than men. [...] And I think that it's also much related to the maternal role and the image of the nurse. They're women.
- I wonder if the fact that we are a profession of women, if that's why we're not paid as well, compared to teachers.

Not one of these 12 women believed that the growing presence of men in the profession was undesirable. In fact, the reasons they cited for wanting men to practise nursing provided a glimpse into their professional concerns and foreshadowed their reactions to the feminizing strategy. Responses indicate that the three primary contributions of men to nursing are: to balance out therapeutic approaches, to increase the political "clout" of the profession (e.g. in labour negotiations), and to enhance the credibility and political weight of the profession. One woman even insisted that the presence of men in the workplace promotes a climate of respect amongst nurses, which she believes has been absent because of the pettiness of women.

The male respondent vacillated between affirmation of historic and current contributions of men to the profession and nuanced remarks on the lack of recognition given to male nurses by their colleagues and their patients.

The majority of participants (8) cited at least one aspect of the hierarchical nature of the healthcare system. They either deplored their subaltern status (being "the doctor's servant") or emphasized the value of their contribution ("when I was a nurse in the hospital, and doctors came to train, I was the one who taught him [sic]"). All of these statements, as well as more oblique references to social and professional hierarchies, reflect a desire for affirming the nursing profession and a preoccupation with its relative powerlessness.

5.2   *Rejection of the feminizing strategy*

Favourable and ambivalent responses to the exclusive use of the feminine were equal in number (5 each). Of the 13 participants, 3 were strongly opposed ("It bothers me, yes. It's not right."). And the majority of nurses who at first reacted favourably to feminization later nuanced their statements. Two even reversed their position after discussing the image, public recognition and future of their profession.

The vacillating and, in some cases contradictory, opinions expressed by respondents were supported by the alternatives they proposed. All stated that the doublet *infirmière/infirmier* and its variants were unwieldy and undermined legibility. Of the 13 respondents, 9 spontaneously proposed the explanatory note as a necessary element of feminized texts, even if they disapproved of the feminizing strategy.

Four nurses expressed the wish that a neutral term be found for the nursing profession, and two of these also believed that the translators should be faithful to the source text and follow the same non-sexist policy.

The majority of respondents (9) linked feminization to the image projected by CNO to its members and their patients. They felt that this strategy perpetuates the feminine image of the profession in the minds of patients and, while they recognize that this image is not a false one, they would express some discomfort with its representation.

Despite the statistically small sample, the data is eloquent. In fact the responses of these 13 nurses are even more revealing than expected, especially with respect to an emerging awareness of the need to ensure current and future recognition of their profession. This imperative supersedes their wish to affirm its predominantly female composition and is demonstrated by the surprising inconsistency in the speech of these nurses and in their opinions.

6.   Conclusions

The ambivalence of respondents to the feminizing strategy is closely linked to their concern for the future of their profession, to their feeling of powerlessness, both within the hierarchy of the healthcare system, and within society at large. Although their own discourse often centred on essentializing views of nursing, and of women, they resisted the foregrounding of these characteristics in discourse.

A majority of respondents consider the feminizing strategy undesirable in the current context. Some even see it as counter to the values of the profession, and detrimental to its advancement. When asked to describe their profession, these nurses speak of rapidly changing technology, new criteria for registration, an alarming decrease in their numbers and a concurrent increase in their workload. These factors, combined with the repercussions of a series of deleterious governmental measures that led, in the 1990s, to a crisis in the healthcare sector, would appear to have exacerbated these nurses' feeling of powerlessness. Some respondents believe that the nursing profession was targeted in part because it lacks political "clout", and that this relative social and political powerlessness is directly attributable to the fact that it is considered a female profession. What would be gained, they ask, from underscoring this fact at a time when nurses are engaged in affirming not their gendered identity, but the value of their profession in a healthcare system that appears to consider nurses as expendable?

Another factor is related to the internal dynamics of the healthcare system. While trying to downplay the gendered nature of their own profession, many respondents refer (explicitly or not) to the medical profession as male when discussing the hierarchical structure in which they work. If most doctors are men, and most nurses are women, at least two motives for oppression can be drawn upon. One respondent was especially articulate in this regard, citing situations where physicians demonstrated more regard for male nurses than for their female colleagues. Men in the nursing profession, she claims, are more likely than women to advance to managerial and research positions. What is the purpose, then, of further feminizing the nursing profession, when the structure and dynamics of the healthcare system is male-dominated?

The surprising reluctance of these nurses to affirm the feminine demonstrates that, although gender may be a salient social category, the complex interweaving of all social and political categories and the pressures they bring to bear on individuals and groups cannot be abstracted. Thus, despite their consistent use of the feminine to name their profession, they maintain that it must be not represented as such. What must be emphasized is the need for greater social, political and economic recognition and power. To accomplish this, they believe that the image of the profession should be desexualized.

Coda: Reactions of the Translators

According to Bassnett and Lefevere (1998:10), "Rewriters and translators are the people who really construct cultures on the basic level in our day and age. It is as simple, and as monumental as that". This is particularly true in the case studied here: we, the translators, were acutely aware of our responsibility toward our readership.

As well-intentioned feminists, we assumed that our interventionist strategy would be perceived by readers as it was intended: affirmation.

When I conceived this project I hoped to hear nurses clearly affirm their professional and gendered identity. I also expected both positive and negative reactions to the feminizing strategy. Yet the results are anything but conclusive. And my surprise at these results was the most enriching outcome of this study. Was it reasonable to seek such polarized positions and expect validation of my choices from the readership? Clearly not. The ambiguity of the results indicates that fluctuating social, political and economic pressures, as well as the internalization of gendered stereotypes on the part of the participants, may be pressuring nurses to question their own identity.

What does this mean, then, for the translators? Sherry Simon (1996:131) states that "inclusive-language translation can potentially do more harm than good, covering over some of the problematic areas and preventing critical engagement with the underlying issues". Should we persist in encouraging critical engagement with the gendered nature of the nursing profession or should we opt for more inclusive strategies?

Despite the ambivalence expressed by the research participants we remain steadfast in our belief that the predominance of women in the nursing profession is a factor that should be foregrounded in discourse. The underlying issues cited by the nurses in the sample are all a function of subalternity and justify the continued foregrounding of the feminine as generic. Indeed, one respondent, who was particularly ambivalent toward feminization, unwittingly provided our *mot d'ordre:* "You have to take a position".

Nonetheless, the translation team has since nuanced its approach in recognition of the varying target audiences of CNO texts. For example, documents whose purpose is to attract high school students to the nursing profession are strictly gender inclusive, whereas those addressed to the membership continue to be feminized. The ambivalence expressed toward this latter practice has not fallen on deaf ears however; we now endeavour to use epicenes when possible.

This study, designed both as an empirical exercise and as a reflective one, demonstrates the crucial role translators can play in the discursive representation of social categories. The results also confirm that the translator "must be able to identify, as much as possible, the institutional pressures hidden behind nationally entrenched public discourses s/he is asked to translate. The translator must also be able to recognize, based on her/his own experience, the considerable influence exerted by analogous pressures being brought to bear in her/his own national context, and more surreptitiously, on herself/himself" (Simeoni 1993:183, my translation).

References

Arrojo, Rosemary (1994) "Fidelity and the Gendered Translation", *TTR: Traduire les sociolectes* VII(2): 147-63.

Bassnett, Susan and André Lefevere (1998) "Introduction", in Bassnett and Lefevere (eds) *Translation, History and Culture*, London: Pinter, 1-11.

Bourdieu, Pierre (1979) *La distinction: critique sociale du jugement,* Paris: Les Éditions de Minuit.

------ and Loïc J.D. Wacquant (1992) *An Invitation to Reflexive Sociology,* Chicago: The University of Chicago Press.

Briggs, Charles L. (1996) *Disorderly Discourse: Narrative, Conflict, and Inequality,* New York, Oxford: Oxford University Press.

Cameron, Deborah (1985) *Feminism and Linguistic Theory*, London: The Macmillan Press Ltd.

Fecteau, T. Joan, Jullane Jackson and Kathryn Dindia (1992) "Gender Orientation Scales: An Empirical Assessment of Content Validity", in Linda A. M. Perry, Lynn H. Turner and Helen M. Sterk(eds) *Constructing and Reconstructing Gender — The Links Among Communication, Language and Gender*, Albany: State University of New York Press, 17-34.

Godard, Barbara (1997) "Writing Between Cultures", *TTR* X(1): 53-99.

Hébert, Lyse (2003) *Pour une traduction-affirmation: les textes de l'Ordre des infirmières et infirmiers de l'Ontario,* unpublished M.A. thesis, Toronto: York University.

Inghilleri, Moira (ed.) (2005) *Bourdieu and the Sociology of Translation and Interpreting*, Special Issue of *The Translator* 11(2).

Lefevere, A. and S. Bassnett (1990) *Translation, History and Culture*, London and New York: Pinter.

Lotbinière-Harwood, Suzanne de (1991) *Re-Belle et Infidèle. La traduction comme pratique de réécriture au féminin /The Body Bilingual. Translation as a Rewriting in the Feminine,* Montréal & Toronto: Les Éditions du Remue-Ménage & The Women's Press.

Nord, Christiane (1997) *Translating as a Purposeful Activity – Functionalist Approaches Explained*, Manchester: St. Jerome Publishing.

Ontario, Government of Direction générale de la condition féminine (1998) *À juste titre: guide de rédaction non sexiste*, Toronto: Office des affaires francophones. www.ofa.gov.on.ca:80/français/splashpage.html.

Ontario, Government of (1990) *French Language Services Act, R.S.O., Chapter F.32.* www.e-laws.gov.on.ca/DBLaws/Statutes/English/90f32_e.htm.

Simeoni, Daniel (1993) "L'institution dans la langue: lexique et pensée d'État", *TTR: L'histoire en traduction* VI(1): 171-202.

------ (1998) "The Pivotal Status of the Translator's Habitus", *Target* 10(1): 1-39.

Simon, Sherry (1996) *Gender in Translation – Cultural Identity and the Politics of Transmission*, London & New York: Routledge

Spivak, Gayatri Chakravorty (2000) "The Politics of Translation", in L. Venuti (ed.) *The Translation Studies Reader*, London & New York: Routledge, 397-416.

Toury, Gideon (2000) "The Nature and Role of Norms in Translation", in L. Venuti (ed.) *The Translation Studies Reader*, London & New York: Routledge, 198-211.

Von Flotow, Luise (1997) *Translation and Gender: Translating in the "Era of Feminism"*, Manchester: St. Jerome Publishing.

------ (1991) "Feminist Translation: Contexts, Practices and Theories", *TTR: Traduire la théorie* IV(2): 69-84.

Court Interpreters' Self Perception
A Spanish Case Study

ANNE MARTIN
GRETI[1] Research Group – University of Granada, Spain

JUAN MIGUEL ORTEGA HERRÁEZ
GRETI Research Group – University of Alicante, Spain

Abstract. *Several authors (e.g. Berk-Seligson 1990; Jansen 1995) have described how court interpreters tend to adopt a more active role than would be expected, and how this can influence the end result of their work. They may perform functions that, in principle, fall within the remit of professionals from other fields: provision of legal advice and, in extreme cases, social work. The aim of this paper is to analyze this active role from the standpoint of the interpreters themselves. It is based on research involving 19 subjects who replied to a questionnaire exploring the perceptions of practising court interpreters in the Madrid region of Spain with regard to their work. The topics covered include controversial issues at the centre of the debate about the court interpreter's role, such as adaptation of language register, cultural explanations, expansion and omission of information and the relationship between interpreter and clients. It was crucial to determine whether court interpreters, at least in Spain, are aware of what their role is, where its limits lie and what reasons may induce them to go beyond their established functions. The results indicate that the majority of practising court interpreters seem to go beyond the remit that codes of ethics stipulate.*

1. Introduction

At the start of any legal proceedings involving interpreting, the interpreter must, under oath, swear to translate "well and faithfully". The implications of this rather cryptic requirement can hardly be said to be clear, lending itself as it does to differing interpretations. Does the word "faithful" imply "literal"? Perhaps the word "well" involves giving priority to communication

---

[1] Research group financed by the Andalusian Regional Government and based in the University of Granada. Name in full: *La interpretación ante los retos de la mundialización: formación y profesión* [Interpreting and the challenges of globalization: training and the profession]. http://www.ugr.es/local/greti

between the parties rather than to literalness? One may wonder whether it is always possible to fulfil both requirements and, indeed, whether it is desirable to do so, bearing in mind that a linguistically faithful translation may end up being an obstacle for communication between the parties involved. Apart from this oath, Spanish court interpreters have no further guidelines of any sort, in the form of codes of ethics or legislation, upon which to model their professional practice.

This study explores the opinions of court interpreters regarding this issue and aims at exploring the strategies they adopt in the absence of such guidelines. Our hypothesis was that many interpreters, either consciously or unconsciously, probably do not restrict their approach to linguistically literal translation. The study is based on a questionnaire completed by 19 court interpreters in Madrid in 2003-2004. The study focuses specifically on court interpreters' self-perception regarding their professional role.

2.   Methodology and profile of respondents

The methodology used in this study is questionnaire-based. The questionnaires were designed using the model described by Oppenheim (1996), which has also been applied by other researchers in translation and interpreting studies at the University of Granada (Calvo Encinas 2001; Foulquié Rubio 2002; Way 2003). As recommended by Oppenheim (1996), the questionnaire used in this study was subjected to pilot testing using a sample group of subjects with identical characteristics to the final group. Due to lack of space we shall not include analysis of the pilot study in the present paper, bearing in mind that, in any case, its main objective was to verify the viability of the questionnaire.

The target population for our final study consisted of practising court interpreters from the Madrid region (*Comunidad de Madrid*). A total of 24 questionnaires were distributed in the different translation and interpreting offices in the various Madrid courts[2] and amongst freelance colleagues,

---

[2] In Spain due to the devolution of powers, the court system may be managed either by the regional or by the national authorities, depending on the region. In the case of Madrid, the regional government oversees those courts with jurisdiction over the province and towns of Madrid: Courts of First Instance and Examination [*Juzgados de Primera Instancia e Instrucción*], Criminal Courts [*Juzgados de lo Penal*], Court of Appeal [*Audiencia Provincial*], Regional High Court of Justice [*Tribunal Superior de Justicia*], Juvenile Courts [*Juzgados de Menores*], among others. Meanwhile the National Ministry of Justice still retains power over those courts with national jurisdiction such

and 19 were returned. The distribution of questionnaires according to main professional activity of respondents is described in Table 1:

Professional activity	No. of respondents	Percentage
Staff interpreters	13	68.42%
Freelance interpreters working exclusively for the courts	5	26.32%
Freelance interpreters working for different departments of public administration	1	5.25%

Table 1: Professional activity of respondents

Regarding gender distribution, 11 of these interpreters were male and 8, female (unlike the pilot sample, which was entirely composed of female interpreters). More than half of the subjects were aged between 31 and 40 and the rest were divided equally above and below this age range. This was a determining factor with regard to years of professional experience, which is reflected in Table 2:

Professional experience	No. of respondents	Percentage
< 3 years	4	21.05%
3 – 6 years	9	47.37%
6 – 10 years	1	5.26%
> 10 years	5	26.32%

Table 2: Professional experience of respondents

Possibly an even more important aspect when analyzing the results is the educational level of the subjects. To date, interpreters working for the Ministry of Justice and the Madrid regional authorities are only required to have reached school leaving certificate level or equivalent.[3] We are not going to discuss this issue here since it has been fully dealt with elsewhere (Ortega

---

as the Supreme Court [*Tribunal Supremo*] or the National Criminal and Administrative Court [*Audiencia Nacional*]. Our research only includes interpreters working for the Madrid regional court system.

[3] Such was the situation when our study was carried out in 2003-2004. However, the situation has changed in some instances, since in 2004 the Madrid Regional Government decided to require a full university degree (*licenciatura*) (in any field) for all staff court interpreters. This requirement does not extend to freelance interpreters.

Herráez *et al.* 2004; Arróniz 2000). Suffice it to say that, despite this requirement, almost 75% of our sample population were university graduates and, in addition, 15.79% were in possession of postgraduate qualifications in translation and interpreting and 5.26% had been awarded a doctorate. It is therefore obvious that the group's level of academic qualification is far higher than the employing administrations' requirements.

However, not all graduates had studied the same degree. The sample included graduates in Social Science and Law (15.79%), Humanities (15.79%), Philology (15.79%) and in Translation and Interpreting (31.58%),[4] together with between 21% and 26% of graduates in possession of an intermediate university diploma.

Language combinations were extremely varied. Indeed, except for three cases, the combinations were all different from each other and included languages such as: English, French, Arabic, Polish, Chinese, Portuguese, Romanian and Russian, in combination with Spanish. However, only two of the respondents had official sworn translator/interpreter status in their working languages.[5] In one case, such status had been achieved as a result of passing the examination set by the Ministry of Foreign Affairs for this purpose and the other as a result of having a degree in Translation and Interpreting. These findings contrast with the pilot study population, 40% of whom were official sworn translators/interpreters for, at least, one of the languages in their working combination.

Before moving on to analyze the theoretical background and results of our study, we should like to point out that the present paper only partially reflects the results of the original study,[6] which was much wider in scope and also included aspects such as professional situation, organization of work, training issues, interpreting techniques and professional image.

---

[4] 21.05% of them only have a university degree in Translation and Interpretation [*Licenciatura en Traducción e Interpretación*], while 10.53% also hold another degree.
[5] The *Intérprete Jurado* (Sworn Translator and Interpreter) is the only accredited professional in the field of legal translation and interpretation that exists in Spain. Accreditation can be obtained by sitting an examination organized by the Ministry of Foreign Affairs each year. The examination focuses mainly on translation (including legal translation), but surprisingly does not include interpreting, just an oral interview. Those who hold a university degree in Translation and Interpretation can also be accredited as Sworn Translators and Interpreters if they have obtained a certain number of credits in legal translation and interpreting during their studies.
[6] Cf. Ortega Herráez (2004).

3. Background

Most codes of ethics and oaths adhered to by court interpreters – in addition to the attitude of many professionals who work with interpreters within the justice system (judges, prosecutors, barristers, etc.) – clearly reflect the philosophy that, to be faithful to the original, the court interpreter must be as literal as possible, without omitting or adding anything and without modifying the register used by either of the intervening parties (González *et al.* 1991:155). This philosophy of court interpreting is what is known in the USA as respecting the *legal equivalent*.[7] This is understandable if we recall that codes of conduct in any profession aim at preventing professionals from going beyond what is understood to be their function (even when these functions may not have been clearly defined), for example translating in a biased or incorrect way in order to benefit one of the parties. Such instruments are based on a hypothetical "ideal translation" which should supposedly be the model professionals aspire to.

However, the idea that only one "correct" translation exists and that the interpreter "only translates" – that is to say, carries out a mechanical code-switching operation in accordance with some previously learned rules – is based on an oversimplified and naïve conception of what translation and interpreting are really about (Jansen 1995:12). In this sense, Pöchhacker (2000:51) suggests that: "'just translating' is little more than a simplistic fiction in an interaction marked by the interlocutors' unequal status and different educational, social and cultural backgrounds".

Court interpreting is a complex process based on norms which evolve and change during the course of the interaction: the different attitudes of the parties and the imbalance in power relations, together with the tension between the priorities of the parties involved, oblige the interpreter to take decisions which are rarely straightforward (Jansen 1995:12).

Indeed, observational studies bear witness to this complexity and show the influence potentially wielded by the interpreter in the interaction, contrary to what is usually imagined. In the field of public service interpreting,

---

[7] For González *et al.* (1991:16) the legal equivalent is "a linguistically true and legally appropriate interpretation of statements spoken or read in court, from the second language into [the language of the court] or vice versa". Therefore, the interpreter is "required to render in a verbatim manner the form and content of the linguistic and paralinguistic elements of a discourse, including all of the pauses, hedges, self-corrections, hesitations, and emotion as they are conveyed through tone of voice, word choice, and intonation".

which shares many of the features of court interpreting, many studies have been carried out showing similar results. The most thorough and emblematic is perhaps the work of Wadensjö (1992) which, amongst other functions, describes how the interpreter assumes a coordinating role in the interaction, and cannot be considered as a mere depersonalized code-switching machine.[8] In the field of court interpreting, the groundbreaking work carried out by Berk-Seligson (1990) analyzes a wide corpus of interpreter-mediated witness testimony. Her analysis demonstrates that the interpreter, despite supposedly being a neutral figure with no capacity to influence the development and result of the interpreted event, in reality influences it in numerous different ways as a result of pragmatic questions such as transmission or omission of certain grammatical mechanisms (verb forms and intransitivity), hedges, double negatives, and politeness forms, etc. In the same vein, Jansen's study (1995) shows that the interpreter tends to modify the register of the defendant and simplify institutional discourse for him/her.

There is a clear contradiction between the behaviour of the interpreters in the studies mentioned and the supposedly ideal definition of the court interpreter's role and such a contradiction cannot be attributed to malpractice or lack of technique on the part of the interpreters.

The issue at the heart of this contradiction is the interpreter's role, its limits and the problems caused precisely by the haziness of such limits. These issues have been given much attention by numerous authors.

The studies mentioned in this paper refer to inherent and non-deliberate interpreter reactions within a given communicative context. However, some authors, especially from within the profession, refer to the range of options open to court interpreters and the difficult decisions they must take in order to resolve certain situations. Most interpreters react instinctively – moved not only by the desire to interpret faithfully what has been said, but also to ensure that their interpretation has been fully understood by the listener. On occasions, especially when dealing with parties from widely differing cultural backgrounds, sticking blindly to a literal translation may actually impede communication.

In this sense, Herrero (1995:108) considers that the function of the interpreter involves not only translating language but also reinterpreting culture. To do this, the interpreter must seek pragmatically equivalent target language renderings. Herrero's opinions are shared by Feria (1999:103) who

---

[8] Reddy (1979) coined the term "conduit metaphor" to restrictively refer to the interpreter as just a linguistic mediator.

also mentions that intervention by the interpreter, in order to save time and effort, should take place on his/her own initiative without express permission being requested from the judge. On occasions, interpreters must take decisions which require reconciliation of contradictory demands of codes of ethics on the one hand and daily practice on the other. This author feels that the interpreter should:

> risking as little as possible, bring the language, the register and the symbolic universe of both participants closer together, intervening if necessary on his/her own initiative, by constructing a parallel metadiscourse which facilitates clarification of those elements the interpreter deems necessary. (*ibid.*, our translation)

It has been argued that adopting this kind of translation strategy may offer a comparative advantage to one of the parties when compared to parties involved in a monolingual trial with no interpreter present to smooth out communication problems between judge and defendant. In a monolingual situation, it is hardly likely that a judge and a defendant from different social classes with widely differing educational levels will always fully understand one another. Indeed, this is precisely what is intended by the *legal equivalent* school, which holds that the interpreter's task is to place the person for whom s/he interprets in a situation similar to that of a native speaker of the language spoken in court, that is to say that the presence of the interpreter should be neither beneficial nor detrimental to the defendant. This school therefore does not believe that it is a function of the court interpreter to ensure that the defendant has actually understood what is said: "The court interpreter's job is to place the non English speaker on an equal footing with, not at an advantage relative to an average layperson who understands ordinary English. The interpreter's task is not to ensure that the defendant understands the proceedings" (Mikkelson 1998:95).

Wadensjö (1997:205), however, argues that the two situations – monolingual interaction and interpreter-mediated interaction – cannot be compared one with another. According to this author, the two constitute different genres of communicative situation – "different systems of social activity" (*ibid.*) – each governed by different rules and parameters: "Interpreter-mediated talk forms a particular type of encounter, with its own specific organisational principles. The question is not then "if?" but "how?" conditions for interaction differ from monolingual situations" (*ibid.*:203).

These considerations form the theoretical backdrop against which the present research took place. We were interested in ascertaining the perception of the interpreters themselves regarding these questions, especially bearing in mind that not all practising court interpreters in Spain have received specific training and are therefore not necessarily familiar with the terms of the theoretical conflict, although evidently they deal with the practical reflection of this conflict on a daily basis through the decisions taken in the course of their interpreting work. In the words of Pöchhacker (2000:50), "These interpreters presumably shape their task according to some implicit norms of translational behaviour as well as expectations on the part of their (professional) clients".

In the newly emerging field of research into public service and court interpreting, several studies have been published which aim at determining the opinion of the participants in interpreted events. However, most of these studies focus on the perception of the primary speakers and very few explore the interpreters´ perceptions. Amongst the latter we find Hale (2004), Pöchhacker (2000) and Lang (1978) amongst interpreters in Papua New Guinea and which is generally considered to be the first study of this kind. Subsequently, Hearn *et al.* (1981) collected the opinions of 65 interpreters in an assessment of two regional interpretation services (quoted by Pöchhacker 2002:99). Tomassini (2002) uses a questionnaire and structured interviews to determine interpreter expectations in the health sector in Italy. Similarly, Angelelli (2003) and Chesher *et al.* (2003) also present interpreter-based studies.

4.   Results of the study

As has been mentioned, our analysis of the interpreter's role revolves around questions such as the adaptation of register, explanation of cultural and procedural issues, amplification or omission of information, and the relation established between the interpreter and the non-Spanish speaker (NSS). Evidently, there is some controversy involved in these issues, both from the standpoint of language and discourse and from the standpoint of the interpreters´ role in comparison to other professionals intervening in the legal proceedings, such as legal advisors or social workers (especially intercultural mediators).

The first of the questions related to the role of the interpreter revolves around the issue of **discoursal techniques** used in their daily practice. As mentioned by some of the studies referred to above, the use of discourse exerts a decisive influence on the parties' perception of each other. Bearing this in mind, our questions dealt with adaptation of register, explanation of cultural differences and legal procedures and finally, amplification, summarizing or omission of information. In the first case (**adapting register**) the vast majority of subjects (78.9%) stated they adapted the language of both the Spanish speaker and the non-Spanish speaker. The reasons justifying such a decision can be grouped into two main categories: firstly to facilitate communication and secondly, to bring the world of each party closer together, in cases where there were wide cultural disparities. This situation does not adhere to the **legal equivalent** model mentioned mainly by American authors, and we do not know to what extent the interpreters are aware of the importance of their decision, especially bearing in mind some of the comments made to justify it: "I usually adapt more formal register when the person is colloquial [sic], believing that this gives him an advantage (though now that I think about it maybe I should question this).

A majority of our subjects also stated they **explained cultural differences and questions of legal procedure** (57.9%), although the figure was lower than in the case of register adaptation. This difference may have been due to the fact that the question also included the explanation of legal procedure, which seems to be clearly understood to be the task either of the solicitor or other court officials. Perhaps in this case the interpreters have a clearer view of the role which corresponds to them. The reasons given by those who answered this question affirmatively include smoothing out cultural asymmetries and procedural issues, especially in some language combinations such as Arabic-Spanish, together with the fact that the non-Spanish speakers themselves often directly ask the interpreter questions about legal procedure which is generally unfamiliar to them.

Exactly the same result (57.9%) was found regarding **amplification, summary and omission of information**, although many respondents specified that they only omit repeated information and that they generally try not to omit anything. This precision would lead us to think that some interpreters are aware of the repercussions their decisions may have. Amongst the reasons justifying their answers we find the following:

- "Depending on the person, I weigh up and filter some information I feel to be unnecessary and I amplify points which need explanation or need placing in context"
- "I may summarize but I try not to omit anything. I don't amplify either because it might be risky"
- "I summarize if the information is too technical for the defendant

or if it is read out, because you have to summarize due to the speed
and lack of consideration of those who read such information out"

Once again, it is quite clear that the interpreters feel their first duty is to
facilitate communication and understanding.

Discoursal techniques applied	Yes	No	N/A
Adaptation of register	78.9%	15.8%	5.3%
Explanation of cultural differences and legal procedure	57.9%	36.8%	5.3%
Amplification, summary and omission of information	57.9%	42.1%	N/A

Table 3: Discoursal techniques applied by respondents

Having established that these practices take place, we wished to determine
how they were undertaken: i.e. whether this active role assumed by the
interpreter was explicit or, as Feria (1999:103) recommends, effected
discreetly without the knowledge of the parties involved. A total of 47.4%
stated they apply such strategies "on their own initiative, without informing the other parties", 21.1% stated that they "first informed the judge and
sought his/her authorisation", and 5.3% did so "on their own initiative but
subsequently informed the judge". The remaining responses were equally
distributed between "other techniques" and "not applicable". The reasons
put forward to justify responses were based on the desire to maintain the pace
and avoid interruption of the proceedings. Thus we find the following:

- "If you tell the judge first, it becomes less agile and holds up the
  proceedings. Judges don't usually think about these things or worry
  about the [translation] procedures we use"
- "When there's an obvious lack of understanding because of a cultural
  concept or practice I inform the judge and request explanation from
  the judge. If it's just a short explanation I add it without permission"
- "It depends on each case and on how serious and important the issue
  is, and also on the kind of trial (jury or not)"
- "It's not necessary to inform anyone"
- "It's not necessary to inform the judge. Many understand English
  and French, not like other languages they can't follow"
- "Once I've explained the details to the person concerned I inform the
  judge so s/he understands I'm not intervening in the declaration"

Assumption of active role	Percentage
On interpreter's own initiative	47.7%
Informing and seeking judge's authorization	21.1%
On interpreter's own initiative and subsequent information to judge	5.3%
Other techniques	10.5%
N/A	15.8%

Table 4: Assumption of active role

Evidently, this involvement on the part of the interpreter may be due to different reasons amongst which we may find **personal identification with the non-Spanish speaker**. In this case, 57.9% of subjects stated they "try to remain impartial", 15.8% stated they "never felt they identified with the persons for whom they interpreted", whereas 26% felt that "on occasions they had felt empathy or had identified with or felt themselves reflected in the person they interpreted for". Amongst the latter, the majority believed their attitude was due to the fact that the non-Spanish speaker was at a disadvantage in the Spanish legal system and on some occasions was even the victim of injustice. Curiously, only one subject linked this identification to the fact that they shared the same language and nobody mentioned common regional or national origins as being the reason for identification.

We now move on to examine **what the interpreters actually believed their functions to be** and to inquire whether they had, on occasions, carried out functions they believed did not correspond to them. In addition to interpreting language content, the following questions referred to functions such as explanation of procedural questions to the non-Spanish speaker (52.6% believed such explanation was the function of the interpreter and 47.4% did not), indication of bodies which the non-Spanish speaker should contact in order to solve his/her problems (78.9% believed this was not the function of the interpreter), explanation to judges, prosecutors, solicitors and officers of the court regarding cultural issues arising in the non-Spanish speakers' discourse (68.4% believed such explanation was not a function of the interpreter whereas 31.6% believed it was). We should like to underline one of the justifications given in this section of the questionnaire, as we feel it may contribute to clarifying both replies to this question and to the following: "I don't do it [everything that is not just interpreting language] because I don't think it's approved of and I haven't been trained to do it [the respondent was a graduate in Translation and Interpreting]. However, I do feel that a quality service would include these functions although that would be moving towards the field of social work (something which is complex and should be dealt with cautiously. I can't see the space or the resources for me to do this)."

Role of court interpreter	Yes	No
Interpreting language content	94.7%	5.3%
Explaining procedural questions to NSS	52.6%	47.4%
Directing NSS to bodies which can solve his/her problem	21.1%	78.9%
Explaining cultural issues in the NSS's discourse to court personnel	31.6%	68.4%
Other functions	10.5%	89.5%

Table 5: The role of the court interpreter

This response leads us on to the **"transgression" of the principal function of the interpreter**, i.e., oral language mediation. Of the respondents, 52.6% considered that, on occasions, they had gone further than their interpreter role permitted, whereas 47.4% stated they had never done so. It is curious that the number of those who admit to adapting register, explaining cultural questions and amplifying or omitting information is higher, especially regarding the question of register, which to a certain extent is related to the breach of their function to the extent that it departs from the **legal equivalent** model. In any case, those who did feel the need to go beyond what they believed were the limits of their role, did so in the following ways: offering legal advice (15.8%); offering cultural information (36.8%) and engaging in social work (26.3%). The results obtained in the pilot phase of this study had been slightly different, as 90% of the pilot study respondents stated they had gone beyond what they believed their role to be. In both the pilot and the final study, respondents stated they had taken this course of action for humanitarian reasons and because of the lack of an adequate structure of legal advice and information, accommodating different cultures and languages.

5.   Conclusions

It would seem that, to a certain extent, our initial hypothesis was confirmed by the results of our study. As occurred in the observational studies mentioned throughout this paper, court interpreters would appear to assume a more active role than is initially ascribed to them. More importantly, the results of the present study would seem to suggest that on many occasions interpreters are fully aware of the decisions they are taking when departing from the **legal equivalent** model prevalent in court interpreting in the USA. As we have mentioned above, the options adopted by Spanish court interpreters should not be attributed to lack of interpreting skills. We must not forget that Spain has no binding norms stipulating the functions and limiting the role of court interpreters, unlike the USA, where specifications are laid down in the *1978 Federal Court Interpreters' Act*. The respondents in the present study seem to clearly feel that their priority is to facilitate communication to which end they use numerous strategies, some of which may not be acceptable to professionals in other countries. This should lead to reflection about the need to produce some form of guidelines to regulate the complex role of court interpreters in Spain, adapting this role to the specificities of the Spanish legal system, which is not adversarial, as in countries with common law systems.

References

Angelelli, Claudia (2003) "The Interpersonal Role of the Interpreter in Cross-Cultural Communication: A Survey of Conference, Court and Medical Interpreters in the US, Canada and Mexico", in Louise Brunette, Georges Bastin, Isabelle Hemlin and Heather Clarke (eds) *The Critical Link 3. Interpreters in the Community. Selected Papers from the Third International Conference on Interpreting in Legal, Health and Social Service Settings, Montreal, Quebec, Canada*, Amsterdam & Philadelphia: John Benjamins, 15-26.

Arróniz, Pilar (2000) "La traducción y la interpretación en la Administración de Justicia", in Dorothy Kelly (ed.) *La traducción y la interpretación en España hoy: perspectivas profesionales*, Granada: Comares, 157-69.

Berk-Seligson, Susan (1990) *The Bilingual Courtroom*, Chicago & London: University of Chicago Press.

Calvo Encinas, Elisa (2001) *La evaluación diagnóstica en la didáctica de la traducción jurídica: diseño de un instrumento de medida*, unpublished Research Dissertation, Dpto. de Traducción e Interpretación, Spain: University of Granada.

Chesher, Terry, Helen Slatyer, Bodin Martinsen, Edda Ostarhild and Yolanda Vanden Bosch (2003) "Community-Based Interpreting: The Interpreter's Perspective", in Louise Brunette, Georges Bastin, Isabelle Hemlin and Heather Clarke (eds) *The Critical Link 3. Interpreters in the Community. Selected Papers from the Third International Conference on Interpreting in Legal, Health and Social Service Settings, Montreal, Quebec, Canada*,

Amsterdam & Philadelphia: John Benjamins, 273-91.

Feria García, Manuel (1999) "El traductor-intérprete en la Administración de Justicia", in Manuel Feria García (ed.) *Traducir para la Justicia*, Granada: Comares, 87-108.

Foulquié Rubio, Ana Isabel (2002) *El intérprete en las dependencias policiales: perspectivas de abogados y estudiantes de Derecho de Granada*, unpublished Research Dissertation, Dpto. de Traducción e Interpretación, Spain: University of Granada.

González, Roseann D., Victoria F. Vásquez and Holly Mikkelson (1991) *Fundamentals of Court Interpretation: Theory, Policy and Practice*, Durham, NC: Carolina Academic Press.

Hale, Sandra B. (2004) *The Discourse of Court Interpreting: Discourse Practices of the Law, the Witness and the Interpreter*, Amsterdam & Philadelphia: John Benjamins.

Hearn, J., Terry Chesher and S. Holmes (1981) "An Evaluation of Interpreter Programmes in Relation to the Needs of a Polyethnic Society and the Implications for Education", [Project notes, questionnaire and summarized responses] [unpublished]

Herrero Muñoz-Cobo, Bárbara (1995) "La interpretación en los juzgados", in Rafael Martín Gaitero (ed.) *V Encuentros Complutenses en torno a la Traducción*, Madrid: Editorial Complutense, 687-92.

Jansen, Peter (1995) "The Role of the Interpreter in Dutch Courtroom Interaction: The Impact of the Situation on Translational Norms", in Jorma Tommola (ed.) *Topics in Interpreting Research*, Turku: University of Turku Centre for Translation and Interpreting, 11-36.

Lang, Ranier (1978) "Behavioural Aspects of Liaison Interpreters in Papua New Guinea: Some Preliminary Observations", in David Gerver and Walter Sinaiko (eds) *Language Interpretation and Communication*, New York & London: Plenum Press, 231-44.

Mikkelson, Holly (1998) "Awareness of the Language of the Law and the Preservation of Register in the Training of Legal Translators and Interpreters", in Isabel García Izquierdo and Joan Verdagal (eds) *Los estudios de traducción: un reto didáctico*, Castellón: Universitat Jaume I, 87-100.

Oppenheim, Abraham Naftali (1996) *Questionnaire Design, Interviewing and Attitude Measurement*, London: Pinter Publishers.

Ortega Herráez, Juan Miguel (2004) *Panorámica de la interpretación judicial en España: un análisis desde la profesión*, unpublished Research Dissertation, Dpto. de Traducción e Interpretación, Spain: University of Granada.

------, Pilar Arróniz, Paloma Aldea and Sonsoles Plaza (2004) "Situación actual de la práctica de la traducción y de la interpretación en la Administración de Justicia", in Susana Cruces and Luna Alonso (eds) *La traducción en el ámbito institucional*, Vigo: Servicio de Publicaciones de la Universidade de Vigo, 85-126.

Pöchhacker, Franz (2000) "The Community Interpreter's Task: Self-Perception and Provider Views", in Roda P. Roberts, Silvana E. Carr, Diana Abraham and Aideen Dufour (eds) *The Critical Link 2: Interpreters in the Community*, Amsterdam & Philadelphia: John Benjamins, 49-65.

------ (2002) "Researching Interpreting Quality: Models and Methods", in Giuliana Garzone and Maurizio Viezzi (eds) *Interpreting in the 21ˢᵗ Century. Challenges and Opportunities. Selected Papers from the 1ˢᵗ Forli Conference on Interpreting Studies, 9-11 November 2000*, Amsterdam & Philadelphia: John Benjamins, 95-106.

Reddy, Michael J. (1979) "The Conduit Metaphor: A Case of Frame Conflict in our Language about Language", in Andrew Ortony (ed.) *Metaphor and Thought*, Cambridge: Cambridge University Press, 284-324.

Snelling, David (1997) "On Media and Court Interpreting", in Yves Gambier, Daniel Gile and Christopher Taylor (eds) *Conference Interpreting: Current Trends in Research, Proceedings of the International Conference on "Interpreting: what do we know and how?" Turku, August 25-27, 1994*, Amsterdam & Philadelphia: John Benjamins, 187-206.

Tomassini, Elena (2002) "A Survey on the Role of the Community Interpreter Conducted in the Region of Emilia Romagna, Italy", in Carmen Valero Garcés and Guzmán Mancho Barés (eds) *Traducción e Interpretación en los servicios públicos: nuevas necesidades para nuevas realidades*, Alcalá de Henares: Universidad de Alcalá Publicaciones. [cd-rom]

Wadensjö, Cecilia (1992) *Interpreting as Interaction*, London & New York: Addison Wesley Longman.

------ (1997) "The Right to Lie: On Interpreter- Mediated Police Interrogations", in Yves Gambier, Daniel Gile and Christopher Taylor (eds) *Conference Interpreting: Current Trends in Research, Proceedings of the International Conference on "Interpreting: what do we know and how?" Turku, August 25-27, 1994*, Amsterdam & Philadelphia: John Benjamins, 202-205

Way, Catherine (2003) *La traducción como acción social. El caso de los documentos académicos (español-inglés)*, unpublished Doctoral dissertation, Spain: University of Granada.

The Pragmatic Significance of Modal Particles in an Interpreted German Asylum Interview

MARIA TILLMANN
Heriot-Watt University, Edinburgh, UK

Abstract. *The pragmatic significance of modal particles in interpreted discourse has not received much attention in dialogue-interpreting research. Particularly in instances of interpretation between languages that differ in the frequency of use of modal particles, the way in which interpreters deal with the pragmatic intention of such discourse markers merits investigation. This study is based on the analysis of five passages from an authentic asylum interview held by the German immigration authorities and interpreted between German and English. The use of modal particles is a prominent feature of the immigration official's questioning technique, which seems designed to reduce distance and improve rapport, while urging the applicant to provide more detailed information about himself. The interpreter is found to introduce pragmatic changes by rendering questions less forceful or reducing the openness of questions. Modal particles used to convey casualness are omitted by the interpreter, as are particles that subtly indicate the immigration official's growing scepticism. The overall effect of the interpreter's deletion of pragmatic content from the official's questions on the discoursal atmosphere may have crucial consequences for the goal of the encounter: to establish the applicant's story of persecution and, above all, the truth of his assertions.*

1. Introduction

This paper examines the linguistic techniques employed by an immigration official questioning an asylum applicant during an interpreted asylum interview and how these techniques are conveyed through the interpretation process. More specifically, it considers how the interpreter deals with the pragmatic meaning expressed by the immigration official through modal particles, downtoning devices used to express the speaker's attitude, in light of the challenges posed by linguistic differences between the two languages of interpretation concerning the frequency of use of modal particles.

The pragmatic significance of modal particles in interpreted discourse has only received a little attention within the growing body of dialogue interpreting research. Knapp-Potthoff and Knapp (1987) in their seminal analysis of intercultural communication enabled by an untrained language mediator observe a tendency on the part of the mediator to delete down-toning devices from the interpretation. In their data, the German speaker, whose role in the exchange is to negotiate conversation topics for a linguistic experiment with a Korean interlocutor, uses an abundance of downtoning particles in order to soften the impositions expressed. Although the mediator regularly omits these particles and their pragmatic content in her interpreta-tion, she is also shown to have a clear interest in making the exchange run smoothly and introduces politeness strategies (Brown and Levinson 1978) on her own initiative, partially in order to save her own face. Amongst other things, she is found to introduce downtoning particles in places where the original utterance did not contain such devices. Knapp-Potthoff and Knapp (1987) suggest that the mediator may gauge the gravity of face threat ex-pressed in each utterance in light of the cultural differences between the two cultures. In order to preserve the discoursal atmosphere, the mediator may consider downtoning particles inappropriate in places where they are used by the German speaker or may judge them to be vital in places where the German speaker expresses a face threat baldly, thus prompting her to introduce changes.

Hale (1999) examines how discourse markers (see Schiffrin 1987) used in courtroom discourse, such as "well", "now" and "you see", are conveyed by interpreters. She finds that lawyers use discourse markers as argumenta-tive and confrontational devices, expressing challenges and disagreement during cross-examination and controlling the progression of talk during ex-amination-in-chief. Like Knapp-Potthoff and Knapp (1987), Hale observes a tendency on the part of interpreters to omit or mistranslate such particles. Interpreters may judge discourse markers as superfluous and thus leave them out or may be prevented by translation difficulties from rendering such lin-guistic devices. However, Hale points out that while the illocutionary point (Searle 1990) of an utterance may remain intact, the illocutionary force is likely to be reduced through such losses, potentially prompting a change in the interlocutor's reaction to the utterance. In a courtroom context, the consequences of even relatively subtle pragmatic changes introduced in the interpreting process can be significant, as has been demonstrated for instance by Berk-Seligson (1990). It can be assumed that the same applies in the related field of asylum hearings. However, not enough evidence exists to date regarding the pragmatic dimension of interpreting in immigration and asylum cases. The aim of this study is to make a small contribution to this area of research by examining data from an authentic German asylum interview, interpreted between German and English.

2.   The data

The data analyzed in this paper were obtained from a recorded asylum interview carried out by the German immigration authorities (former *Bundesamt für die Anerkennung Ausländischer Flüchtlinge*), which was broadcast as part of a TV documentary.[1] The five passages broadcast were transcribed and subsequently analyzed. Present at the interview were the asylum applicant (A), a young male from Sierra Leone, whose first language is not English, the female immigration official (D), the so-called "individual decider" (*Einzelentscheider*), and a female African interpreter (I) for English. The decider is a higher-ranking civil servant who makes a decision on whether or not an applicant will be granted asylum under the German Basic Constitutional Law (*Art. 16 Grundgesetz*) and whether obstacles to deportation exist under German Immigration Law (*§53 Ausländergesetz*). The decider is free from any instructions from superiors (at least under German law applicable at the time of recording) and therefore makes her decisions independently like a judge. The applicant can file an appeal against the decision taken, resulting in court proceedings before an administrative court (*Verwaltungsgericht*). The official language of the hearing is German and an interpreter is legally required when an applicant does not have sufficient command of this language. However, applicants are not necessarily entitled to be heard in their mother tongue if they can speak a more common language such as English or French, as can be gleaned from the German Asylum Procedure Law (*§ 17 (1) Asylverfahrensgesetz)*. The rationale for having an interpreter present is thus to enable communication in a way that is acceptable from the point of view of the institution in the pursuit of its goals, and not to allow the applicant to express himself in his own language.

3.   The asylum hearing as an instance of institutional talk

The asylum hearing can be described as instance of institutional talk (Drew and Heritage 1992). The speech event is goal-oriented in that the main purpose of the hearing is to determine whether or not the applicant fulfils the criteria to be entitled to asylum in the host country. In addition, there may be subordinate goals, deriving, for instance, from the current

---

[1] *Menschen Hautnah, 'Die Entscheider'*, broadcast on 3 Sat, 23 April 2001 and on WDR, 25 April 2001.

political or institutional climate, as well as intermediate goals within the interview, such as establishing a particular fact. The decider is guided by a list of questions (which in themselves are goal-oriented, the goal being to determine the truth). The questions provide the structure of interaction: the decider has the right and the obligation to ask, the applicant replies, resulting in an asymmetrical distribution of questions and answers. The relationship between the three participants of the hearing is hierarchical. The power differential derives, above all, from the roles inherent in the genre "asylum hearing". The asylum seeker is in the role of applicant, requesting permission to stay from the host country, so his power is extremely constrained. The decider, despite being bound by the asylum regulations applicable in the host country, has the right and the obligation to decide on the applicant's fate on behalf of the host country and is therefore in a very powerful position. The interpreter is less powerful than the decider in that she has little institutional power. However, this institutional power must be distinguished from the power within the exchange (Thompson and Thetela 1995). By nature of her task in a key position and as the only participant to understand both languages, the interpreter holds considerable power within the exchange. In her role as language-mediator she has, amongst other things, control over how talk evolves between the two participants, although this power is not explicitly endowed to her, and the institution may not be aware of or have sanctioned this power.

An initial analysis of the data revealed some interesting insights into the decider's questioning technique. As will be shown below, questions were often posed in a way that would give the applicant an opportunity to provide more information than is explicitly requested. *Hammer's German Grammar and Usage* (Durell 2002:184) states that modal particles "alter the tone of what is being said and make sure that the speaker's intentions and attitudes are clearly understood". Some languages, such as German and Greek, are rich in such downtoning particles, while others, for instance French or English, are not. However, speakers of languages that feature fewer such particles have other means of expressing the same pragmatic meaning, for instance through intonation, tag questions or through the use of modal verbs (e.g. "er ist *wohl* ohne uns abgefahren" can be expressed as "he must have left without us"). In order to convey the pragmatic meaning of an utterance in the other language, the interpreter's technique would therefore need to involve this transfer. However, there is a clear tendency in German to use such downtoning particles much more extensively than in English. The question thus arises of if and how interpreters compensate for this difference in linguistic behaviour.

As will be demonstrated below, in the data at hand modal particles are employed abundantly by the immigration official in order to reduce distance, improve rapport and achieve the overall goal of determining the applicant's life story, his story of persecution and escape and the truth of his assertions. The particular questions arising are therefore whether the interpreter is sensitive to the pragmatics expressed, and if so, how this is conveyed in the interpretation. Is an expression found that represents the illocutionary force of the modal particles used in the source language, are modal particles substituted or even omitted, and what is the likely outcome of the interpreter's respective choices for the interaction? In order to address these questions empirically, three short excerpts (excerpts [1], [2] and [4]) and one longer excerpt (excerpt [3]) have been selected from the five transcribed sections and subsequently analyzed in more detail. It should be noted that the approach taken here is a purely descriptive one, leaving normative judgements aside.

4. Data limitations

When considering the evidence presented here, some of the limitations of the data should be borne in mind. First of all, it was not possible to observe the unfolding exchange in its entirety, as only five extracts from the entire interview were included in the documentary and the unedited material could not be obtained. Also, only one participant could be observed visually at any time due to the editing of the material for broadcasting, while the applicant's face remained concealed throughout in order to protect his confidentiality. Furthermore, the applicant's utterances were often difficult to hear or entirely inaudible. Nevertheless, the data obtained are an invaluable source of evidence, especially considering the difficulties commonly encountered when seeking permission to record authentic data in sensitive areas such as this.

The notation adopted for data transcription follows transcription rules adapted from Wadensjö (1998) and Mason (2001). In order to make the data accessible to a wider audience, utterances that were expressed in German have been translated and integrated into the transcript in italics. This translation does not represent a suggestion for an optimal or ideal interpretation. In its aim to reflect the original utterance as closely as possible, it tries to strike a balance between conveying the pragmatics expressed, while remaining as literal as possible. In some cases, two alternative translations (separated by a backslash) were provided in English to reflect the range of interpersonal meanings that were possible.

5. Data Analysis

In the first example, taken from the initial stages of the interview, the applicant (A) has just replied "no" to the question of whether he has any kind of identification document. The decider (D) now enquires if he has ever had any such document:

Excerpt [1]

5   D: (3) °mhm° (.) **Hatten** Sie denn jemals irgendein Ausweispapier zu Hause?
        *Did you ever **have** any kind of identification paper at home?*

6   I: have you had any kind of identification paper at home?

7   A: °no no no no°

8   I: [nein
                [no

9   D: nein, keine? (schreibt) (5) mhm. (.) Wissen Sie Ihr Geburtsdatum?
        no, none? (writes) (5) mhm (.) Do you know your date of birth?

10   I: Do you know **your** birth date?

The decider puts particular stress on "*Hatten*", emphasizing that the question refers to the past. This stress is further underlined by the modal particle "*denn*", which would be impossible to render with exact equivalence in English, and which is in fact left out by the interpreter without compensation. Finally, D uses "*jemals irgendein*" ("ever any kind of"), of which only "any kind of" is rendered by I. The colouring of the question as quite probing has therefore been reduced in the process of interpretation and the illocutionary force of the question as referring to all previous times lost. It can only be speculated as to what motivated this change. The interpreter may not have been aware of the decider's pragmatic intentions or she may have found it too difficult to find a pragmatic equivalent in English. The second explanation can be found in Hale's study on courtroom questions, where "the main reason for the interpreters' omissions of certain features was a lack of syntactic and semantic equivalence" (Hale 2001:48). However, in the example here, the only feature that would present such a difficulty is the pragmatic content of the modal particle "*denn*", where an alternative expression would have to be found. The loss of pragmatic content, however, also extends to other features, as could be seen.

The following example is from the same passage and follows the applicant's reply to the question about where he was born:

Excerpt [2]

16   D: mhm (.) Is' das 'ne größere Stadt oder ein Dorf, was ist Waterloo?
           mhm (.) Is that a bigger town or a village, what is Waterloo?
17   I: is it a big town or a village?
18   A: a village
19   I: ist ein Dorf
           is a village

D now requests more detailed information about A's place of birth, tagging
on the open question "what is Waterloo?". This can be interpreted as summons directed at A to provide more information and not just a brief reply.
D's questioning technique here is likely to be led by her objective to get A
to talk freely about his life in his home country in order to be able to draw
conclusions regarding his credibility. However, the tagged-on question is
left out in the interpretation, making the question a closed one, and the
pragmatic objective is not fulfilled.

The next example is taken from the following passage of the transcript.
The initial phase of taking the applicant's personal details has apparently
been completed, and the decider now tries to obtain some background information on the asylum seeker's life. The decider's question again features
a modal particle, "*eigentlich*", conveying a certain casualness, in some way
similar to the English expressions "actually" or "by the way". In terms of
politeness theory (Brown and Levinson 1987) this could be interpreted as
a negative politeness strategy, expressing the speaker's intention not to
impose on the hearer by reducing the weight of the question. By making
the question sound less threatening, the speaker at the same time increases
the likelihood of receiving a reply:

Excerpt [3]

1   D: was ham' Sie eigentlich/ womit haben sie sich ihr Leben lang beschäftigt?
          what did you actually/ what did you occupy yourself with throughout your life?

          Sie sind **nicht** zur Schule gegangen. Was haben Sie anstelle getan?
          *You did **not** go to school. What did you do instead?*
2   I: mhm you didn't go to school.   What did you do?
3   A: °No° (mumbles)   I read Arabic

It can be easily seen that the interpreter does not preserve D's strategy. The
initial question is omitted altogether and the propositional content ("what
did you occupy yourself with throughout your life?") is lost. The summons
to provide some more information is therefore omitted. The question is

asked baldly, after the statement "you didn't go to school", which is left without preface and thus quite a considerable face-threat, considering that A is applying for asylum in a country where attending school throughout childhood is the norm. The final question "What did you do?" consequently sounds quite reproachful.

The reply given by the asylum seeker is very short, clearly not fulfilling the decider's expectation to be given some more information on his life story, so a longer question-answer sequence follows, which, as we will see, fails altogether to generate information to D's satisfaction. The apparent mismatch between the decider's expectation when formulating the question and the applicant's response is reminiscent of the findings by Roberts *et al.* (1992) where linguistic and cultural differences in an intercultural job interview prevent the interviewee from arriving at the correct interpretation of questions posed in that particular setting. Mason (2004) presents similar evidence from interpreted data in a British immigration context, and in his data the interpreter is found to compensate for the perceived mismatch, a type of interpreter behaviour directed at protecting the interest of the client. The interpreter in the data presented here, however, does not compensate. On the contrary – any indication as to the significance of the question is lost in the interpreting process.

The next question in this sequence contains three modal particles in combination, again conveying casualness. The German question clearly conveys the decider's wish to find out more and, although in this respect it is probing, the imposition is weakened through the informality introduced by the modal particles. In particular the particle "so" conveys the decider's wish to be given some examples of the reading material in order for her to gain a more general impression of how A used to spend his time:

Excerpt [3] contd.

4   I: mhm   ich habe Arabic gelesen.
         mhm   *I read Arabic*

5   A: [(mumbles)

6   D: (3) mhm (2) Was ham' Sie denn da so gelesen?
         (3) mhm (2) What did you read in this respect\ for instance?

7   I: what did you read?

Again, the question is put baldly by the interpreter, without compensation for the modal particles. The applicant provides a short reply, whereby he may have wanted to say more, but was interrupted by the interpreter:

Excerpt [3] contd.

8   A: ah we/ we read how to pray.   how to/
9   I: [mhm   wir haben gelesen, wie man betet.
             [mhm   we read how to pray.
10   D: (2) hmhm (.) Sie ham den ganzen Tag nur **gelesen**⌈? ((klingt herausfordernd))
             *(2) hmhm   (.)   you were just **reading** all day   ⌈?((sounds challenging))*
11   I: so the whole day you were reading?
12   A: the whole day (.) any time we did do our morning (.) and evening time
13   I: [mhm   hmhm   wir
             [mhm   mhm   we
      haben das morgens und abends gelernt.
      learned that in the mornings and evenings.

Once more, the reply given does not coincide with the decider's idea of a proper preoccupation. Like in the above example, the interpreter is not found to compensate for the lack of appropriate information provided by the applicant. On the contrary, the illocutionary force of the decider's renewed question, conveying a challenge to the truth of his assertions, is not conveyed by the interpreter and it is no surprise that the applicant's reply following the challenge sounds rather factual.

The decider makes one more attempt at eliciting some concrete information about the applicant's daily reading practice, in a way reiterating the question from line 6 above. In his reply, the applicant does not provide any new information; however, he offers to recite some of the religious texts that formed the basis of his daily practice, an indication of his eagerness to cooperate. The passage ends with the decider laughing in a rather sarcastic and condescending manner at the applicant's offer:

Excerpt [3] contd.

14   D: und **was** haben Sie da gelernt?
             *and **what** did you learn there\ in this respect?*

15   I: and what did you learn?
16   A: ah we learn how to pray. I can say something.
17   I: wir haben gelernt, wie man betet. Ich/ ich kann Ihnen auch etwas vorsagen.
             we learned how to pray. I/I can recite something for you.

18   D: nein, ((lacht sarkastisch)) vielen Dank.
             no, ((laughs sarcastically)) thank you very much.

The decider's behaviour at this point in the interview points to her growing scepticism and she may already have come some way in forming her judgement on the applicant's truthfulness and his case in general, issues she addresses in a statement given for the documentary after completion of the interview. There, she clearly judges the applicant's story to be manufactured, his story diverging quite considerably from those expressed by Sierra Leonean asylum seekers she has heard in the past and assessed as "genuine". Whether or not this can be directly or indirectly attributed to the process of interpreting is something that is of course impossible to judge and clearly goes beyond the remit of this study.

The data nevertheless also contain evidence of an awareness of modal particles on the part of the interpreter. In these cases the interpreter chooses expressions in English that approximate the pragmatic meaning expressed through the modal particles in German by the decider. Two small data samples have been selected to demonstrate this point. At this point in the interview, the decider is establishing the events that forced A to flee from his home country:

Excerpt [4]

9   D: ((schreibt)) (5) also wurden doch nicht alle umgebracht.
           ((writes)) (5) thus not everybody was killed.

10   I: so it means (.) actually not everyone was killed.

[......]

20   D: ((schreibt)) (4) mhmh (11) jetzt stell'n sich 'mal vor, *ich war nicht dabei*
            *((writes)) (4) mhmh (11) now imagine, *I was not there**

21   I: you just imagine I wasn't present there. I was **not** there.

In her interpretation of the decider's remark containing the particle "*doch*" (line 9), the interpreter uses the word "actually", conveying the overall pragmatic meaning of the utterance fairly successfully (line 10). A few interventions later, in line 20, the decider uses the modal particle "*mal*" ("*einmal*"). In this context, the particle seems to strengthen the illocutionary force of the utterance by more strongly appealing to the asylum seeker to understand that the decider will not be able to know what happened in his home country unless he comes forward with more information. Again, the interpreter uses a word to approximate the meaning of the German particle ("just" in line 21), evidence of her awareness of the pragmatics expressed.

6.   Discussion

In the above data analysis the process of interpretation was shown to result in pragmatic changes with regard to the decider's questioning techniques and her use of modal particles. It could be seen that the immigration official uses subtle indicators and prompts to elicit information from the applicant and to determine the truth of his assertions. The interpreter was shown to change the illocutionary force of questions by rendering them less forceful or reducing the openness of questions designed to invite the applicant to provide information. One salient feature of the analysis was the finding that modal particles used by the decider to convey a certain casualness were omitted by the interpreter, which again affected a speech style employed to invite the applicant to speak. At the same time, speech features that subtly indicated a growing scepticism on the decider's part were not conveyed in the target language. Although there are instances in the data where the interpreter is found to render German modal particles fairly accurately in the English interpretation, in the majority of instances this is not the case, and the cumulative effect of such pragmatic changes introduced in the interpreting process may be significant, as various authors have shown (e.g. Berk-Seligson 1990; Hale 1999).

One can only speculate as to the interpreter's reasons for the losses in pragmatic meaning. One possible explanation relates to her capacity to retain information. The interpreter active in this case does not take any notes and therefore has to rely exclusively on her memory. With all the interpreter's concentration focused on the factual content of each utterance, she may be unable to retain and subsequently convey the actual speech style employed by the primary interlocutors. An indication of the strain the interpreter's memory and concentration may be under is provided by evidence in the data of frequent interruptions by the interpreter. She often interrupts the applicant in the middle of an utterance, adopting a staccato-like interpreting technique, where only individual chunks of speech are interpreted at one time. This particular interpreter behaviour would warrant further investigation that goes beyond the scope of this paper.

Two equally likely explanations of the interpreter's behaviour go back to Hale (1999, 2001). Firstly, the interpreter may find it difficult to identify a pragmatic equivalent in English due to differences inherent in the two languages, leading her to utter questions baldly. This problem might be enhanced by the fact that some of the interpersonal meanings of the particles expressed might simply escape her as a non-native speaker of German. Secondly, the interpreter may judge the particular speech style employed to be unimportant and therefore regard pragmatic devices employed by the immigration official as superfluous, a plausible explanation given that modal particles are used much more abundantly in German than in English.

From this angle, the interpreter's behaviour could even be interpreted as an attempt to make communication more efficient. This second explanation is also linked to Knapp-Potthoff and Knapp's (1987) notion of cultural speech style differences being gauged by the mediator throughout the encounter and the resulting deletion or addition of polite particles in the interpreting process.

In some ways linked to both the notion of interpreter interruptions as well as the interpreter's discretion regarding the conveyance of pragmatic intent is the concept of interpreter role, or the interpreter's "participation status" (Goffman 1981; Wadensjö 1998). Throughout the encounter presented here, the interpreter seems to be a relatively involved participant. Evidence of the interpreter's possible over-involvement is, for example, provided by an instance where she is unable to utter the verb "to piss" expressed by the applicant, and instead converts it into "to pass water". This finding is reminiscent of a study by Cambridge (1999), where the interpreter is found to be unable to express certain taboo words used by the primary interlocutors during an interpreted medical consultation. As an over-involved participant, the interpreter in such a situation may feel the need to protect her own face by avoiding the use of taboo language, as she could be regarded as being personally responsible for the utterance. An interpreter who is over-involved might also subconsciously tend to express utterances in her own personal speech style rather than reflect the speech styles expressed by the primary interlocutors.

Although the impact on the interaction of pragmatic changes introduced in the interpreting process cannot be judged with absolute certainty, one can assume that such changes become particularly significant when they occur repeatedly. One cumulative effect of the loss of pragmatic meaning in the data at hand, particularly of changes in the illocutionary force expressed, is that the decider's growing scepticism is not conveyed. A less forceful questioning style and a reduction in the openness of questions may, in turn, impact on the applicant's replies. It would be in the applicant's interest to receive all the contextualization cues (Gumperz 1982) given by the decider, especially since he is removed from D through the language barrier and affected by cultural differences regarding the appropriate behaviour in the speech event. This would aid his understanding of the significance of the speech situation and each particular utterance expressed therein and allow him to respond appropriately by adapting his own communicative behaviour and possibly become more forthcoming with information. It must be stressed, however, that the decider's difficulty in obtaining coherent information from the applicant may be attributable to a number of reasons unrelated to the interpreting process, for instance to the applicant's individual communicative style and his willingness or ability to come forward with the required information. In order to be able to draw more general conclusions on the interpretation of modal particles and the effects of the interpreter's choice on the interaction, it would be necessary to study a larger number of interpreted events involving different interpreters and other language combinations.

7. Conclusion

This study may give the impression of a ruthless account of interpreting errors. It should therefore be pointed out that the aim of this analysis was in no way to advocate a verbatim style of interpreting where equivalence is aimed for on a word-by-word level. Although the general assumption that pragmatic equivalence is desirable and achievable in dialogue interpreting underlies this study, a purely descriptive stance was adopted. The aim was to provide some insight into the reality of interpreting in a German asylum interview rather than to provide a critique on the performance of one particular interpreter. What should perhaps be mentioned in this context, however, is that the interpreter active in this case will in all probability have received little or no interpreter training and that interpreters working for the *Bundesamt* are likely to be amongst the lowest paid public service interpreters in Germany.

It should also be noted that this analysis contains short extracts from one asylum interview only and that no general conclusions can be drawn with regard to the behaviour of all interpreters or the effectiveness of interpreting in German asylum hearings *per se*. However, the findings of this study, limited as they may be, point to a number of issues worth further investigation. Controlled experiments would be useful in order to gain more insight into the consequences of pragmatic changes introduced through the interpreting process. More specifically, it would be revealing to study whether or not different interpreting styles, for instance, including or excluding the pragmatic content of modal particles, do, in fact, make a difference to the interlocutors' perceptions of one another and the ultimate outcome of the speech event.

Most importantly, however, it would be necessary to study a larger corpus of authentic data in order to be able to gather more evidence on the reality of interpreting in authentic asylum interviews and shed more light on the three-way exchange in this setting. Such studies, however, will only become possible through an increased awareness of the importance of opening the "black box" of dialogue interpreting, thus resulting in access to data being granted by institutions like the *Bundesamt* that rely on the services of interpreters in providing those in need of protection with a fair hearing.

References

Berk-Seligson, Susan (1990) *The Bilingual Courtroom: Court Interpreters in the Judicial Process*, Chicago: The University of Chicago Press.

Brown, Penelope and Stephen C. Levinson (1978) "Universals in Language Usage: Politeness Phenomena", in E.N. Goody (ed.) *Questions and Politeness: Strategies in Social Interaction*, Cambridge: Cambridge University Press, 56-289.

------ (1987) *Politeness. Some Universals in Language Usage*, Cambridge: Cambridge University Press.

Cambridge, Jan (1999) "Information Loss in Bilingual Medical Interviews through an Untrained Interpreter", *The Translator* 5(2): 201-19.

Drew, Paul and John Heritage (1992) *Talk at Work: Interaction in Institutional Settings*, Cambridge: Cambridge University Press.

Durell, Martin (2002) *Hammer's German Grammar and Usage*, London: Arnold, 4th edition.

Goffman, Erving (1981) *Forms of Talk*, Philadelphia: University of Pennsylvania Press.

Gumperz, John (1982) *Discourse Strategies*, Cambridge: Cambridge University Press.

Hale, Sandra (1999) "Interpreters' Treatment of Discourse Markers in Courtroom Questions", *Forensic Linguistics* 6(1): 57-81.

------ (2001) "How are Courtroom Questions Interpreted? An Analysis of Spanish Interpreters Practices", in Ian Mason (ed.) *Triadic Exchanges: Studies in Dialogue Interpreting,* Manchester: St. Jerome Publishing, 21-50.

Knapp-Potthoff, Annelie and Karlfried Knapp (1987) "The Man (or Woman) in the Middle: Discoursal Aspects of Non-professional Interpreting", in Karlfried Knapp, Annelie Knapp-Potthoff and Werner Enninger (eds) *Analysing Intercultural Communication*, Berlin: Mouton de Gruyter, 181-211.

Mason, Ian (ed.) (2001) *Triadic Exchanges: Studies in Dialogue Interpreting*, Manchester: St. Jerome Publishing.

------ (2004) "Discourse, Audience Design and the Search for Relevance in Dialogue Interpreting", in G. Andruolakis (ed.) *Translating in the 21st Century: Trends and Prospects*, Proceedings of an international conference held at the Aristotle University of Thessaloniki, Greece: September 2002, 354-65.

Roberts, Celia, Evilyn Davies and Tom Jupp (1992) *Language and Discrimination: A Study of Multiethnic Workplaces*, London: Longman.

Schiffrin, Deborah (1987) *Discourse Markers*, Cambridge: Cambridge University Press.

Searle, John (1990) "A Classification of Illocutionary Acts", in D. Carbaugh (ed.) *Cultural Communication and Intercultural Contact*, New Jersey: Lawrence Erlbaum Associates, 349-72.

Thompson, Jeff and Puleng Thetela (1995) "The Sound of One Hand Clapping: The Management of Interaction in Written Discourse", *Text* 15(1): 103-27.

Wadensjö, Cecilia (1998) *Interpreting as Interaction*, London: Longman.

Legal Texts

Asylverfahrensgesetz

Gesetz über die Einreise und den Aufenthalt von Ausländern im Bundesgebiet (Ausländergesetz – AuslG) vom 9. Juli 1990 (BGBl. I S. 1354) zuletzt geändert durch Gesetz vom 09.01.2002 (BGBl. I S. 361 – Terrorismusbekämpfungsgesetz)

Grundgesetz für die Bundesrepublik Deutschland

Forging Alliances

The Role of the Sign Language Interpreter in Workplace Discourse

JULES DICKINSON & GRAHAM H. TURNER
Centre for Translation and Interpreting Studies in Scotland, Heriot-Watt University, Edinburgh, UK

Abstract. *This paper examines the role of the sign language interpreter in workplace settings and outlines the case for the interpreter as an integral, visible and active part of the communication process. We argue that, in order to work effectively and successfully in any setting, sign language interpreters must continue to move away from the pervasive "interpreter as conduit" norm and must consider working in a more transparent and open way, involving and informing all parties in the communicative interaction. The workplace is a complex environment, with its own specific rules and cultural norms. People present different social identities at work and these identities are continually negotiated and constructed through interaction with their colleagues. Sign language interpreters have to be aware of all these complexities and must act as cultural mediators, working in a participatory way with both Deaf and hearing clients in order to co-construct a shared understanding of discourse and accurately reflect and replay the shifting, hybrid identities within that discourse. Drawing upon data from a study into the experiences of sign language interpreters in the workplace environment, the article explores the ways in which all primary participants can contribute to a more successful interpreted outcome.*

1. Introduction

For well over a decade, it has been clear that the development of the sign language interpreting profession in the UK – as is true for community interpreting in general – depends to a considerable extent upon maintaining a mutually supportive, though constructively critical, relationship between service providers and consumers (Pollitt 1991; Scott Gibson 1991). The aim of developing and practically realizing the key features of an interpreting profession which will fully meet the needs of both service users and practitioners, underpinned by shared understandings of "good practice", and involving the kind of give and take which will enable interpretation of real quality to occur, has been central to the field in various forms for many years.

We believe that it is only by forging alliances with all those involved in the interpreted event that sign language interpreters (SLIs) can share some of the responsibility for achieving successful communication, a task that has sometimes been seen as their remit and theirs alone.

Reviewing how interpreters work with others will help us to bring a co-participatory or triadic model of interpreting to the foreground. Whilst there has clearly been a late 20th century "turn" towards a model of the interpreter as a co-ordinator and negotiator of meanings in a three-way interaction (Mason 1999, 2000), we feel there is much scope for developing our understanding of how triadic, multi-layered interpreted interactions work.

Taking as a starting point Turner's (2007) characterization of the interpreter as a "weaver-together" – someone who connects people, shedding light on their narratives and enabling them to share their stories – we want to develop and extend the point that making meaning is a co-operative venture. As such, it should be seen as an integral part of the interpreter's responsibility to draw the practicalities of their role to the attention of all those involved in the communicative event. The key to this is in acknowledging the **interdependence** of participants within the process, and it is only with the active "uptake" or appreciation of the interpreter's role by the primary participants (PPs) that it is fully "made real" as effective communication. What we are working towards is pushing beyond our understanding that interpreting takes place through a triadic relationship between the interpreter and the primary participants, and going on to examine the re-distribution of responsibilities within the interpreting triad in an attempt to define exactly where those responsibilities lie. We suggest that it is a legitimate part of the interpreter's professionalism to seek to bring an overt and active appreciation and understanding of the interpretative work to the attention of the PPs. Drawing PPs into a deeper and more detailed understanding of what the interpreter is doing will enable them to become consciously active in the interpretation process itself. In other words, making transparent the influence of the interpreter in such a way as to enable the consumer to be aware of it and thus to react "knowingly" and not "naively". We will illustrate these propositions with reference to the SLI's role in the workplaces of Deaf people and examine what they might mean in practical terms.

2.   Deaf people's experience of work

Very few Deaf people work in environments that are "Deaf friendly" or in workplaces where most of their colleagues are also Deaf. The common situation for a majority of Deaf employees is that they are the only Deaf person in a hearing dominated environment and that their work practices conform to the norms of hearing culture (Turner *et al.* 2002). As a result, communication problems are frequently cited as one of the main difficulties that Deaf people experience in the workplace environment. In some workplaces, signing is not allowed or is actively discouraged, resulting in Deaf employees being isolated from their hearing peers. The general lack of awareness regarding the need for SLIs in meetings and at training events, coupled with the current national shortage of BSL/English interpreters (Brien *et al.* 2002), means that Deaf employees can experience great difficulty in accessing information. In addition to all of these issues, Deaf people also face the problem of trying to fit into a workplace and build relationships with colleagues through a barrier of linguistic and cultural differences. It is no wonder then that these rifts and gaps result in Deaf people feeling frustrated, angry, devalued and oppressed. Sign language interpreters, often seen as one solution to addressing some of these issues, are confronted with the emotional and practical realities resulting from these underlying factors and are expected to deal with them in the course of their work.

3. Sign language interpreters in the workplace: the research study to date

This paper draws on research conducted into the experience of BSL/English interpreters working in office-based or *Access to Work* type settings. Access to Work is a Government funded scheme, whereby Deaf and disabled people can apply for assistance for support at work, be that in the form of personal assistants, sign language interpreters, technical support or the modification of materials. Deaf people are assessed by Access to Work and are subsequently allocated a number of interpreting hours, according to their needs. They can then book sign language interpreters (SLIs), either on a freelance or agency basis, to work with them for the support hours that have been agreed. This means, that generally, SLIs are employed to work with Deaf people who use British Sign Language as their first or preferred language, on a part time basis, in what are mainly hearing dominated workplace environments. The consistency of the work can vary, depending on the availability of the SLI and the preference of the Deaf client, but most SLIs will work with the same Deaf person on a regular basis (over 90% of SLIs responding to this question in the research study stated that they worked regularly with the same client).

The research project takes an ethnographic approach to collecting video data of authentic work-based interpreted interaction, in what is primarily a qualitative study.

In the preliminary stage of data collection, SLIs working in this domain had their views solicited through the use of questionnaires. One hundred and ten questionnaires were issued, distributed mainly via interpreter e-groups, and a total of 57 questionnaires were returned. At the end of the questionnaire a request was made for SLIs to participate further in the research by volunteering to keep a journal of their workplace experiences over a three month period. Forty interpreters volunteered to do so and 24 journals were completed and returned. Some of the themes and commonalities identified from this secondary data are highlighted in this paper, linked to underpinning ideas about the need for the interpreter to work with the PPs. A number of quotes have been selected from the journals, thus allowing us to explore the relevance of these ideas with reference to the workplace setting.

4.   The reality of the workplace

Workplaces are complex environments, with their own specific rules and cultural norms. In work settings, people present different social identities and these identities are continually negotiated and constructed through interaction with their colleagues. Sign language interpreters have to be aware of all the complexities of workplace communication, acting as cultural mediators and working in a participatory way with both Deaf and hearing clients in order to co-construct a shared understanding of discourse and accurately reflect and replay the shifting, hybrid identities within that discourse. From the research data analyzed so far, a number of common concerns have emerged.

The lack of clarity about the role of the SLI in the workplace, telephone interpreting, managing and maintaining appropriate client/interpreter boundaries, dealing with the subtleties and shifting allegiances in workplace politics and hierarchies, and "doing collegiality" through the process of small talk, have all been raised by SLIs in this particular setting.

> I tackle those (issues) that I am aware of, again and again, but they often remain unchanged (simply going underground for a while, to resurface again). Power dynamics, group dynamics, status, ownership, identification, self-suppression, over-reactions, prejudice, an endless list of subtleties that often overwhelms me. (J10:2)[11]

---

[1] 'J' denotes journal data (e.g. J14:4 signifies Journal 14: entry 4).

Whilst all of the issues raised warrant individual attention and detailed exploration, for the purpose of this paper we have focused on the issue of interpreter visibility, developing with reference to one particular interpreting arena – the workplace – recent suggestions (see Turner 2007) as to how interpreters can work more effectively *with* all those involved in order to maximize the efficacy of interpreted communication.

5.   The invisible interpreter

In examining the role of the sign language interpreter in the workplace setting, we are focussing on the SLI as an active third participant in the communicative event. Models in our field have moved (Pöchhacker 2004) towards a robust understanding that effective "dialogue interpreting", the prototype for many community or liaison settings, commonly requires an interactive or participatory stance on the part of the practitioner.

As Inghilleri (2004:72) states, the term "dialogue interpreting" reflects the shift in interpreting research to view all interpreting contexts, excepting conference interpreting, as having a shared interpersonal communicative structure, suggesting that all interpreted exchanges are at least triadic in nature and contain "significant communicative shifts" in the interpreter's embedded role. This has been elegantly theoretized and illuminatingly described with reference to spoken language interpreting (e.g. Berk-Seligson 1990; Wadensjö 1998; Anderson 2002) and sign language interpreting alike (e.g. Metzger 1999; Roy 2000).

Whilst agreeing with Mason (2000) and others (see Baker-Shenk 1991; Roy 1993; McIntire and Sanderson 1995) that the "conduit" or machine model of interpreting is deeply flawed and has little value in relation to dialogue interpreting, we would state that the concept of the interpreter as a neutral and detached "passer on" of information is still the most commonly held understanding of the interpreter's role by of those outside the profession.

Invisibility, non-involvement and **conduit** are also words that are pervasive throughout interpreting literature and training and are not only still the strongly-held beliefs of Deaf and hearing clients, but are also deeply embedded in the SLI's self-perception. Current interpreter training for SLIs *is* moving away from the uninvolved, unthinking model of interpreting practice and is progressing towards and embracing the realization that SLIs are an active part of the communicative process.

However, it is still common for SLIs to encourage their clients to "imagine that I am not here" and to "just ignore me", covering themselves with an imaginary "Cloak of Invisibility". In doing so, they are suppressing their own human needs for recognition and acceptance in what we believe is an effort to make their Deaf client more visible. If we can illustrate this with an example:

> I was recently accused of being "off hand" and "frosty" in my Deaf
> client's workplace. I was deep in (signed) conversation with the
> Deaf client, the hearing staff had walked in and I voiced over the
> Deaf client's greeting. Because I personally didn't say hello to the
> staff or make eye contact they said I was stand-offish. (J50:1)

The reality is that SLIs very rarely produce their own greeting or respond as though they are being personally addressed alongside their Deaf client. If we look at what underpinned this decision we can see some of the reasoning that influenced their choice. The SLI did not respond to the hearing staff members, either verbally or through eye contact, as in their experience this would lead to the Deaf client being ignored. Hearing people often prefer to make eye contact with and talk directly to the SLI, rather than the Deaf person, because they feel more comfortable communicating with another hearing person.

> I am aware that often the hearing person who is happy to chat with
> the SLI may well be the same one that won't talk to the Deaf person,
> and when we get too friendly with the hearing person we can end
> up colluding with the communication imbalance within the work
> or training setting. (J51:2)

Sign language interpreters have also experienced confusion when they do respond in their own right, due to the lack of clarity as to who is actually speaking.

As a result of all these experiences, SLIs have developed strategies that include behaviours such as not making eye contact with the hearing participants, not responding when addressed directly and never venturing any personal comments. None of these actions are made clear or overtly explained, but instead the SLI hopes that the hearing participant will understand their behaviour. On the occasions when SLIs have the opportunity to brief participants about what to expect, they frequently find that this can add to the confusion. Instructions to "ignore me, make eye contact with the Deaf person" are insufficient when the hearing participant has never met a Deaf person before. They are generally disconcerted, unsure and embarrassed when confronted with a Deaf employee and an SLI, feeling uncertain as to whom to address and where to look.

Hearing participants are unprepared when the Deaf client makes no eye contact with them, but instead focuses on the SLI, and often cannot quite understand why the interpreter is speaking in the first person. The SLI's motivation for behaving in this way – avoiding eye contact and attempting to disengage from direct contact with the hearing client – is not intentional, but stems, we believe, from the confusion over their role and responsibilities within the interpreted event.

There are wide ranging and deep implications if SLIs persist in this type of behaviour without any explanation to the other participants. Their actions will reflect upon the Deaf client, as those participants who are inexperienced in working with interpreters may assign the interpreter's characteristics to the Deaf person. It also encourages all participants to view the sign language interpreter as a communication machine.

One interpreter, reflecting on the reasons for their (regular) Deaf client not introducing them in a meeting, wrote in their journal:

> Is it a fixed view that the Deaf person has of interpreters that we are just vessels of communication? Or do I promote the idea by behaving in such a self-sufficient manner that I may not appear to have needs like other humans? Perhaps I give the impression that I don't need to be recognized as a person as I do not interact with other staff that often where I work. My role as an interpreter seems to prohibit my humanistic needs from surfacing. (J1:3)

Spencer-Oatey (2000:14-15), in her exploration of "sociality rights", states that people fundamentally believe that they are entitled to an association with others, and this belief is connected to the type of relationship that they have with other people. As a result of this right to association, people feel that they are "entitled to an appropriate amount of conversational interaction and social chit-chat with others". If this is the case, then we can see that SLIs are presented with a very complex task. Not only are they managing the "association rights" between their Deaf and hearing clients, but in addition, when recognized as person in their own right, they are expected to acknowledge that they are present and engage in an appropriate amount of interaction.

Putting these examples under the microscope, it can be seen that SLIs have an extremely complex task. Not only are they expected to ensure that the conversation flows, that turn-taking happens in an ordered manner and that all the participants understand each other, but they will also be busy making decisions about the relationship between the participants and their corresponding "appropriate amount of social interaction".

They are also trying to mediate across three different cultures: that of the Deaf client, the hearing client and the culture of the specific workplace. In the midst of this cultural divergence, the SLI has to try and balance the needs of all parties, making decisions about what constitutes an acceptable and appropriate amount of "chit chat" in this particular interaction, trying to negotiate a compromise that suits both the Deaf and hearing client, and at the same time attempting to deal with his/her own needs and trying to diminish his or her "identity face" in this multifaceted scenario. It is no wonder that SLIs report difficulties in dealing with the complexities that they face:

> I am a sponge that is dipped and soaked in the undercurrents. I am sure that I am not the only person who goes home from this workplace with a surfeit of complicated and indigestible feelings and thoughts!! (J10:2)

6. Changing practice – a team approach

SLIs are often seen as an irritant when they are first introduced to the communicative event. Initially viewed as a solution to the problem, addressing the language and cultural needs of all the participants, it can be something of a shock when SLIs seem to magnify and draw attention to the communication difficulties, by asking for clarification, breaks, preparation material and so forth.

Results from the research to date show that Deaf clients themselves will try to minimize the impact of the SLI on the proceedings, requesting that they do not interrupt too often and that they play down their role in the event. The reactions to the intrusion of the SLI can be varied.

Some participants will try to avoid creating situations where an SLI might be required, or alternatively suggestions are made that the Deaf client could "manage without" an SLI. Occasionally, participants can see the positives that can be achieved by working through the difficult period and it is these reactions that SLIs need to foster and encourage in others.

The solution to the problem lies in the mismatch between consumer expectations and the actual reality of interpreted events, referred to by Mason (2000). There is no easy answer; SLIs cannot give their clients a "whistle-stop tour" of the developments in dialogue and sign language interpreting over the past twenty years. They may perhaps have to start small, e.g. in a particular practitioner-client relationship, and seek to develop this across a whole workplace, with the long-term target of raising awareness of what interpreters do and how they do it, throughout the relevant language communities. We are suggesting then that SLIs can make small but significant changes that will have a ripple effect.

7. Working with the deaf community

It is difficult to imagine the frustration for Deaf people of witnessing hearing people commenting to SLIs about "how lovely sign language is and what a wonderful skill to have" when it is these same employees that routinely ignore and exclude them because of their difference or "otherness" (Ladd 2003). Ladd (1988:37), referring to the declaration that BSL really was a language, stated "Deaf people officially had something positive and attractive which made them equal to hearing people".

However, from the evidence provided in this research project it still seems that hearing people only find sign language attractive when they do not have to deal with the problematic and thorny issue of having to actually communicate through it. SLIs have to find ways of sensitively directing the focus back to the Deaf employee. Working with the Deaf client, raising their awareness and keeping them informed is an imperative. For some Deaf employees, their lack of awareness of the wider issues embedded in workplace culture, practices and hierarchical structures might mean that they perceive their requirements as being deliberately dismissed or devalued. By working **with** the Deaf community, SLIs have the opportunity to plant some seeds and get across the concepts that we are exploring and at the same time, see the issues from the "other side of the fence".

Practitioner researchers can discuss the intricacies of workplace culture, distribution of power and the importance of access to small talk with some degree of dispassion, but listening to Deaf people's everyday experience of being dismissed, ignored and treated as outcasts in the workplace is a very painful and salutary experience and a useful reminder as to why such research is undertaken. It is vital that Deaf clients' perspectives are included. If this does not happen, then the oppression of Deaf people is perpetuated and, as Ladd (2003:21) states, only minor adjustments will be made to how "We" treat "Them" – and Deaf people will continue to be treated as objects of linguistic or psychological analysis (Ladd 2003).

8.   Informing the hearing participants

SLIs must work with the hearing consumer to develop their understanding of the interpreted event. By highlighting what is actually happening during the interpreting process and making clear the linguistic and cultural differences between Deaf and hearing people they can contribute to making people aware of the benefits when Deaf employees form an integral part of the workplace environment. From the perspective of the hearing staff, when working with a Deaf employee, through a SLI, they are expected to make considerable adjustments to various aspects of their communicative behaviour, such as turn-taking, making eye contact with the Deaf person, speaking clearly and at an even pace, as well as giving thought to more practical considerations such as seating, lighting and ensuring interpreter availability (Lichtig *et al.* 2004).

Given the stress, competing demands and workloads of many modern day organisations, it is easy to see how the communication needs of Deaf employees can be seen as a low priority, if not ignored altogether. SLIs have to find ways of raising awareness of the needs of Deaf employees and ensuring that they are included more fully in the workplace.

9.   Acceptance of role and developing a framework

If SLIs begin to accept that they are not invisible, that they are going to have an effect on the interpreted event, then they will start to think about how they are going to deal with the issues that arise during those events.

It only takes small alterations in their professional practice to have a significant knock-on effect – changing the way that they introduce themselves, making themselves more visible in the interpreting process, being honest about the fact that this is not "just a conversation between two people" and feeling comfortable with the reality that sometimes they will have to interrupt, adjust and manage the discourse. SLIs frequently find themselves in positions where their own social identities and desires for recognition as human beings are submerged and the needs of their clients are placed foremost. This struggle between the interpreter's needs and those of their clients is the source of much of the discomfort, irritation and loss of control that interpreters frequently experience. SLIs need to be encouraged to develop a deeper understanding of their role in the context of the workplace, which will in turn enable them to feel more confident within that role. If SLIs are stating that: "The freedom to develop a broader working relationship is undercut by the panic of no framework to refer to when it all goes awry (or threatens to)" (J10:5), then they clearly need a safety net, some guidance of a non-prescriptive nature and an underpinning framework or model to work from that empowers them to operate in the most effective way for all participants and for themselves.

Bergson and Sperlinger (2003:20) confirm this when they refer to the need for a clear framework for thinking about the personal responses that arise in the interpreting context, in order to alleviate some of the "unnecessary stress and even distress" that SLIs can experience.

10. Conclusion – In the real world

We have referred throughout this paper to the role of the SLI in the workplace. We see this as being just one aspect of public service interpreting, but our recommendations for this approach to the interpreter's role apply to the wider public service interpreting domain. It is going to be very difficult to negotiate changes – even examining the roles and needs of interpreters and initiating discussions of power and control can bring to the surface some very long-held and very real fears, frustrations and resentments.

> It struck me recently when a Deaf friend, who is not having a good time at work, (particularly with some of his colleagues) told me how bad it felt to see the interpreter getting on like a house on fire with members of his team....and the interpreter's inability to understand why this was upsetting. (J15:1)

The sensitivity of the sign language interpreter's task is immense. In attempting to fit in with the hearing employees they can easily be seen to be siding with the majority. Sign language interpreters are all too aware of the fine line of oppression/advocacy on which they continually balance and will have to tread a delicate path in terms of making themselves more visible in the workplace.

However, if all participants accept from the outset that there are bound to be elements of difficulty and confusion when an SLI is introduced to the workplace, or indeed to any discourse setting, then all will be better equipped to anticipate those problems and work out positive strategies for addressing them. The crux of the matter in educating hearing employees and employers is that a team approach is vital.

We are not saying that this will be easy; in fact the reality is that it will no doubt be a painful and difficult process. People are certain to complain that it is not always possible to work with PPs in such an intensive way. This is true, but it cannot continue to be used as an excuse to avoid making changes; the fact that it may not apply to some particular setting or situation does not mean that it should be ruled out as unachievable in principle. By making the effort to encourage practitioners to work together to bring about changes to their practice, we hope to begin to see the broad cultural shifts that are needed in the ways in which participants work with interpreters. This in turn will lead to a more successful and satisfying communication outcome for all those involved.

References

Anderson, R. and W. Bruce (1976/2002) "Perspectives on the Role of Interpreter", in Richard W. Brislin (ed.) *Translation: Applications and Research*, New York: Gardner Press, 208-28; reprinted in Franz Pöchhacker and Miriam Shlesinger (eds) *The Interpreting Studies Reader*, London: Routledge, 2002, 209-17.

Baker-Shenk, Charlotte (1991) "The Interpreter: Machine, Advocate or Ally?", in Jean Plant-Moeller (ed) *Expanding Horizons: Proceedings of the 1991 RID Convention*, Silver Spring MD: RID Publications, 120-40.

Bergson, Mo and David Sperlinger (2003) "'I Still Don't Know What I Should Have Done': Reflections on Personal/Professional Dilemmas in Sign Language Interpreting", *Deaf Worlds: International Journal of Deaf Studies* 19(3): 6-23.

Berk-Seligson, Susan (1990) *The Bilingual Courtroom: Court Interpreters in the Judicial Process*, Chicago: Chicago University Press.

Brien, David, Richard Brown and Judith Collins (2004) "Some Recommendations Regarding the Provision and Organisation of British Sign Language Interpreters in England, Scotland and Wales", *Deaf Worlds: International Journal of Deaf Studies* 20(3): 282-98.

Inghilleri, Moira (2004) "Aligning Macro- and Micro- Dimensions in Interpreting Research", in Christina Schäffner (ed.) *Translation Research and Interpreting Research: Traditions, Gaps and Synergies*, Clevedon: Multilingual Matters Ltd., 71-76.

Ladd, Paddy (1988) "The Modern Deaf Community", in Susan Gregory and Gillian. M. Hartley (eds) *Constructing Deafness*, London: Pinter Publishers Ltd., 35-44.

------ (2003) *Understanding Deaf Culture*, UK: Multilingual Matters Ltd.

Lichtig, Ida, Bencie Woll, Maria S. Cárnio, Renata Akiyama and Mariana Gomes (2004) "Deaf Staff Members Participation in a Brazilian Intervention Programme for Deaf Children and Their Families: Impacts and

Consequences", *Deaf Worlds: International Journal of Deaf Studies* 20(3): 282-98.

McIntire, Marina and Gary Sanderson (1995) "Who's in Charge Here? Perceptions of Empowerment and Role in the Interpreting Setting", *Journal of Interpretation* 7(1): 99-114.

Mason, Ian (1999) "Introduction", *The Translator* 5(2): 147-60.

------ (2000) "Models and Methods in Dialogue Interpreting Research", in Maeve Olohan (ed.) *Intercultural Faultlines: Research Models in Translation Studies 1– Textual and Cognitive Aspects*, Manchester: St. Jerome, 215-31.

Metzger, Melanie (1999) *Sign Language Interpreting: Deconstructing the Myth of Neutrality*, Washington DC: Gallaudet University Press.

Pöchhacker, Franz (2004) *Introducing Interpreting Studies*, London: Routledge.

Pollitt, Kyra (1991) "Rational Responses", *Signpost* 4(2): 24.

Roy, Cynthia (1993) "The Problem with Definitions, Descriptions and the Role Metaphors of Interpreters", *Journal of Interpretation* 6(1): 127-54.

------ (2000) *Interpreting as a Discourse Process,* Oxford: Oxford University Press.

Scott Gibson, Liz (1991) "Sign Interpreting: An Emerging Profession", in Susan Gregory and Gillian M. Hartley (eds) *Constructing Deafness*, London & Milton Keynes: Pinter Publishers in association with the Open University, 253-58.

Spencer-Oatey, Helen (2000) "Rapport Management: A Framework for Analysis", in Helen Spencer-Oatey (ed.) *Culturally Speaking: Managing Rapport Through Talk Across Cultures*, London: Continuum, 11-46.

Turner, Graham H. (2007) "Professionalisation of Interpreting *with* the Community: Refining the Model", in Cecilia Wadensjö, Birgitta Englund Dimitrova and Anna-Lena Nilsson (eds) *The Critical Link 4: Professionalisation of Interpreting in the Community*, Amsterdam: John Benjamins, 181-92.

------, Jen K. Dodds and Lisa A. Richardson (2002) *"Always the Last to Know": Institutionalised Audism and Linguistic Exclusion of Deaf People from Workplace Communities*, Preston, England: University of Central Lancashire.

Wadensjö, Cecilia (1998) *Interpreting as Interaction*, London: Longman.

ABOUT THE EDITORS

Raquel de Pedro Ricoy is a Lecturer in the Department of Languages and Intercultural Studies at Heriot-Watt University, where she teaches Spanish written composition, translation (theory and practice) and interpreting. After completing a degree in Philology at the University of Valladolid (Spain), she was awarded a PhD by the University of Edinburgh for a thesis on translation. Her research interests lie in translation theory (mainly cultural issues in translation and translation and the media) and cross-cultural communication.

Isabelle Perez is a Professorial Fellow in the Department of Languages and Intercultural Studies at Heriot-Watt University. Her specialist language is French and she teaches courses on interpreting (both conference and liaison) and French for business. She is a practising conference interpreter and her research interests include liaison/public-service interpreting, quality assessment in interpreting and interpreter-mediated interviews.

Christine Wilson is a Lecturer in the Department of Languages and Inter-cultural Studies at Heriot-Watt University, where she teaches French and English (translation, interpreting, and related aspects of linguistics and area studies). She also teaches with colleagues in the Arabic, British Sign Language, Chinese (Mandarin), German and Spanish sections. Her main research interests are translation theory and interpreting studies – with particular reference to public service and remote (telephone and video-conference) interpreting – as well as lexicography, cross-cultural survey methodology and kinesics.

ABOUT THE AUTHORS

Dr. **Hanneke Bot** is a sociologist and Dutch registered psychotherapist. She works in a psychiatric clinic for asylum seekers and refugees. The patients often speak very limited Dutch, so she often works with interpreters in their treatments. This inspired her to engage in research to get a better insight into the communication processes at work in interpreter-mediated psycho-therapeutic talk. This resulted in a PhD degree at the University of Utrecht, The Netherlands, in 2005. Since 2006 she is also self-employed as a trainer, researcher and consultant on interpreter-mediated communication.

Pedro Jesús Castillo Ortiz completed an MA in Translation and Interpreting at the University of Granada (UGR), Spain in 2003, specializing in Conference and Liaison Interpreting. He also holds an MA in Communication and Media from the same university, which he completed in 2005. In 2002 he was awarded a research scholarship by the Department of Translation and Interpreting at UGR as part of a project entitled *Language Assistance Needs for Immigrants in Andalucía* and in 2003 he was a researcher on the *Teaching Innovation and New Technologies in Interpreting Classes* project, under the supervision of Professor Jesús de Manuel Jerez. He is currently completing his PhD on *Interpreting in the Media and Liaison Interpreting in Radio settings* at the UGR. He has worked as freelance translator and interpreter and is currently working at Heriot-Watt University.

Jules Dickinson has worked as BSL/ English interpreter for a number of years, and is currently in the final year of a PhD research project at Heriot-Watt University, examining the impact and implications of sign language interpreters in workplace settings. She is a member of the Centre for Translation and Interpreting Studies in Scotland (CTISS).

Lyse Hébert is a course director at the Glendon College School of Translation (York University, Toronto, Canada). She has extensive experience as a translator and community interpreter in the public and academic sectors. Her current research interests focus on cultural and socio-political dimensions of translation.

Anne Martin has a PhD in Translation and Interpreting Studies from the University of Granada, Spain. She is a practising conference interpreter and Senior Lecturer in interpreting at the FTI, University of Granada, where she teaches a doctoral course on community interpreting. She is a member of the GRETI research group funded by the Andalusian Regional Govern-ment and based at the University of Granada. One of the group's main fields of research is public service interpreting. She is co-editor of the journal *Puentes: Hacia Nuevas investigaciones en la mediación intercultural*.

From 1994 to 2005, **Ian Mason** was Professor of Interpreting and Transla-tion at Heriot-Watt University and Director of the Centre for Translation and Interpreting Studies in Scotland. Now retired, he has taught translating and liaison interpreting for many years and has been involved in the validation and accreditation of degree programmes in interpreting and translating in Spain, Hong Kong, Kuwait, Ireland and the United Kingdom. In addi-tion to collaborations with Basil Hatim – *Discourse and the Translator* (Longman, 1990) and *The Translator as Communicator* (Routledge 1997) – he has published on various aspects of the linguistics and pragmatics of interpreting and translating. In recent years he has focused on face-to-face interpreting and was guest editor of a special issue of *The Translator* (Vol. 5, no. 2) entitled *Dialogue Interpreting* and editor of *Triadic Exchanges: Studies in Dialogue Interpreting* (St. Jerome, 2001). His most recent studies are of 'Projected and Perceived Identities in Dialogue Interpreting' (*IATIS Yearbook* 2005), 'Ostension, Inference and Response' (*Linguistica Antver-piensia* 5, 2006) and of participant gaze in interpreter-mediated exchanges (forthcoming).

Raffaela Merlini is Associate Professor of English language and transla-tion at the University of Macerata, Italy, where she teaches English-Italian dialogue and consecutive interpreting. From 2000 to 2005, she held a post as lecturer in English-Italian simultaneous and consecutive interpreting at the School of Modern Languages for Interpreters and Translators (SSLMIT) of the University of Trieste, Italy. She was Head of the Italian Section in the Department of Modern Languages at the University of Salford, England, where she lectured full time from 1996 to 1999. She has published in the field of interpreting studies, particularly on consecutive and dialogue in-terpreting topics. Her research interests currently focus on the interactional dynamics of interpreter-mediated talk in healthcare and other community settings. Raffaela Merlini also worked as conference interpreter in high-level institutional settings.

Bernadette O'Rourke lectures in Spanish and General Linguistics at Heriot-Watt University, Edinburgh. She is a graduate of Dublin City University and holds a BA in Applied Languages (1998) and a PhD in Applied Language and Intercultural Studies (2005). In 2007 she was awarded a Visiting Research Fellowship to the National University of Ireland, Galway. Her research focuses on the role of language in the construction of social difference and social inequality and she explores these issues as they unfold in the case of two minority languages – Irish in the Republic of Ireland and Galician in Spain. Although her research to date has looked mainly on these indigenous language cases, more recently her work has involved an analysis if migrant language communities in Ireland and Scotland. Apart from these active interests, she is also interested in general issues of language planning and language policy, language rights and language ideologies. In 2006 she acted in an advisory capacity to the Irish delegation of the Committee of the Regions in the drafting of an opinion paper on the European Commission's *New Framework Strategy for Multilingualism.*

Juan Miguel Ortega Herráez holds a PhD in Translation and Interpreting from the University of Granada, where he presented his thesis on court interpreting in Spain and the role of the interpreter. He has been a staff court and police interpreter in Madrid and Alicante and is currently lecturing in translation and interpreting at the University of Alicante, Spain. He has been involved in different EU GROTIUS and AGIS projects on legal translation and interpreting and is a member of the GRETI research Group funded by the Andalusian Regional Government and based at the University of Granada, Spain. One of the group's main fields of research is public service interpreting.

Hanne Skaaden is a Dr. in Art with a thesis on first language attrition in the speech of adult migrants (University of Oslo, 1998). Her research interests include studies on bilingualism and migration and the screening of interpreter students. She has taught interpreting both on-campus and online to a variety of language groups, and is now Professor in the Department of Interpreting Studies at Oslo University College. Skaaden has extensive experience as an interpreter in the public sector (Serbian/Norwegian), and engaged in policy development of public sector interpreting when working for the Norwegian Directorate of Integration and Diversity.

Maria Tillmann teaches German, conference and liaison interpreting at the Department of Languages and Intercultural Studies at Heriot-Watt University, where she has also been involved in research at the Centre for Translation and Interpreting Studies in Scotland. She is particularly interested in the pragmatic dimension of interpreted communication in a variety of fields, including asylum hearings and medical settings. She is also a freelance translator and interpreter and, because of her background in public service interpreting in the German system, has a special interest in teaching public service interpreting and improving interpreter training, as well as in the public perception of PSI in Germany.

Professor **Graham H Turner** is the Director of the Centre for Translation & Interpreting Studies in Scotland at Heriot-Watt University, Edinburgh. He has been a teacher and researcher in applied sign linguistics for 20 years, and now focuses on interactional approaches to interpreting. Graham currently conducts and supervises a number of research and knowledge exchange projects in applied bilingualism and sign language studies. He has published widely, co-authoring *Interpreting Interpreting: Studies and Reflections on Sign Language Interpreting* (2001, Douglas McLean), and is the Founding Editor of *The Sign Language Translator & Interpreter*.

Maria Wattne holds an MA in International Studies and a BA in Thai Studies. During 2004 she was a project consultant at the University of Oslo, facilitating an Internet-based course on interpreting. Wattne has worked as an interpreter (Thai/Norwegian) and journalist in Norway and Thailand, and as an advisor for the online Register of Interpreters of the Norwegian Directorate of Immigration (currently IMDi). As an independent researcher, Wattne studied quality control measures of Norwegian interpreting service providers (2006). She is currently working as a communications advisor to the Norwegian Union of Municipal and General Workers (Fagforbundet), which also organizes interpreting services.

Index